Critical Thinking within the Library Program

Edited by John Spencer and Christopher Millson-Martula

Routledge
Taylor & Francis Group
LONDON AND NEW YORK

First published 2009 by Routledge
2 Park Square, Milton Park, Abingdon, Oxon, OX14 4RN

Simultaneously published in the USA and Canada
by Routledge
270 Madison Avenue, New York, NY 10016

Routledge is an imprint of the Taylor & Francis Group, an informa business

Typeset in Times by Value Chain, India
Printed and bound in the United States of America on acid-free paper by IBT Global.

British Library Cataloguing in Publication Data
A catalogue record for this book is available from the British Library

ISBN10: 0-415-99838-7
ISBN13: 978-0-415-99838-3

CONTENTS

Introduction

Critical thinking skills are important for students at all levels of their college and university careers. For librarians and faculty, there has been a resurgence of interest in teaching critical thinking skills to students. Part of the reason for revived attention to critical thinking skills is today's new generation of students, the millennials or Generation Y.

Why has critical thinking resurfaced as an important skill for students to develop? While there are many reasons, a primary reason is the skill set which millennial students in college exhibit. Their skills include an emphasis on using technology in any form, but the Internet in particular. In fact, millennials may be using Internet resources to the exclusion of more traditional resources, such as books, periodicals, and other materials found in libraries that could actually possess greater value for students. In terms of library instruction, these students present many challenges for librarians who want to encourage them to use a multitude of appropriate resources, not just those found on the Internet.

While students today are obviously very adept at finding resources on the Web using search engines like Google, other skills such as evaluating and assessing the best resources to use are skills they need to develop. Since using library resources can be a challenge for millennial students, a primary goal for librarians is to enable students to evaluate sources they locate and develop critical thinking skills to identify appropriate resources in the discipline they are studying.

In addition to being Net savvy, millennials also naturally like multitasking and being surrounded by technology in all its forms. Listening to their iPod, working on a paper, chatting on a social networking site, and text-messaging their friends at the same time is not uncommon for students of the Net generation. The missing link for students may be the critical thinking skills which would help them assess their information options and determine the best resources to use.

In this book twelve chapters present a wide range of instructional options for consideration to enable and encourage students to think critically. To see how far we've come, read the annotated bibliography by Ellis and Whatley, which includes a sample of articles published on critical thinking and library instruction over a twenty-year period. The bibliography illustrates how librarians have worked successfully with teaching faculty to address critical thinking skills as part of a larger movement toward developing information literacy competencies.

How to teach critical thinking skills is a central question for librarians. A constructivist approach to teaching and learning places students at the center of the learning environment, and the instructor is the guide or facilitator; this is a natural model for online learning. Allen's article, "Promoting Critical Thinking Skills in Online Information Literacy Instruction Using a Constructivist Approach," clarifies how this approach works in the online environment, which has exploded in the last ten years. Using a classical approach to teaching, Schiller explores and demonstrates how librarians can effectively use Socratic techniques to improve and refine the critical thinking skills of students in a library instruction classroom.

First year students are a very important target audience for librarians and faculty who teach critical thinking skills. At Oregon State University, Deitering and Jameson write about their university's approach to a collaborative library and writing faculty project to promote critical thinking skills and embed information literacy in first year composition classes. They advocate and explain how to use Graff and Birkenstein's innovative approach to modeling scholarly writing and use conversation to illustrate the connections among critical thinking, writing and learning, and information literacy.

Integrating critical thinking and information literacy skills in a freshman skills program that combines innovative uses of student Wikis and student collaboration at Gonzaga University is explored by Alfino, Pajer, Pierce, and Jenks. In addition, Gruber, Knefel, and Waelchli's article, "Modeling Scholarly Inquiry: One Article at a Time," clarifies how complex ethical questions can encourage students to present different perspectives within a scholarly research framework as part of a beginning composition class at the University of Dubuque. For many librarians, teaching critical thinking skills is also an important element of subject-specific library instruction, and this issue provides examples of how librarians approach critical thinking skill development in course-integrated instruction. In a hospitality management setting, Berger integrates student-oriented active learning into a library workshop that presents students with "real-life" problems to solve. In the field of business, Taylor's article, "Information Literacy in Subject-Specific Vocabularies: A Path to Critical Thinking," discusses a skill-building workshop approach to improving business students' abilities in identifying, researching, and analyzing business information. Nentl and Zietlow present their work with business students to enhance critical thinking by using Bloom's taxonomy as a diagnostic framework for engaging business students in higher order thinking.

Ways to teach critical thinking reflect a wide range of pedagogical techniques. Librarians and psychology faculty (Hayes-Bohanan and Spievak) at Bridgewater State College collaborated to create a course called "The Psychology of Academic Success," based upon what psychology has to say about learning and problem solving. Mathson and Lorenzen of Central Michigan University write about how they challenge their students to evaluate hoax and historical revisionist Websites in a library credit class. They emphasize critical thinking skill development and address assessment of student learning using pre- and post-testing on research readiness with a self-assessment instrument.

Campus-wide efforts in librarian and faculty collaboration are also important ways to reach students by teaching critical thinking and enhancing information literacy across the curriculum. At Washington State University, Johnson, Lindsay, and Walter's article, "Learning More About How They Think: Information Literacy Instruction in a Campus-Wide Critical Thinking Project," presents models for collaboration, which include a critical thinking focus in the WSU Freshman Seminar Program and their Information Literacy Project.

In each of the articles, librarians are exploring new ways to meet their instructional goals and the goal of teaching critical thinking skills to students across the curriculum. Collaboration, innovation, and active learning techniques are evident elements of successful approaches to teaching students how to develop critical thinking skills essential for today's Internet-based society.

John S. Spencer
and Christopher Millson-Martula

The Evolution of Critical Thinking Skills in Library Instruction, 1986–2006: A Selected and Annotated Bibliography and Review of Selected Programs

Erin L. Ellis
Kara M. Whatley

INTRODUCTION

Academic librarians are continually evaluating and seeking to improve the library instruction and information literacy programs offered by their institutions. To do this, it is increasingly important to understand the needs of students as information consumers in a technology-driven world and to understand how critical thinking as a key component of information literacy has evolved in library instruction.

Since the mid 1980s, academic libraries have viewed their expanding instruction programs not just in terms of teaching particular library tools, but in terms of teaching students to be knowledgeable information consumers who are information literate. Accommodating critical thinking in higher education has required many pedagogical changes across campuses. As library instruction and information literacy programs have expanded, critical thinking skills for students have been increasingly emphasized. In accordance with the Information Literacy Competency Standards for Higher Education (2000), academic librarians have taken leading roles to support and complement curricula that focus on improving critical thinking skills.

This annotated review will highlight research and case study literature that focuses on critical thinking in library instruction programs at the college and university levels in the last twenty years (1986–2006). It will categorize the literature by:

- successful implementations/collaborations,
- ILC standards impact,
- current trends,
- and new/future directions.

The goal is to track the evolution, value, and effectiveness of critical thinking in library instruction and information literacy programs. Using library literature indices and databases, the reviewers will analyze the correlations and connections found among the literature. Also, the reviewers will comment on the changing nature of critical thinking within library instruction and information literacy programs. Additionally, the annotated review will include Websites for library instruction programs that have incorporated critical thinking into their instruction plans and activities as part of an organized and integrated campus-wide effort. These Website references will provide a snapshot of latest trends and new directions in critical-thinking best practices in academic libraries.

METHODS

This review of literature regarding critical thinking and library instruction included basic searching in the following databases: Library Literature, Library, Information Science & Technology Abstracts (LISTA), Emerald Insight, and Web of Science. Search terms included: "critical thinking," "bibliographic instruction," "library instruction," and "information literacy." The reviewers eliminated results that were not library focused and fell outside the 1986–2006 publication timeframe. Selected articles provide an overview of critical thinking in the context of library instruction or information literacy, introduce readers to the evolving argument about where critical thinking belongs within the library profession, and demonstrate the value or effectiveness of critical thinking. Many of these articles have become key works in the library instruction canon.

ANNOTATED BIBLIOGRAPHY

Atton, C. 1994. Using critical thinking as a basis for library user education. *The Journal of Academic Librarianship* 20: 310–313.

This study builds upon the work of Bodi and Wesley in developing critical thinking skills during library instruction. However, Atton takes their work further, asserting that critical thinking skills should be emphasized above library skills. In this study, Atton provided undergraduate biological sciences students with paragraphs on a variety of life sciences topics. These paragraphs contained both jargon and acronyms that might impede the students' ability to fully comprehend the information presented. After a brief discussion on critical thinking and communication as well as a short lecture on non-academic information sources such as newspapers, the students were divided into groups. These groups were given a series of six questions to guide them through the research process. As they worked, all group members assessed the students to ensure full participation, and the progress of each group was monitored. Groups completed their work by turning in a written list of information sources consulted and then delivering an oral report to their classmates. Each group was then asked to reflect on this research process, and these reflections were used to develop a list of recommended research practices for the students. In analyzing both the work process of the groups and the list of recommended research practices, Atton concludes that this instructional approach engaged the students to such a degree that the instruction was highly effective, and that the students learned both transferable critical thinking skills and library research practices. Atton further reflects that this approach to teaching library skills places a great demand on librarians as teachers to promote active learning and encourage full student participation. Atton suggests that librarians work with both course instructors and other librarians to team-teach such sessions, integrating them into the curriculum as critical thinking skills must likewise be integrated.

Bodi, S. 1992. Collaborating with faculty in teaching critical thinking: The role of librarians at North Park College, IL. *Research Strategies* 10: 69–76.

Because faculty may believe librarians only focus on finding resources, librarians may be excluded from research-based courses. This article explains the importance of librarian-faculty collaboration and how the librarian role can be developed through creating course-integrated bibliographic instruction that promotes critical thinking. Bodi uses Ruggiero's "Five Stages to Teaching Critical Thinking" to illustrate where librarians should enter the student research picture. At stage three—investigation—librarians will be most helpful. Rather than at the beginning of a term, it is at this point where librarians should become involved and where they can be most effective. The author also gives a brief description of Kuhlthau's stages of the cognitive and affective aspects of student research. With Ruggiero and Kuhlthau in mind, librarians can adapt instruction accordingly. The author calls upon librarians to articulate their role in instructing students to be autonomous learners. Bodi cites Breivik, who said that librarians keep much of their expertise secret, and that many faculty members believe library instruction is removed from the rest of the curriculum. Although there may appear to be a disparity of focus, critical thinking can become a bridge to reaching complementary goals through effective collaboration. The article concludes with successful examples of collaboration for critical thinking at North Park College, a small liberal arts college, and it explains the opportunities and strategies used.

Bodi, S. 1988. Critical thinking and bibliographic instruction: The relationship. *Journal of Academic Librarianship* 14: 150–153.

Sonia Bodi discusses the lack of a general definition of critical thinking but describes at length what critical thinking is not. It is the author's contention that bibliographic instruction (BI) should be focused on critical thinking and evaluative skills in support of course content. The author argues that, as critical thinking is a commonly held goal of general education curricula, bibliographic instruction can be a teaching strategy incorporated into those curricula to encourage and reinforce critical thinking development. Through awareness of Perry's "Four Developmental States," instruction librarians can develop sessions that fully support critical thinking in the curriculum at the appropriate stage in student careers. The article concludes with a case study from an education course at a small, private liberal arts college that used class debate to begin a discussion on search strategies. This technique has taught students the complexity of most issues, that there are few easy answers, and that they must search widely to form a balanced view.

Cody, D. E. 2006. Critical thoughts on critical thinking. *Journal of Academic Librarianship* 32: 403–407.

Cody's article is a critical response to many others who have written about, and attempted to define, critical thinking over the past 25 years. The author argues that a review of the various views over this time period reflects a significant inability to articulate a definition of critical thinking. Thus, librarians should be instructing patrons on database control. The article uses examples from the work of Ennis, McPeck, Gibson, and Bodi, among others, to demonstrate the numerous obstacles critical thinking faces in terms of library instruction. The crux of the article's argument is that, since many librarians have only one shot at instruction, these sessions should emphasize the importance of controlling systems such as databases and catalogs. Cody suggests that this should be the new focus of instruction—controlling searches in a variety of platforms and interfaces. Attempting to tackle critical thinking in limited time is ineffectual, according to Cody. Cody believes that by controlling systems, users are employing critical thinking skills, consciously or not, and that a focus on control should replace critical thinking in the library instruction classrooms.

Dickstein, R. and K. B. McBride. 1998. Listserv lemmings and fly-brarians on the wall: A librarian-instructor team taming the cyberbeast in the large classroom. *College & Research Libraries* 59: 10–17.

This article chronicles the team-teaching experiences of a librarian and women's studies professor at the University of Arizona. While the article focuses mainly on how the two successfully used listservs to elicit participation and discussion among students in a large course filled with general-interest students, a significant by-product of this project was the greater critical evaluation of information sources achieved by the students via this medium. In this project, the authors required the students as part of a group to submit a "Listserv Research Report," detailing their research process for a given topic and evaluating the information they retrieved. By completing this report and reading the reports of other groups, students learned to think critically about the information sources they encountered in both print and newly emerging electronic formats.

Engeldinger, E. A. 1988. Bibliographic instruction and critical thinking: The contribution of the annotated bibliography. *RQ* 28: 195–202.

This article promotes the use of annotated bibliographies in teaching critical thinking skills. Instructors often assume that students are learning these skills on their own, but, like library research skills, teaching critical thinking skills often falls through the cracks. The author suggests that librarians can fill the void in both of these areas. Annotated bibliography assignments can allow students to become familiar with research resources, the literature of a discipline, and critical thinking skills all at once. To guide students through this process, the librarians at the University of Wisconsin-Eau Claire developed an annotated bibliography assignment, instruction curriculum, and a list of questions that would lead students step-by-step through evaluating an information source. To be successful, students need to employ both subject knowledge and critical thinking skills when evaluating information. Collaboration between the instructor, the subject expert, and the librarian, the critical thinking maven, is key in teaching these skills. With such collaboration, librarians at UW-Eau Claire have successfully used this approach to promote research skills and critical thinking in a variety of courses across the curriculum.

Gibson, C. 1989. Alternatives to the term paper: An aid to critical thinking. *Reference Librarian* 24: 297–309.

This article decries the time-honored term paper and calls on librarians to create and offer alternatives that encourage better use of library materials, stimulate interest, and facilitate growth in critical thinking. The author describes term papers as lacking a meaningful learning experience that fails to develop good research habits in undergraduates. Due to a variety of reasons, the term paper pervades and is tolerated. He goes on to explain that, though librarians are often overlooked, they see assignment problems as they occur, and librarians possess the training and experience to develop other types of activities. The author calls on librarians to be change agents, to become active developers of alternative assignments that facilitate critical thinking. Librarians are uniquely positioned to assist in revitalizing critical thinking in the general education curriculum.

The article argues that librarians already facilitate some critical thinking development through reference interviews. Gibson describes Ennis's "Illinois Critical Thinking Project" and identifies twelve abilities that apply to library instruction. Gibson and Ennis both stress that critical thinking development should move along a continuum and be developmental. The author concludes with several examples of alternatives to the term paper from Lewis-Clark State College. These examples focus on the critical use of sources in relation to contemporary issues where students must consider multiple perspectives and apply evaluative scrutiny.

Gibson, C. 1995. Critical thinking: Implications for instruction. *RQ* 35: 27–35.

In this article, Gibson makes the case for including critical thinking in library instruction. Through the review of three central controversies surrounding critical thinking and critical thinking theories, Gibson addresses the need for library involvement in critical thinking instruction. Citing several philosophers and psychologists, the author examines the commonly held controversies regarding critical thinking, including whether critical thinking is a part of rational, human thought or has a motivational or emotional dimension, and whether critical thinking is a general set of skills or needs to be taught within a subject context. Gibson concludes by providing something of an FAQ regarding critical thinking in terms of information skills. Questions addressed include: Does critical thinking equate only with evaluation of sources? Can critical thinking be taught in a one-shot bibliographic instruction session? And, how can a bibliographic instruction environment for critical thinking be created?

Herro, S. J. 2000. Bibliographic instruction and critical thinking. *Journal of Adolescent & Adult Literacy* 43: 554–558.

In this article, the author makes a strong case for the interconnection of information literacy and critical thinking. Citing not only how our definition of literacy has evolved but also how information has proliferated and changed, Herro argues that the critical evaluation of resources is an even more valuable part of the research process. The author feels that this argument is of particular importance due to several articles that had been recently published refuting the need for information literacy instruction over traditional bibliographic instruction sessions. With this argument thoroughly made, Herro focuses on profiling library instruction programs that have successfully integrated critical thinking skills with information literacy instruction. This article serves almost as a review of the literature, detailing articles that demonstrate the success of teaching critical thinking skills in library education courses and sessions.

Jacobs, M. 2001. Speakeasy Studio and Cafe: Information literacy, Web-based library instruction, and technology. *Information Technology and Libraries* 20: 66–71.

This article focuses on using online student discussion as a method to encourage critical thinking skills in students who are increasingly interacting with information in digital formats. Librarians at Washington State University have incorporated this technique in their one-credit course on the library research process. Using Speakeasy, a locally developed course management system, they are asking their students to hold online discussions on topics such as their research questions, choosing search terms and sources to search, and the validity of the information retrieved. These discussions foster critical thinking skills in these students, and the online environment provides unique opportunities that are lacking in the traditional classroom. For example, there is a record of these discussions preserved in the Speakeasy system which allows both students and instructors to reflect on how the students' understanding of library research and critical evaluation skills have evolved over the course of the semester. Additionally, the online discussion environment encourages participation by students who may not feel comfortable speaking up in the traditional classroom setting.

Julien, H. 2000. Information literacy instruction in Canadian academic libraries: Longitudinal trends and international comparisons. *College & Research Libraries* 61: 510–523.

This article details the results of a January 2000 survey of instructional practices, opinions, and objectives in Canadian academic libraries. Much of the data from this survey was compared to a similar survey conducted by the author in 1995. During this five-year period, the author notes that teaching critical evaluation of resources has become more prominent in library instruction programs in Canada. In fact, 94% of all survey respondents in 2000 indicated that teaching these skills was key to teaching information literacy, although 80% agreed that librarians are not solely responsible for imparting critical thinking skills. Additionally, many survey respondents indicated that technology had impacted the content of their instructional sessions, noting that the trend toward online sources meant that librarians take a lesser role in the selection of resources for students and a greater role in teaching students to evaluate and select resources for themselves.

Krest, M. and D. O. Carle. 1999. Teaching scientific writing—A model for integrating research, writing, & critical thinking. *American Biology Teacher* 61: 223–227.

Building upon previous works that teach research and writing skills in the sciences, these authors from the University of Colorado collaborated to develop a course introducing students to scientific writing. This course does not assume that students have prior experience with writing or research. Rather, it aims to equip the students with these skills, which they can then apply in more advanced courses. The authors created a matrix of assignments and learning outcomes in three areas: writing skills, research skills, and critical thinking skills. Critical thinking skills are developed by asking students to analyze article abstracts, write their own article abstracts, and write their own article reviews that included their own evaluations of the article's content complete with support from outside sources. These skills are reinforced through in-class discussions in small groups. The authors emphasize the importance of the collaboration between librarian and instructor in this project and the importance of integrating critical thinking skills into any instruction in writing and the research process.

McGuigan, G. S. 2002. Exorcising the ghost from the machine: Confronting obstacles to critical thinking through library instruction. *Internet Reference Services Quarterly* 7: 53–62.

This article identifies computer/technology illiteracy, hypertext as distraction, and information overload as obstacles to critical thinking in the electronic environment. The author offers several techniques for demonstrating these obstacles to users and eliminating them. The author contends that, if librarians can demystify these obstacles, users will have the ability to interact with information resources more critically and effectively. It is the author's belief that computer literacy is a requirement for critical thinking in the current information environment, and information literacy skills hinge upon critical thinking; therefore, information literacy assumes some basic skill in computer literacy. The issue of hypertext as distraction is also a major obstacle that leads many users to interruptions in the research process. Finally, the vast amount of information available has paradoxically decreased success in finding usable research for many users. The author calls for tool analysis as a new paradigm in bibliographic instruction.

Sonntag, G. and D. Ohr. 1996. The development of a lower division, general education, course-integrated information literacy program. *College and Research Libraries* 57: 331–38.

In the midst of higher education reform, this article discusses the oft-mentioned, yet rarely dealt with, topic of information literacy. The authors go on to describe the model used at California State University-San Marcos (CSU-SM), the process used to establish a successful information literacy plan, and observations. Responding to reports from the mid 1980s, asking higher education institutions to provide critical thinking and problem-solving skills to students, the librarians at CSU-SM found themselves in a position to contribute to changes in the campus's general education program. With a growing need for students to be critical consumers of information, the authors and their colleagues recognized the need for building partnerships with teaching faculty. The authors contend that the library should be a vital resource for students in making informed decisions. Using the library as a gateway, the library becomes a learning lab critical to teaching and learning on campus. This was the fundamental idea behind the Information Literacy Program (ILP), developed by librarians at CSU-SM, and based on the *ACRL Model Statement of Objectives for Academic Bibliographic Instruction*. The authors acknowledge that getting administrative support on campus is often a major obstacle for most libraries; however, a major asset to CSU-SM was provost support from the outset. A general education program task force advanced the ILP in a report given to the academic senate, where it was ultimately approved. Librarians received development funds to create workshops focusing on lower-division general education courses. In addition to the provost support, the ILP was a success because of the high profile of librarians on campus committees, the teaching faculty's acceptance of librarians as colleagues, and extraordinary library administrative support.

Whitmire, E. 1998. Development of critical thinking skills: An analysis of academic library experiences and other measures. *College & Research Libraries* 59: 266–273.

This article discusses the influences that affect the development of critical thinking skills in undergraduates. Using data from the 1992–1993 College Student Experiences Questionnaire (CSEQ), in addition to employing Astin's IEO model and Pace's quality of effort, the author sets out to determine what aspects of the college experience influence critical thinking; in particular, what role the library plays in this development. The author identifies library "probing activities" that appear to marginally affect critical thinking development. The author concludes that, in order for students to fully achieve critical thinking-related student-learning outcomes, faculty and librarians need to work together. In the author's analysis, more significant impacts can be made through students meeting with faculty more often and students being more active in class.

INTEGRATED CRITICAL THINKING AND INFORMATION LITERACY—ORGANIZED CAMPUS-WIDE EFFORTS

Many universities across the United States are implementing projects, pilots, and programs that incorporate information literacy and critical thinking into the college curriculum. As evidenced by the scholarly research over the last twenty years, the concepts of information literacy and critical thinking have increasingly become co-mingled, and, in many cases, interchangeable. This list includes those universities that have made great strides in developing campus-wide support and integration of critical thinking and information literacy. Though not all-inclusive, this list represents universities that have created engaging, sustainable, and strategic programs that emphasize critical thinking in the undergraduate experience.

California State University Information Competence Project

http://www.calstate.edu/ls/infocomp.shtml

The California State University (CSU) system has, in many ways, led the way for the integration of critical thinking and information literacy skills into the curriculum. Beginning in 1993, the CSU system has strategically addressed critical thinking and research skills on all of its campuses through active programming and grant-funded projects. For-credit research courses are offered on some campuses, while other campuses have integrated critical thinking and information competencies into existing courses. Additionally, the system as a whole has made great strides in advocating assignment redesigns. Currently, system universities are addressing a number of issues including assessment using Educational Testing System's Information, Communication, and Technology (ICT) Literacy Test, information competency and programming with first-year experience courses, and several discipline-focused integrations.

University of California-Berkeley

http://www.lib.berkeley.edu/mellon/index.html

The University of California-Berkeley has taken advantage of a Mellon Foundation grant in order to create faculty fellowships in support of undergraduate research. Berkeley has developed collaborative implementation teams with discipline faculty, created Mellon Library/Faculty Fellowships on undergraduate research, and established ongoing partnerships with academic support units. As a result of these collaborations and partnerships, fifty-six courses have been redesigned to include information competencies and research skills. Through the Mellon Foundation, Berkeley has made significant strides toward creating a campus environment that embraces and integrates critical thinking and information competency skills in the undergraduate curriculum.

University of Connecticut

http://geoc.uconn.edu/geocguidelines.htm

http://www.lib.uconn.edu

As part of new general education requirements implemented in 2005, the University of Connecticut (UConn) set information literacy as one of five competencies for undergraduates. To address the gap that exists developmentally between the required English courses and courses within a major, undergraduate services librarians have advocated the use of research portfolios on campus. Additionally, the university libraries have created interactive learning modules for use in many first-year experience and other composition courses. Beyond basic information literacy competency, departments will determine what information literacy competencies are required of its graduates and build those expectations into the upper-level research and writing requirements in the major. Departments are also required to develop exit expectations for their graduates and a programmatic plan for information literacy to be approved by the school or college. The information literacy competency program at UConn is based upon critical thinking as a concept, among others, to "enhance the intellectual power of those who learn the skills."

Five Colleges of Ohio

http://collaborations.denison.edu/ohio5/grant/

The Five Colleges of Ohio have also benefited from the Mellon Foundation. In 1999, the colleges were awarded a three-year grant to strengthen information literacy instruction in the curriculum. To do this, the colleges established faculty curriculum development grants. Applicants for the grants were encouraged to incorporate information literacy skills into their courses in substantive ways in order to foster critical thinking in the undergraduate. Additionally, travel grants were provided so that faculty and librarians could share their work at conferences and workshops. A wide variety of departmental faculty took advantage of the grant opportunities, and, consequently, several courses have been redesigned at all of the colleges. The liberal arts curriculum has been reshaped in many ways and reflects the institutions' dedication to promoting the critically thinking graduate.

Florida International University

http://www.fiu.edu/~library/ili/

An information literacy requirement for lower- and upper-division students at Florida International University (FIU) was approved by the faculty senate on November 10, 1998. This requirement is met through courses that have integrated information literacy components. Additionally, in collaboration with the Academy for the Art of Teaching, FIU Libraries commenced an information literacy initiative "to promote excellence in the teaching and learning of critical thinking and information literacy skills as a fundamental component of higher education." Through seminars, workshops, and individual consultation, this initiative set out to assist faculty with incorporating information literacy and critical thinking into their assignments and assessments. This effort continues with libraries as a part of the teaching and learning collaboration with the Academy.

Washington State University

http://www.wsulibs.wsu.edu/ile/

http://wsuctproject.wsu.edu/

With a renewed focus on improving the undergraduate experience, as well as new measures assessing those efforts, Washington State University (WSU) has dedicated itself to "Six Learning Goals of the Baccalaureate." First among these six goals is critical and creative thinking. Information literacy, also one of the six goals, is separate and distinct. In support of the critical and creating thinking goal, a collaboration between the writing programs, the general education program, and the center for teaching, learning, and technology was established to create the "Critical Thinking Project." Of particular interest, the project has generated data revealing actual critical thinking levels of undergraduates. This data has informed the critical and integrative thinking rubric. Criteria in this document relate to information literacy, as well as several other dimensions of critical thinking. The rubric has been widely used across the WSU campus. With information literacy being institutionalized in the undergraduate curriculum, the libraries have recently been awarded an internal grant for the "creation, maintenance, and promotion of the Information Literacy Education (ILE) project." The ILE project goal is to collaborate with departmental faculty to build information literacy skills into existing research papers and projects.

DISCUSSION

While information literacy instruction has been part of the academic library landscape since the 1980s, the role of critical thinking has become increasingly important in instruction. In the past twenty years, several themes have emerged in the literature regarding critical thinking in library instruction. First, librarians have had a difficult time defining exactly what critical thinking actually is (Cody 2006), along with grappling with how to include it in their instruction. Depending on their definitions of critical thinking, some librarians have concluded that it is not the role of an instruction librarian to teach critical thinking, or, at least, it is not as effective when a librarian assumes this role (Cody). However, other librarians take a slightly different view of critical thinking in information literacy instruction. They feel that critical thinking is not mutually exclusive to teaching information literacy to students, but they feel that teaching such skills is not the sole responsibility of librarians (Julien 2000). This idea highlights a second important theme to emerge from the growth of critical thinking in information literacy instruction, that of subject and curriculum integration.

Librarians writing on the subject of critical thinking in information literacy instruction most often are writing to describe successful instruction programs that integrate critical thinking skills into course curricula. Many note that collaboration with the instructor, the subject expert, is key to teaching these skills (Engeldinger 1988; Krest and Carle 1999; Whitmire 1998). This collaboration often goes farther than simply sharing teaching time between the librarian and instructor: librarians are working with instructors to develop alternative assignments for students that encourage the development of critical thinking skills (Bodi 1988; Gibson 1989; Dickstein and McBride 1998; Krest and Carle). Additionally, many collaborations reported in the literature focus on teaching critical thinking skills to undergraduate students, a third theme to emerge from this review of the literature.

The push for higher education reforms that took place in the early 1990s challenged universities to provide students with critical thinking skills as part of information literacy instruction programs. Many librarians responded to this challenge by examining their roles in undergraduate education and its unique demands (Sonntag and Ohr 1996). For example, undergraduate students first confronting the literature of their disciplines may encounter jargon and acronyms that might impede their ability to completely understand the information they are finding (Atton 1994). Librarians are addressing these needs with tools such as guided discussions, listservs, writing assignments, and online discussions via course management software (Atton; Dickstein and McBride; Krest and Carle, Jacobs 2001). Additionally, many universities, including the University of California-Berkeley, are creating extensive undergraduate research programs. The ability to respond to the needs of undergraduates in general, as well as to the specialized needs of undergraduate researchers, is the impetus behind the development of information literacy instruction programs in libraries—programs that address the essential critical thinking skills of their undergraduates. The instruction programs included in this review, as well as many others, are tackling these issues with advocacy for critical thinking and information literacy on the university level, research and development fellowships and grants, online instructional modules, and much more.

Finally, many librarians are discussing the impact of dynamic and rapidly changing technology. The development and adoption of new and ever-changing technologies has a profound effect on the teaching of critical thinking in information literacy instruction. While some librarians are experimenting with the use of new technologies in their information literacy instruction, others are confronting the impact that technology has had on their approach to teaching critical thinking skills. For example, a recent survey of Canadian academic librarians indicated that many librarians felt that technological changes were significantly impacting the content of their instructional sessions (Julien). Librarians responded to these impacts by emphasizing the importance of evaluating and selecting resources to undergraduates, which meant including critical thinking skills in their instruction sessions. Additionally, librarians are confronting the obstacles technological changes present to critical thinking in the electronic environment (McGuigan 2002). These technological changes require students to be computer and technology literate even before librarians can begin teaching critical thinking skills, and technology and its distractions cannot be allowed to impede the teaching of these skills.

Increasingly across university campuses, critical thinking is becoming a goal or focus within departments and programs. The questions that must be asked after this review is: what role will librarians play in teaching critical thinking skills in information literacy instruction? How will they measure the effectiveness of this instruction? This review of selected current instruction programs seems to indicate that they are working, just as they always have, to support the curriculum of the university—just in more integrated and online ways. Critical thinking assessment, assessment of learning outcomes, and overall program assessments need to be done in order to truly measure the success of library instruction programs. Without the information gained in such assessments, future librarians cannot effectively continue to respond to student needs, develop effective strategies for teaching critical thinking skills, or identify ways for information literacy to become a part of a general education plan.

Promoting Critical Thinking Skills in Online Information Literacy Instruction Using a Constructivist Approach

Maryellen Allen

INTRODUCTION

As academic libraries fully embrace the concept of information literacy and attempt to apply its concepts to library instruction programs, the emphasis upon critical thinking skills emerges at the forefront of these efforts. Combined with this trend, libraries are increasingly finding it necessary to take their traditional library instruction (or information literacy) efforts into the online environment in order to reach the ever-increasing numbers of students who are choosing to pursue their education via Web-based means. Munro observes in her discussion of pedagogical styles, ". . . as universities and other institutions evolve to give students more autonomy, flexibility, and seamless access to tools and resources, libraries must evolve too" (Munro 2006, 53). The question arises then of how library instructional materials can best be designed for online asynchronous or self-paced instruction while promoting the critical thinking skills that will allow students to become lifelong learners. We find ourselves now at the crossroads of information literacy, with trends toward exclusive online delivery of instructional materials and the need for effective instructional design methods that will deliver the skills necessary to promote lifelong learning. "Gaining skills in information literacy multiplies the opportunities for students' self-directed learning, as they become engaged in using a wide variety of information sources to expand their knowledge, ask informed questions, and sharpen their critical thinking for still further self-directed learning" (American Library Association 2006, 5).

We may look to instructional design theories to provide us with the guidance we need in order to produce effective online library instruction. In particular, constructivist approaches to online library instruction hold a great deal of promise for effective online learning. Manifestations of constructivist-based learning can be seen in problem-based learning, cooperative and collaborative learning, and discovery learning. Instructional materials designed using a constructivist approach may include case studies or scenarios, and very often they involve students working within groups, although this is not a requirement. Moreover, in a constructivist environment, the instructor assumes a more passive role as facilitator and guide rather than lecturer. Although not an advisable approach in every setting, constructivist learning environments can offer students the kinds of learning experiences that will foster the development of critical thinking skills, possibly leading to higher levels of overall achievement.

This article will provide a philosophical discussion regarding the logic of using a constructivist-based instructional design approach in online library instruction incorporating critical thinking skills within the framework of the Association of College and Research Libraries' (ACRL) information literacy standards. The author presents a firm argument advocating this instructional design model as an appropriate means of reaching online students while supporting the goal of creating successful lifelong learners who have the ability to apply critical thinking skills to real-world problems.

Information Literacy, Critical Thinking Skills, and Library Instruction

First, we must resolve some of the confusion that can arise when comparing the concepts of information literacy and critical thinking. While the distinction between what constitutes information literacy skills and those skills that describe critical thinking is somewhat ambiguous, the two terms are often used as synonyms. The Association of College and Research Libraries, citing the American Library Association's *Presidential Committee on Information Literacy*, defines information literacy as "... a set of abilities requiring individuals to 'recognize when information is needed and have the ability to locate, evaluate, and use effectively the needed information'" (American Library Association, 2). For the purposes of this discussion, we will define critical thinking as the intellectual and mental process by which an individual successfully conceptualizes, analyzes, synthesizes, evaluates, and/or applies information in order to formulate judgments, conclusions, or answers. It is apparent that both the definitions of information literacy and critical thinking skills share similar meanings. Scholars in the field of librarianship and education have noticed the apparent ambiguity and have sought to resolve it. After surveying the education and library-related literature, Albitz concludes that "... the education field has labeled a series of attributes as critical thinking, and librarianship has done the same with information literacy" (Albitz 2007, 98). Furthermore, she explains, "In the library literature, the phrase 'critical thinking' is often used but not clearly defined" (99). Albitz addresses this apparent ambiguity and attempts to distinguish one concept from the other. Citing Ennis' twelve elements of critical thinking, Albitz notes, "Certainly, some of these points are similar to elements of information literacy, and accomplishing some would depend on information literacy skills. For example, in order to make many of the judgments articulated above, the critical thinker would need the skills to locate and evaluate the appropriate information. Not all, however, would require a student to be able to capture and synthesize outside information gathered through research—thus, we see a difference between the two concepts" (100). Albitz contends that, while critical thinking skills are always an essential component of information literacy (i.e., research), information literacy is not always a component of critical thinking skills. Keeping with this same reasoning, Ward writes: "Critical thinking is not always sufficient in itself as a strategy for navigating through the information universe. Being information literate requires more than the ability to work analytically with information. It also demands that we know how to manage information in more creative and meaningful ways" (Ward, 2006/7, 396). Citing Breivik, Albitz sums up the discussion nicely, asserting "Information literacy is a kind of critical thinking ability: often the terms are used interchangeably. But a person who is information literate specifically uses critical thinking to negotiate our information-overloaded existence" (101). Nonetheless, most scholars in the field of librarianship agree that critical thinking skills are a necessary part of any library instruction program.

The emphasis upon teaching critical thinking skills in library instruction is not a new concept. In 1983, McCormick and Lubans made reference to the teaching of critical thinking skills as a part of a traditional bibliographic instruction program so that students would be able to make "informed decisions, to evaluate applications of knowledge, to find truth" (339). Later in 1988, Bodi emphasizes the importance of teaching critical thinking techniques in bibliographic instruction sessions. Citing the overall primary goal of the American education system to develop independent and competent adults who have the ability to make informed decisions, Bodi asserts that bibliographic instruction programs have an obligation to contribute to the development of critical thinking skills in students. "Critical thinking in higher education can be encouraged and reinforced by certain kinds of course structures and assignments that require the use of library resources. It is commonly agreed that the primary goal of an academic library is to support the curriculum of the institution. Contributing to this goal is bibliographic instruction (BI)—which helps students find information, encourages flexibility of thought as they discover conflicting points of view, and acquaints them with ways of evaluating the expertise and bias of an author" (150).

Nevertheless, there have been a few critics of the trend to incorporate critical thinking skills into library instruction programs. Gibson reports on the reluctance of many librarians to engage in teaching critical thinking skills: "In one sense, ideas about critical thinking seem too global, too removed from the specific skill clusters that most librarians would associate with learning to use the library. Some think only of a mechanistic, tool-based approach to library skills and will consider critical thinking outside the scope of their responsibilities" (1995, 13). He goes on to cite LaGuardia's 1992 article in which she strongly criticizes the practice of teaching students abstract concepts concerning information retrieval. In LaGuardia's experience, the vast majority of college undergraduates needed to learn the very basics of using the library, citing their lack of familiarity with the physical layout of the library and its organizational systems. LaGuardia advocates a "back-to-basics" approach instead. ". . . most bibliographic instruction (BI) literature is aimed at instructing only a small percentage of our constituency—those relative few who need to learn conceptual frameworks to deal with esoteric information concepts" (53). LaGuardia's argument has merit, especially during a time when most students were still locating much of the information they needed in print-based formats. In fact, this problem has not gone away and will likely continue to persist. There are still many print-based sources and many students, whether directed by instructors or not, still go looking for books and articles in print. And yet, with the proliferation of online resources supplementing or sometimes replacing what the library offers in its physical collections, teaching critical thinking skills is perhaps more important than ever. In 1998, Whitmire observes, "The combination of a new generation of computer-literate undergraduates and the vast amount of information available by way of computers and electronic resources has increased the necessity for the development of critical thinking skills" (266). Indeed, as Internet use among students has grown steadily since the 1990s, development of critical thinking skills in research and library instruction has become a topic of primary importance. Quoting a study by Grimes and Boening, Wills reports that the investigators "discovered that most students are satisfied with their abilities to judge Web-based information, although they evaluate on a superficial level, if at all. The students in their study assumed that any resources which fit their topic were appropriate to use" (2002, 11). Here lies the strongest argument for incorporating critical thinking skills into a library instruction program. What's more, since so many students use the library's online databases and/or the library's portal as their primary point of departure when conducting research, it makes even more sense to bring that instruction online as well, perhaps housing it side-by-side with the online resources.

In 1999/2000, the Association of College and Research Libraries published their *Information Literacy Competency Standards for Higher Education (The Standards)* to serve as a guide for library instruction programs. One of the primary goals of implementing *The Standards* was to involve librarians in promoting the types of skills that would enable students to become lifelong learners. "Developing lifelong learners is central to the mission of higher education institutions. By ensuring that individuals have the intellectual abilities of reasoning and critical thinking, and by helping them construct a framework for learning how to learn, colleges and universities provide the foundation for continued growth throughout their careers, as well as in their roles as informed citizens and members of communities" (American Library Association, 4).

Although much more developed and rounded out, the components of critical thinking are quite evident. If one examines the definition of information literacy as outlined in *The Standards* and compares the list of abilities attributed to the information-literate individual to those factors defining critical thinking skills, a close relationship can be seen. *The Standards* themselves, however, suggest that the information-literate individual comes to possess a measure of critical thinking skills resulting from the individual's exposure to a curriculum emphasizing information literacy. In her article chronicling the assessment of the level of information literacy among undergraduates, Maughan makes a distinction between individual tasks to be addressed as a part of library instruction versus the whole concept of "information literacy," observing, "In contrast, information literacy is a far more comprehensive concept, encompassing abilities such as critical thinking, synthesis, communication, and research methodologies" (2001, 74). However, one could argue that critical thinking skills and the competencies are correlative and that it would not be possible to achieve any one of the competencies without engaging in critical thinking for each. For example, one might argue that Standard 1 of the ACRL standards, "Determine the extent of the information needed," (American Library Association, 2) would necessitate having the already-existing ability to analyze and conceptualize, with the act of "determining" being part and parcel of analysis and conceptualization. Figure 1 attempts to link the information literacy competencies with the associated critical thinking skill(s).

Thus, it is evident that critical thinking skills are not just an outcome of a curriculum centered on the competencies and standards, but also an ever-present, essential component of *The Standards*. Any library instruction

FIGURE 1. Side- y-Side Comparison of the Dening Characteristics of Information iteracy vs. Critical Thinking Skills

Information Literacy Defined by ACRL	Defining Features of Critical Thinking Skills
Determine the extent of information needed	Conceptualizes/analyzes information
Access the needed information effectively and efficiently	Synthesizes
Evaluate information and its sources critically	Analyzes/evaluates
Incorporate selected information into one's knowledge base Use information effectively to accomplish a specific purpose	Applies
Understand the economic, legal, and social issues surrounding the use of information, and access and use information ethically and legally	Formulates judgments/conclusions/answers

program that seeks to impart the information literacy competencies outlined in *The Standards* must also effectively convey those critical thinking skills that enable learner acquisition of this new knowledge.

Library Instruction Online

The effort to incorporate critical thinking and information literacy skills into a library instruction program can be complicated by the need to take the instruction program to an online environment. Colleges and universities continue to offer online courses in ever-increasing numbers. In a report from the National Center for Education Statistics from 1999, it was determined that in 1997–1998 "about one-third of the nation's two-year and four-year postsecondary education institutions offered any distance education courses during the 12-month 1997–98 academic year . . ." (National Center for Education Statistics 1999, iii). Several years later, the same body issued another report for 2000–2001 and found "56 percent (2,320) of all two-year and four-year Title IV-eligible, degree-granting institutions offered distance education courses for any level or audience (i.e., courses designed for all types of students, including elementary and secondary, college, adult education, continuing and professional education, etc.)" (National Center for Education Statistics 2003). At present, with enrollment in distance education programs continuing to be in high demand, there seems to be no reason to assume that the trend will continue in any other direction except up. The question remains of how to best design library instruction so that critical thinking skills and their resulting information literacy competencies can be effectively delivered in a Web-based setting that incorporates self-paced or asynchronous learning.

In response to the mass migration in higher education to Web-based, online, or distance learning, libraries are (and have been for some time) following suit to meet students at their point of need for library instruction. Yi cites the demand from both non-traditional students who see online educations as their only means of furthering their education along with more traditional students who are increasingly mandating, through the courses for which they choose to register, that instructional materials be placed online where they can access them at any time and place (2005, 48). Most libraries offer a certain degree of online instruction via Web-based tutorials, subject guides, or help pages while some are incorporating subject-specific and even entire information literacy modules into course management systems (CMS). Many academic libraries are taking their traditional BI activities, and even credit-earning library research courses, to the Web. Outlining a rationale for moving library instruction to the online environment, Hoffman writes, "Of course, there were expected benefits in migrating Library 110 to an electronic environment. Among them: ... accommodation of different students' learning styles; . . . increased interactivity . . ." (2002, 200). Hoffman goes on to quote Tobin and Kesselman who "astutely observe, it needs to include an interactive component wherein the '. . . user inputs to the system and the system provides feedback that either reinforces the user or provides guidance for learning"' (2000, 67–75). Viggiano and Ault describe their efforts using chat software to provide information literacy instruction to distance learners in Florida through the Reference and Referral Center (RRC), a state funded project of the Florida Distance Learning Library Initiative (DLLI). They pose the question, "If librarians are responsible for the information literacy training of distance learners, how will they reach this geographically diverse community?" (2001, 135). Their answer was simply to reach out to distance students using the technologies that were at their disposal. "The RRC has conducted over 14 chat instruction sessions for 130 distance learners from several of Florida's universities" (137). The instruction sessions that the RRC held online were similar in structure to the one-shot bibliographic instruction sessions that are often held face-to-face and were deemed fairly successful. If nothing else, libraries should be applauded for making the transition to online instruction quite early in the overall migration of education to Web-based environments. Indeed, libraries were one of the first pioneers in delivering information through electronic means, and, more often than not, electronic "help pages" accompanied many of those early electronic interfaces that were delivered via dumb terminals from mainframes. Thus, for libraries and librarians, online delivery of instruction is nothing new. What is novel, however, is the reliance upon electronic means to deliver the entire educational experience, referring, of course, to the explosion in demand for distance or online learning programs.

As demand has grown for this kind of education, many academic libraries have employed librarians devoted solely to needs of distance or online learners. These librarians are often charged with the task of developing online instructional materials aimed specifically at these audiences. Some have been tasked with the development of a complete online instructional environment for the delivery of library instruction.

The advantages to porting entire instructional programs into online environments are many. A student can work at his or her own pace and access the instruction at a time that is most convenient. The ability to include multi-media and hyperlink text can make the instruction accessible to a wide variety of learning styles. However, the most effective instructional design model for effectively reaching online students and providing the most complete educational experience is an often debated issue. Most often, librarians opt for a static method of information delivery where the learner is asked to read about the key points of information literacy: search methodologies, information retrieval, information evaluation, etc. He/she may then be asked to demonstrate knowledge acquisition by completing an online quiz or activity. Yet, many would argue that this instructional model is not effective in creating long-term skills in online learners. Rather, many librarians engaging in instructional design for Web-based audiences advocate other methods such as problem-based learning, discovery learning, or learner-centered models, all under the umbrella of constructivism and constructivist approaches to instructional design.

Constructivism Defined

The Swiss philosopher and psychologist Piaget is widely known as the father of constructivist theory. Piaget developed his theory as a result of his disagreement with both the empiricist and nativist schools of thought. While empiricists hold the belief that knowledge results from the accumulation of experiences, the nativists contend that children are born "with an innate set of ideas that form the basis for knowledge" (Driscoll 2000, 187). Piaget believed that the acquisition of knowledge lay somewhere in the middle and labeled his theory constructivism, ". . . because he firmly believed that knowledge acquisition is a process of continuous self-construction. That is, knowledge is not out there, external to the child and waiting to be discovered. But neither is it wholly preformed within the child, ready to emerge as the child develops" (188). It was Piaget who had a strong influence upon other psychologists and educational theorists who expanded upon his theories. Most notably, Bruner and Vygotsky concentrate on the importance of the individual's interaction with the environment to resolve the conflict between what is believed and what is observed as the path to knowledge acquisition. Other educational psychologists took these theories of cognitive development and applied them to models of instructional design.

Constructivist approaches to instruction combine some theories of cognitive psychology with ideas of behavior modification to produce a theory proposing that learners build knowledge and skills upon their already-existing constructs of the world based upon individual experience. Constructivist theory contends that the learner brings to the learning environment knowledge from past experience, and that knowledge has a strong influence upon how the learner constructs meaning and acquires new knowledge from new experiences. Additionally, advocates of constructivist approaches believe that the process of knowledge acquisition and creation, in order to become stored in long-term memory, must be active rather than passive, and must also be applicable to the learner's everyday world and experiences. Within constructivist learning approaches, there are several subsets of pedagogical techniques, including inquiry-based learning, discovery learning, and problem-based learning. All of these rely firmly upon the learner taking an active role in the learning process while the instructor serves as more of a facilitator or guide.

Unfortunately, many instructors believe that simply providing hands-on experiences for learners, such as recreating a database search after watching the instructor do a similar activity, qualifies as active learning. As Cooperstein and Kocevar-Weidinger observe, ". . . these theorists meant much more by active learning than providing hands-on activity, encouraging class participation, or having students move around the room. Active learning as prescribed by these theorists, and more appropriately called constructivist or discovery learning, moves from experience to learning and not the other way around. Constructivist learning is inductive. Constructivist learning dictates that the concept follow the action rather than precede it. The activity leads to the concepts; the concepts to do not lead to the activity" (2004, 141). Rather, in order to provide a true constructivist-based learning environment, instructors and instructional designers must plan carefully from the beginning of the instruction to the end. "At the core of inquiry-based learning is the idea that complex problems may be vehicles for learning. Complex problems compel students to think about the many issues and alternatives inherent in the problems. This technique leads them to recognize that there may be multiple solutions. Inquiry-based learning challenges students with complex situations that have multiple solutions. Each student participating in the exercise may arrive at a different answer and in a different way" (Thompson et al. 2003, 187).

Thompson's reference to the complex problem is one of the core principles of constructivist learning and may also be referred to as an "ill-structured" problem. This type of problem, conceived of by the instructor or designer, may be a case study, scenario, or ultimate desired goal statement that provides the learner with important component information, but offers no direction and no obvious solutions to the stated problem. The use of the ill-structured problem is typically used in instructional settings where the learner already possesses a great deal of prior knowledge. Thus, the learner must use his or her previous skills and apply them to the proposed situation to formulate a plausible solution.

Critical Thinking Skills, Online Instruction, and a Constructivist Approach

Critical thinking skills are a necessary component of constructivist instruction designed using an inquiry-based, problem-based, or discovery learning approach. Due to the ill-structured nature of constructivist-based learning activities, the learner must continually question the information that is presented. Then, upon reaching conclusions or making decisions, the student is forced to reevaluate his or her conceptual pathways that led to these conclusions or decisions. He or she must then compare what they believe to be true versus what is actually observed. If they are in conflict, the learner is forced to rethink the problem. "To develop critical thinking in students, course work must encourage discussion, questioning, evaluation, and reflection" (Thompson et. al., 190, quoting Myers *Teaching Students to Think Critically* 1986). Cooperstein and Kocevar-Weidinger describe library instruction sessions employing online resources where students are asked to locate scholarly articles on very specific topics. The students are not instructed to search in particular databases, nor are they prohibited from using the World Wide Web. However, in the planning stages for the instruction, the designers have taken great pains to insure that the solution cannot be found using a general Web-based search engine such as Google. Once the students become frustrated at not finding the answer on the Internet, the instructors then step in as guides to steer the students to the correct resources. Once the students discover the online databases, the authors report, "Students are usually amazed at how much more quickly and easily they can get exactly what they need" (Cooperstein and Kocevar-Weidinger, 147). Cooperstein and Kocevar-Weidinger admit that they have used a modified constructivist-based approach in their face-to-face sessions rather than a true unbounded constructivist learning module in order to accomplish their learning goals in an allotted time period, as well as to assist those students who may be lacking the necessary skills that would allow them to engage in the instructional session.

For effective online library instruction (and, indeed, library instruction in any venue), a concentration upon the transference of critical thinking skills to the learner necessitates a modified constructivist-based approach—point that has not been lost on the authors of *The Standards*. A further analysis of ACRL's standards document will reveal this intent.

The Constructivist Nature of the Standards

Let's revisit ACRL's statement contained within *The Standards*. It reads, "Developing lifelong learners is central to the mission of higher education institutions. By ensuring that individuals have the intellectual abilities of reasoning and critical thinking, and by helping them construct a framework for learning how to learn, colleges and universities provide the foundation for continued growth throughout their careers, as well as in their roles as informed citizens and members of communities" (American Library Association, 4). Most importantly, notice the phrase ". . . construct a framework for learning how to learn. . . ." This sentiment represents the very essence of constructivism and demonstrates ACRL's advocacy of a constructivist-based approach. By stating that the ultimate goal of higher education is to produce lifelong learners, and that providing a "framework for learning how to learn" is the proper methodology through which institutions can achieve this goal, we can conclude that online library instruction programs may be best designed using a constructivist model.

However, creating true constructivist-based instructional materials and online learning environments can be difficult, time-consuming, and not warranted in every situation. In environments where students are so inexperienced that they have very little prior knowledge to build upon, a constructivist-based approach would likely overwhelm them. It may, in such cases, be more advisable to provide a more straightforward, objectivist approach like the one advocated by LaGuardia. Furthermore, some learners simply do not thrive in a constructivist environment. As Bostock observes, "Some students will enjoy the challenges of constructivist learning while others will sometimes find them uncomfortable and need more objectivist instruction. A radically constructivist course would be more difficult to implement within the constraints of large numbers, resources and institutional culture, so it is cheering to think that a partial implementation of constructivist principles may actually be optimal for the majority of students" (1998, 236). Finally, designing a series of instructional modules that utilize constructivist-based approaches can take more time and manpower than many libraries can afford. As Cooperstein and Kocevar-Weidinger observe, "Designing suitable activities requires careful planning and greatly increases preparation time. Finding perfect examples and problems that will lead students to an appropriate "Aha!" experience is difficult and requires a great deal of intense, time-consuming work" (145). However, as these authors go on to comment, for those who decide to redesign their library's instruction program using constructivist techniques, "Although difficult and time consuming, constructivist learning has many benefits. In a modified constructivist approach, carefully planned, structured, directed activities lead students to discover concepts and develop skills. Abstract concepts become meaningful, transferable, and retained because they are attached to performance of an activity" (145).

The "structure" to which Cooperstein and Kocevar-Weidinger refer is not in conflict with the idea of the overall ill-structured problem cited earlier as a pillar of constructivist-based instruction. Rather, these authors are making reference to the extreme care that must go into planning the sort of ill-structured problem that will result in the types of learning outcomes desired by the instructor. Indeed, the problem as presented to the learner is ill structured, as it provides little in the way of direction. However, from the instructional designer's point of view, the problem must actually be very well structured to insure that the learner cannot stray too far afield of the learning goals while attempting to achieve the desired learning outcomes.

DISCUSSION

Although there has been much discussion in the professional literature regarding the pros and cons of constructivist-based pedagogies, most would agree that a well-planned program centered around a constructivist framework is effective for the transference of critical thinking and information literacy skills in online learning environments. Furthermore, the ACRL standards, to which many academic libraries strive to adhere, appear to support a constructivist-based approach to fulfill the goal of creating lifelong learners who possess the ability to conceptualize, analyze, synthesize, evaluate, and ultimately apply information to everyday problems. On the other hand, many librarians responsible for designing online library instructional materials would contend that adhering strictly to a constructivist-based approach is time-consuming, difficult, and perhaps unwarranted, given the brevity of many library instructional sessions. Additionally, some scholars in the field of librarianship have commented that many students lack the necessary basic skills needed to serve as a proper foundation upon which constructivist-based instruction must be built.

The solution may be found in a mixed approach to online library instruction. In an asynchronous online environment, it is easier to address the array of learner needs from those who require very basic skills to those advanced learners who are more sophisticated. For the former, basic online tutorials that address foundation skills such as using online catalogs versus databases, navigating a library's Website, evaluating online information, or the mechanics of searching online, are fairly simple to construct using static Web pages or Screenshot software packages such as Macromedia's Captivate or Techsmith's Camtasia. For librarians who do not have access to these resources, or for those who do not have the time needed to create tutorials from scratch, it is often possible to find other institutions that have already created the kind of basic online instructional modules that are required. Most institutions are happy to share these resources with other librarians who may wish to link to the tutorial or modify the code for their individual needs. However, it is very important to seek permission from the originating institution prior to linking to or downloading these instructional materials.

Creating constructivist-based online library instruction that emphasizes critical thinking skills for the more advanced learner will require a more concentrated approach, and it is less likely that other institutions will already have created the exact type of instruction that will fit your needs. For librarians who are considering the development of online library instructional programs, it is advisable to consult the literature, including articles, Web pages, and books within the areas of online instructional design, constructivist theory, and teaching critical thinking skills. A list of additional suggested readings may be found at the end of this article.

Ultimately, those who choose to create an online library instruction program using a modified constructivist framework to address the transference of information literacy and critical thinking skills to online learners will no doubt find the process of designing, delivering, and providing feedback a rewarding one for both instructor and student.

FOR FURTHER READING

Agostinho, S., J. Meek, and J. Herrington. 2005. Design methodology for the implementation and evaluation of a scenario-based online learning environment.*Journal of Interactive Learning Research* 16:229–242.

Asselin, M. 2005. Teaching information skills in the information age: An examination of trends in the middle grades.*School Libraries Worldwide* 11:17–36.

Bangert, A. W. 2004. The seven principles of good practice: A framework for evaluating on-line teaching.*Internet & Higher Education* 7:217–232.

Brooks, J. G. and M. G. Brooks. 1993. *In search of understanding: The case for constructivist classrooms*. Alexandria, VA: Association for Supervision and Curriculum Development.

Bruner, J. S. 1966. *Toward a theory of instruction*. Cambridge, MA: Belknap Press of Harvard University.

Curtis, D. 2002. *Attracting, educating, and serving remote users through the web: A how-to-do-it manual for librarians*. New York: Neal-Schuman Publishers.

Dupuis, E. A. 2003. *Developing web-based instruction: Planning, designing, managing, and evaluating for results*. New York: Neal-Schuman Publishers.

Ennis, R. H. 1996. *Critical thinking*. Upper Saddle River, NJ: Prentice Hall.

Flavell, J. H. 1963. *The developmental psychology of Jean Piaget*. Princeton, NJ: Van Nostrand.

Fosnot, C. T. 1996. *Constructivism: Theory, perspectives, and practice*. New York: Teachers College Press.

Gradowski, G., L. Snavely, and P. Dempsey. 1998. Association of College and Research Libraries, Instruction Section, and Teaching Methods Committee. *Designs for active learning: A sourcebook of classroom strategies for information education*. Chicago: The Association.

Grassian, E. S. and J. R. Kaplowitz. 2001. *Information literacy instruction: Theory and practice*. New York: Neal-Schuman.

Hung, D., S. Tan, and T. Koh. 2006. From traditional to constructivist epistemologies: A proposed theoretical framework based on activity theory for learning communities. *Journal of Interactive Learning Research* 17:37–55.

Leonard, D. C. 2002. *Learning theories, A to Z*. Westport, CT: Oryx Press.

Loertscher, D. 2006. Constructivist learning design: Key questions to teaching to standards. *Teacher Librarian* 33:43–44.

Nilsen, H. and S. Purao. 2005. Balancing objectivist and constructivist pedagogies for teaching emerging technologies: Evidence from a Scandinavian case study. *Journal of Information Systems Education* 16:281–292.

Phillips, D. C. and National Society for the Study of Education. 2000. *Constructivism in education: Opinions and second opinions on controversial issues*. Chicago: National Society for the Study of Education: Distributed by the University of Chicago Press.

Phye, G. D. 1997. *Handbook of academic learning: Construction of knowledge*. San Diego: Academic Press.

Rovai, A. P. 2004. A constructivist approach to online college learning. *Internet & Higher Education* 7:79–93.

Smith, L. and J. T. Dockrell. 1997. *Piaget, Vvygotsky and beyond: Future issues for developmental psychology and education*. London/New York: Routledge.

Taija, S., K. Tuominen, and R. Savolainen. 2005. "Isms" in information science: Constructivism, collectivism, and constructionism. *Journal of Documentation* 61:79–101.

Whitmore, M. P. and S. B. Archer. 1996. *Empowering students: Hands-on library instruction activities*. Lancaster, PA: Library Instruction Publications.

Woo, Y. and Reeves, T. C. 2007. Meaningful interaction in web-based learning: A social constructivist interpretation. *Internet and Higher Education* 10:15–25.

REFERENCES

Albitz, R. S. 2007. The what and who of information literacy and critical thinking in higher education. *Portal: Libraries and the Academy* 7:97.

American Library Association. 2006. *Information literacy competency standards for higher education.* http://www.ala.org/acrl/ilcomstan.html.

Bodi, S. 1988. Critical thinking and bibliographic instruction: The relationship. *Journal of Academic Librarianship* 14:150–153.

Bostock, S. J. 1998. Constructivism in mass higher education: A case study. *British Journal of Educational Technology* 29:225–240.

Bruner, J. S. (1966). *Toward a theory of instruction.* Cambridge, MA: Belknap Press of Harvard University.

Cooperstein, S. E. and E. Kocevar-Weidinger. 2004. Beyond active learning: A constructivist approach to learning. *Reference Services Review* 32:141–148.

Driscoll, M. P. 2000. *Psychology of learning for instruction,* 2nd edition, Boston: Allyn and Bacon.

Gibson, C. 1995. Critical thinking: Implications for instruction (library literacy) (column). *RQ* 35:27–35.

Hoffman, P. S. 2002. The development and evolution of a university-based online library instruction course. *Reference Services Review* 30:198–211.

LaGuardia, C. 1992. Renegade library instruction. *Library Journal,* October 1:51–53.

Maughan, P. D. 2001. Assessing information literacy among undergraduates: A discussion of the literature and the University of California-Berkeley assessment experience. *College & Research Libraries* 62:71–85.

McCormick, M. and J. Lubans. 1983. Library literacy (critical thinking and library bibliographic instruction). *RQ* 22:339–343.

Munro, K. 2006. Modified problem-based library instruction: A simple, reusable instruction design. *College & Undergraduate Libraries* 13:53–61.

National Center for Education Statistics. 1999. *Distance education at postsecondary education insitutions: 1997–98* (Statistical Analysis Report No. NCES 2000-013). Washington DC: U.S. Department of Education Office of Educational Research and Improvement.

National Center for Education Statistics. 2003. *Distance education at degree-granting postsecondary institutions: 2000–2001* (No. NCES 2003-017). Washington DC: U.S. Department of Education Institute of Education Sciences.

Thompson, S. D., L. Martin, L. Richards, and D. Branson. 2003. Assessing critical thinking and problem solving using Web-based curriculum for students. *Internet and Higher Education* 6:185–191.

Tobin, T. and M. Kesselman. 2000. Evaluation of Web-based library instruction programs. *INSPEL* 34:67–75.

Viggiano, R. and M. Ault. 2001. Online library instruction for online students. *Information Technology and Libraries* 20:135–138.

Vygotskii, L. S. and Kozulin, A. (1986). *Thought and language* (Translation newly rev. and edited/by Alex Korzulin ed.). Cambridge, MA: MIT Press.

Ward, D. 2006/7. Revisioning information literacy for lifelong meaning. *The Journal of Academic Librarianship* 32:396–402.

Whitmire, E. 1998. Development of critical thinking skills: An analysis of academic library experiences and other measures. *College & Research Libraries* 59:266.

Wills, D. 2002. Critical thinking and instruction: Exploiting the possibilities of the internet. *PNLA Quarterly* 67:11–13.

Yi, H. 2005. Library instruction goes online: An inevitable trend. *Library Review* 54:47–58.

Finding a Socratic Method for Information Literacy Instruction

Nicholas Schiller

INTRODUCTION

Do you suppose that he would have attempted to look for, or learn, what he thought he knew, though he did not, before he was thrown into perplexity, became aware of his ignorance, and felt a desire to know?—Meno 84d

Instruction librarians have many tools at their disposal for teaching information literacy. Still, they continually look for innovative ways to increase the quality of instruction, engage students, and facilitate student learning. There are situations where looking backward can reap just as many benefits. If librarians look back to Athens in the years preceding 399 BCE to Plato's Socrates, they will find a pedagogy that can inform their current practice in information literacy instruction. The method Socrates employed to seek truth, stimulate the intellectually lazy, and help his students use critical reasoning to uncover flaws in their knowledge can be a valuable skill in the instruction librarian's repertoire. When appropriately applied and supported by other pedagogical techniques, teaching with the Socratic Method can increase the effectiveness of existing instruction programs by guiding students to critically examine their existing information skills and practices, by providing active learning techniques, and by critically engaging them in thinking about information issues.

THE SOCRATIC METHOD

The label Socratic Method has been applied to a wide range of pedagogical techniques. The Oxford Companion to Philosophy gives a general definition of the Socratic Method as: "Any philosophical or pedagogical method that disinterestedly pursues truth through analytical discussion." Discussion is key, but the kind of discussion used is central to understanding what makes a discussion particularly Socratic in nature. More narrowly defined, the Socratic Method involves an instructor using questions to prod students into critically examining their opinions. This technique of guided questioning and answers is often referred to as *dialectic*, a Greek term that means discourse, or *elenchus*, which can be roughly translated as refutation. However, not every pedagogy that uses questions or cross-examination can be called Socratic. Phillips, who is attempting to recreate Socrates' style of popular philosophy, explains in *Socrates Cafe* that "it is a type that reveals people to themselves, that makes them see what their opinions really amount to" (Phillips 2001, 20). Another useful definition of Socrates' method can be found in Copleston's *History of Philosophy*.

> . . . Socrates would lead the conversation in that direction, and when the other man had used the word 'courage,' Socrates would ask him what courage is, professing his own ignorance and desire to learn. His companion had used the word, therefore he must know what it meant. When some definition or description had been given him, Socrates would express great satisfaction, but would intimate that there were one or two little difficulties which he would like to see cleared up. Accordingly he asked questions, letting the other man do

> most of the talking, but keeping the course of the conversation under his control, and so would expose the inadequacy of the proposed definition of courage. The other would fall back on a fresh or modified definition, and so the process would go on, with or without final success. (Copleston 1985, 106)

This kind of Socratic instruction includes certain key elements: it begins with students expressing an opinion or factual claim. The instructor asks probing questions, guiding the student to critical reflection of their stated opinion. As they answer the questions, the students identify and reject bad reasoning and false claims to knowledge. If successful, students end up with a clearer understanding of the topic. They will have shed themselves of incorrect or mistaken ideas and thus will be ready to seek out better ideas to replace them.

Instruction using this Socratic Method differs from expository or lecture-style instruction in three key ways. First, the Socratic Method does not involve the instructor bringing a body of expert knowledge to impart to students. In *Theaetus,* Socrates compares the instructor's role to that of a midwife (Plato and Cairns 1961, 150a–d), i.e., the instructor helps the student through the process, but it is the student who gives birth to knowledge. Second, the learning that takes place under the Socratic Method involves the shedding of false knowledge, rather than adding correct knowledge. Third, there are no pre-existing "correct" answers to Socratic questions.

The instructor using the Socratic Method focuses on the students' existing knowledge. The questions serve to help students refine their existing knowledge and rid themselves of poorly conceived opinions. The questions asked clear the ground and set a solid foundation for building future knowledge. Unlike other models of instruction, the instructor's role is not to add any new knowledge during the class. Socrates did not claim to have any knowledge to give to his students, but by using dialectic to help them examine their ideas he did them a great service. As he said in the *Meno*: "Now notice what, starting from this state of perplexity, he will discover by seeking the truth in company with me, though I simply ask him questions without teaching him" (Plato and Cairns, 84c–d). This is the role the instructor has under the Socratic Method: helping students realize what they don't know and preparing them to discover answers to their questions.

The learning that takes place under the Socratic Method is often destructive rather than constructive. Students will realize that there is much that they do not know and that much of what they thought they knew was incorrect. The value of ridding students of their false claims to knowledge is at least as valuable to the learning process as providing them with new knowledge. In many cases, new knowledge cannot be properly assimilated until existing false conceptions are removed. By guiding the students to critically evaluate their existing understanding on a given topic, the Socratic Method can help students identify problems and contradictions in their views. When students discover for themselves the flaws in their opinions, they will be motivated to correct them, more so than if the flaws had not been pointed out and their confidence left unshaken.

When questioned by an instructor, a student provides an answer that traditionally has been assessed by how closely it corresponds to the instructor's expert knowledge. The point is to give the "correct" answer. When using the Socratic Method, answers to questions are assessed by the level to which they critically reflect on their claims to knowledge. Under this system, for students to discover that their answers are "wrong" is an achievement and a success! The goal of Socratic instruction is to stimulate critical thinking and self-awareness, not to enforce the authority of a particular "correct" answer or set of answers. The *Encyclopedia of Philosophy* describes this as follows.

> For Socrates, knowledge was not acceptance of secondhand opinions which could be handed over for a sum of money like a phonograph record (or encyclopedia) but a personal achievement gained through continual self-criticism. Philosophy involved not learning the answers but searching for them—a search more hopeful if jointly undertaken by two friends, one perhaps more experienced than the other, but both in love with the goal of truth and reality and willing to subject themselves honestly to the critical test of reason alone. (Edwards 1967, s.v. "Socrates")

Problematic Interpretations of the Socratic Method

Not everyone shares this view of Socrates' Method. Some identify trickery, humiliation, and entrapment as the defining characteristics of the Socratic Method. The film *The Paper Chase* and its terrifying Professor Kingsfield provides a very different model of the Socratic Method from the one outlined above. It is possible to use dialectic methods to enforce a certain viewpoint and to punish those who cannot supply the "correct" answer. Some define the Socratic Method in exactly that manner. *A New Dictionary of Eponyms* (1997) describes the Socratic Method as:

> . . . a form of cross-examination which tangled his students in a network of errors. When asking questions, Socrates feigned ignorance (which is known as Socratic irony), luring the students to feel free to speak their minds. Through a series of questions, the students were led to the conclusion that Socrates had reached long before the class convened. (Freeman 1997, s.v. "Socrates")

Socrates did make free use of irony, and occasionally people who challenged him were humiliated. He admitted that some younger students may have attended his lectures "because they enjoy hearing me examine those who think they are wise when they are not—an experience which has its amusing side" (Plato and Cairns, 33c). An attempt to modernize the Socratic Method needs to account for this. In the context of contemporary information literacy instruction, humiliation and entrapment are not desired outcomes, nor are they recommended practices. Students should not be treated in such a manner. Modern practitioners of the Socratic Method have found ways to abandon the model of Professor Kingsfield and build a better one. Elizabeth Garrett of the University of Chicago Law School notes that "the day of the relentless Socratic professor who ended every sentence with a question mark is over." She describes their method as "a cooperative one in which the teacher and students work to understand an issue more completely." Humiliation and entrapment can only come into play when answers are the most important responses to question. Following Socrates' model, the process of answering is much more important than the actual answer. This means that realizing that an answer can be improved upon is a success, not a failure. As Garrett says, "we are teaching reasoning skills, and the process of discovering a right answer is often more important than the answer itself."

What do we make of the fact that several of Socrates' dialog partners *were* humiliated? He was put to death by the very citizens he claimed to serve. Socrates described his work as performing the civil service of rousing, persuading, and reproaching the population when they become intellectually lazy (Plato and Cairns, 30e). Not everyone who received this so-called service from him was grateful for the experience, but it would be another mistake to assume that because Socrates acted as a gadfly to the people of Athens, that his teaching method is necessarily unpleasant to endure. Copleston explains in his *History of Philosophy:*

> This dialectic might, of course, prove somewhat irritating or even disconcerting or humiliating to those whose ignorance was exposed

> and whose cocksureness was broken down—and it may have tickled the fancy of the young men who congregated round Socrates to hear their elders being "put in the sack"—but the aim of Socrates was not to humiliate or to disconcert. His aim was to discover the truth, not as a matter of pure speculation, but with a view to the good life: in order to act well, one must know what the good life is. (Copleston 1985, 107)

In the end, it is this unwavering commitment to uncovering the truth that rescues the Socratic Method from accusations of humiliation or images of unpleasant instructors toying with students and intentionally tripping them up. What makes a dialog-based instruction method specifically Socratic in nature is the ultimate goal of student learning. The student discovers knowledge, insight, or truth in the process of the dialog. It is about the honesty of the search and participation in uncovering answers. Methods of instructions that use dialectic, cross-examination, or refutation that forgo this disinterested search for truth and instead are used to enforce the domination of a particular set of answers are not Socratic in nature.

The Problem of Socratic Irony

Another problematic aspect of the Socratic Method is *Socratic irony*—the pretense to ignorance affected by the instructor. How can instructors committed to the disinterested pursuit of uncovering the truth claim ignorance about matters for which they clearly possess expertise? Some scholars diffuse the apparent contradiction by pointing to the dual nature of the Greek understanding of knowledge (Brickhouse and Smith 1994, 31). Others claim that Socrates was sincere in professing ignorance. Copleston thought the profession of ignorance was honest: "his 'irony' then, his profession of ignorance, was sincere; he did not know, but wanted to find out, and he wanted to induce others to reflect for themselves and to give real thought to the supremely important work of caring for their souls" (107). For library instructors looking for ways to engage their students in thinking critically about the research process, it isn't necessary to conclude the debate on the nature of Socratic irony. It should be enough to understand that in order for the students to go through the process of examining their personal understanding of the research process and then to critically examine the ramifications of their claim, the instructor's expert knowledge must be removed from the question. If it is not, then the entire dialectic process may appear to the students to be the unpleasant sort of trickery discussed above. If instructors make the goal of the discussion to have the students adopt their expert opinion, this robs students of the opportunity to critically examine their own answers. By bracketing their expertise and making the discussion about what the students think they know, Socratic irony allows students to experience the process of discovering answers for themselves. Phillips describes it this way: "the Socratic Method is a way to seek truth by your own lights" (2001, 18). Instruction using the Socratic Method is a participatory process. If an instructor steers the class toward a specific answer, the students lose the chance to honestly examine the issue and reach the conclusion for themselves. From this perspective, the Socratic irony is seen as a technique that frees students to participate in the learning process. The process of discovering an answer is more important than the answer itself. Feigning ignorance is not a disingenuous trick, rather it is a gift that gives students freedom and space to explore and learn for themselves.

Examples from Plato's Socratic Dialogs

In order to create a model for how Socrates' method of stimulating the intellectually lazy can be used in information literacy classrooms, let us look at some historical examples of how Socrates practiced his method. Socrates left no written record of his ideas. However, his contemporaries Plato, and, to a lesser extent, Xenophon and Aristophanes, did record some of Socrates' dialogs. Their writings present a view of how Socrates practiced his craft (Copleston, 99).

Plato's Socratic dialogs are a body of literature that record a series of conversations between Socrates and people who professed to have knowledge on a certain subject. For example, Gorgias professed to know the greatest good for humankind, Meno claimed to know something of human virtue, and Euthyphro claimed to know the nature of piety. In these conversations, Socrates took a position of ignorance—he claimed to know nothing about the subject at hand and asked his conversation partner to teach him. In the course of the exposition, Socrates asked a series of questions that lead his partner in conversation to reject or rethink his earlier claims to knowledge. Looking at how Socrates did this may be useful in developing techniques to use in information literacy classrooms.

Gorgias

For the first example, examine sections of *Gorgias*. In this dialog, Socrates talks with the rhetorician Gorgias about the greatest good of humanity. Gorgias claims to be a master of rhetoric and defines rhetoric as having to do with the good of humanity. Socrates is prodding him to define what the rhetorician does that other experts do not do. Prior to this section, Gorgias admitted that the nature of the rhetorician's art is persuasion. In the excerpt below, they discuss the difference between being informative and being persuasive. Socrates has asked: "Of what kind of persuasion is rhetoric the art, and what is its province?"

Gorgias: The kind of persuasion employed in law courts and other gatherings, Socrates, as I said just now, and concerned with right and wrong.

Socrates: Then let us consider the next point. Is there a state which you call "having learned"?

Gorgias: There is.

Socrates: Now do you think that to have learned and to have believed, or knowledge and belief, are one and the same or different?

Gorgias: I consider them different, Socrates.

Socrates: You are right, and you can prove it thus. If anybody were to say to you, can there be both a false belief and a true, Gorgias? You would, I think, say that there is.

Gorgias: Yes.

Socrates: But can there be both a false and a true knowledge?

Gorgias: By no means.

Socrates: Then it is obvious that knowledge and belief are not the same.

Gorgias: You are right.

Socrates: But both those who have learned and those who believe have been persuaded.

Gorgias: That is so.

Socrates: Shall we lay it down then that there are two forms of persuasion, the one producing belief without knowledge, the other knowledge?

Gorgias: Certainly.

Socrates: Now which kind of conviction about right and wrong is produced in the law courts and other gatherings by rhetoric? That which issues belief without knowledge, or that which issues in knowledge?

Gorgias: Evidently, Socrates, that which issues in belief.

Socrates: Then rhetoric apparently is a creator of a conviction that is persuasive but not instructive about wrong and right (Plato and Cairns, 454c–455).

In this section, Gorgias states that rhetoric is employed in legal affairs and is the art of determining right from wrong. Through a series of probing questions, Socrates helped Gorgias critically examine his assertion, and in the end Gorgias discovered that rhetoric is concerned primarily with persuasion and not necessarily about right and wrong. Along the way, they discussed the difference between knowledge and belief. This kind of conversation could be extremely valuable in an information literacy classroom. Substituting academic writing for rhetoric provides an excellent example of how information literacy can be advanced by using Socratic questioning.

A librarian could follow the model of this dialog by asking students questions about their use of sources. Starting with a broad question such as "when you write a paper, are you trying to teach your reader something, or are you trying to persuade them to adopt your opinion?" The librarian and students can begin a conversation about why we choose certain sources and how we use them. A general question like this one works well to start a conversation; just about any answer will get students talking and move the dialog forward. Whether the students say "to persuade" or "to inform" or even "both" or "it depends on the circumstance and the assignment," the conversation is started and the stage is set for the next question. "What is the difference between persuading your audience and informing them?" In order to answer this question, students have to grapple with the issue toward which Socrates steered Gorgias: the relationship between opinion and truth. More than likely, a library instruction session is too small a context for in-depth discussions of epistemology, but it is an ideal setting to raise the issue and move on to practical questions such as "what kind of sources would an attempt to inform cite" and the same question asked for an attempt to persuade. Using the Socratic Method to direct the students to question their rhetoric can lead to critical examination of the research process. If the students honestly ask themselves "what am I doing when I look for sources," no matter how they answer that question, they will have learned something about their research process and be equipped to be far more intentional about their research choices. They will also be better prepared to receive future instruction about research and library services after having broached the questions in the first place.

The next logical question in this dialog is to ask whether it is better to persuade or inform. Socrates and Gorgias certainly take their dialog in that direction. Given sufficient time, it could be a very instructive conversation. Unfortunately, time is a finite resource for many information literacy instructors. It may be that to continue that discussion would require certain compromises, such as limiting student discussion or artificially maneuvering the students toward the desired learning outcomes. One of the dangers of using the Socratic Method for information literacy instruction is that time limits may make some of the tricks or manipulations discussed above seem justified. In order to reach a desired outcome, it may seem necessary to focus more on answering a question in a certain way rather than critically examining the answers that arrive naturally. In these situations it is advisable to remember that the process of answering a question is more important (at this point) than the answer itself. Starting the critical thinking process, engaging students in thinking about how they go about research, and exposing some flawed assumptions are all worthy outcomes. It may be more conducive to student learning to cut off a Socratic dialog without arriving at a satisfactory answer than to artificially force the discussion to a pre-determined conclusion.

When a Socratic discussion ends with students critically evaluating their writing and thinking about the role that research and their sources play in how they are communicating with their audience, then the class is in a very fertile place for several information literacy learning goals. After using the Socratic Method to rid students of misconceptions about the research process and academic writing, the class may be much more receptive to subsequent non-Socratic lessons instruction about concrete content. This content includes source evaluation and selection, the difference between scholarly and popular sources, and introductions to the services and resources an academic library has to offer students. As seen in the *Meno*, confusing students by giving them questions they cannot (at this point) satisfactorily answer can in some cases be a gift that stimulates their curiosity and appetite to learn.

Meno

In the dialog *Meno*, Socrates and Meno discussed whether or not virtue can be taught. This discussion does not directly apply to teaching information literacy, but in the course of the dialog Socrates explained his pedagogy in a clear fashion. He made a case for Socratic irony, or the claim of ignorance on the part of the teacher, and explained that by not teaching, he helped his students learn. Out of all of the dialogs, this section of the *Meno* gives the clearest picture of Socrates' pedagogy. Instruction librarians can use it to contrast instruction or teaching with a focus on student learning or "not teaching" as Socrates calls his method. In this dialog, Meno, a teacher (sophist) by profession, has asked Socrates for an explanation of what he means by not teaching. In response, Socrates asked Meno to call over one of his household slave boys and presented the boy with a geometry problem. Starting with a two-foot by two-foot square, the boy was able to explain that the area of the square is four feet. Next Socrates asked the boy to image a square double the area, an eight-foot square, and also how long each side would be. The boy answers, with great confidence (and incorrectly) that the sides of an eight-foot square would be double the length of the sides of a four-foot square. Socrates proceeded to demonstrate to the boy how the area of a square has an exponential relation to the length of the sides. Then he asked his question again:

Boy: It's no use, Socrates, I just don't know.

Socrates: Observe, Meno, the stage he has reached on the path of recollection. At the beginning, he did not know the side of the square of eight feet. Nor indeed does he know it now, but then he thought he knew it and answered boldly, as was appropriate—he felt no perplexity. Now, however, he does feel perplexed. Not only does he not know the answer, he doesn't even think he knows.

Meno: Quite true.

Socrates: Isn't he in a better position now in relation to what he didn't know?

Meno: I admit that, too.

Socrates: So in perplexing him and numbing him like the sting ray, have we done him any harm?

Meno: I think not.

Socrates: In fact, we have helped him to some extent toward finding out the right answer, for now not only is he ignorant of it but he will be quite glad to look for it. Up to now, he thought he could speak well and fluently, on many occasions and before large audiences, on the subject of a square double the size of a given square, maintaining that it must have a side of double the length.

Meno: No doubt.

Socrates: Do you suppose that he would have attempted to look for, or learn, what he thought he knew, though he did not, before he was thrown into perplexity, became aware of his ignorance, and felt a desire to know?

Meno: No.

Socrates: Then the numbing process was good for him?

Meno: I agree.

Socrates: Now notice what, starting from this state of perplexity, he will discover by seeking the truth in company with me, though I simply ask him questions without teaching him. Be ready to catch me if I give him any instruction or explanation instead of simply interrogating him on his own opinions (Plato and Cairns, 82b–e).

Information literacy librarians may find this section of the *Meno* of particular interest. Meno represents a content-heavy approach to library instruction. If Meno were a librarian, he would have a lot of experience and expertise with search interfaces, resources, and library services. His instruction would center on the transfer of his expert knowledge to students. Socrates suggested and described an alternative to this approach. Although he denied the label, this might be called a learning-centered or student-centered approach. Rather than focusing on the instructor's expert knowledge, Socrates focused on what the student knows and understands. He had full confidence that when students are guided through clear examples, they have the critical thinking capacity to reach logical conclusions. He referred to this process as recovery (Plato and Cairns, 85d) and built an argument for the immortality of the soul on it. Today we are more likely to refer to this experience as *discovery,* and, while we may not link it to arguments about the soul, discovery-based learning does have proponents in the academy.

One area of library instruction for which Socratic questioning and this kind of student-centered discovery-based library instruction might have a great effect is when students over-estimate their information skills. Competency theory teaches that persons with low levels of information literacy are frequently unable to accurately assess their information needs; "the incompetent do not know they are incompetent" (Gross 2005). Some of our students may be very much like Meno's slave boy. They may think they can speak well and fluently on many occasions and before large audiences on the subject of information literacy. Without a Socratic gadfly to numb them and sting them into perplexity, they might not realize the extent of their ignorance or incompetence. Being unaware of their ignorance, they are not likely to seek the remedies available or take advantage of instruction when offered. Library instruction sessions may be an ideal setting for librarians to give students the gift of numbing perplexity.

Socrates used a counter-intuitive principle of geometry to expose (and remedy) the ignorance of Meno's slave boy. Librarians can use examples from their experience to provide students with the same lessons. For example, imagine an instructor requests a library instruction session because students are relying too heavily on non-scholarly sources found on the Internet and not taking advantage of the library's scholarly materials for their research. Rather than lecturing on the differences between popular and scholarly materials or on the academic communication and publication systems, a librarian could lead the class through a Socratic discussion of sources. The librarian could divide the class into groups and ask half of the groups to research a topic using an Internet search engine and ask the other half to use a full-text database of scholarly articles. Each group could then be questioned about the sources they found. Questions such as "Who wrote the information in your source?" "Where did the author of your source get their information?" "What makes the author of your source an expert?" and "Why should we respect the opinions or findings of your article?" will guide students to critically examine their information sources. Answering these questions will require the students to subject their information sources to a level of critical examination that will reveal much about the appropriateness of sources. Students who discover for themselves that they cannot determine the authority of a Web page or establish the bona fides of an author may compare their experience with a classmate who can quickly (with a little guidance) find an author's affiliation and read the reference list used to research the article. Students who are guided to critically examine their research strategies will discover on their own the advantages and disadvantages of search strategies. If they see deficiencies in how they prefer to search or advantages in other strategies, they will be motivated to make changes. As Socrates said, "In fact, we have helped him to some extent toward finding out the right answer, for now not only is he ignorant of it but he will be quite glad to look for it" (Plato and Cairns, 84b). In this example, students are not taught *how* to find appropriate scholarly sources through the library. If they are led to realize that simple keyword searches on Google don't work well for academic research, they have started on the path to greater information literacy.

Euthyphro

In the *Euthyphro*, Socrates had a dialog with a young man very much convinced of the rightness of his cause. Euthyphro accused his father of murder over the death of a worker in his care. Socrates noted that Euthyphro, who is a very young man, must be very sure of his understanding of piety (or holiness) in order to pursue so severe a course. Since Euthyphro must know the difference between piety and impiety, Socrates asked to be instructed in the nature of piety. Euthyphro gave his definition of piety and Socrates revealed flaws in the definition. Euthyphro refined his definition to "holiness is what the gods all love, and its opposite is what the gods all hate, unholiness." In response, Socrates asked a very key question, the kind of question students should ask of their own opinions:

Socrates: . . . Is what is holy holy because the gods approve of it, or do they approve of it because it is holy?

Euthyphro: I do not get your meaning.

Socrates: Well, I will try to make it clearer. We speak of what is carried and the carrier, do we not, of led and leader, of the seen and that which sees? And you understand that in all such cases the things are different and how they differ?

Euthyphro: Yes, I think I understand.

Socrates: In the same way, what is loved is one thing, and what loves is another.

Euthyphro: Of course.

Socrates: Tell me now, is what is carried 'carried' because something carries it, or is it for some other reason?

Euthyphro: No, but for that reason.

Socrates: And what is led, because something leads it? And what is seen, because someone sees it?

Euthyphro: Yes, certainly.

Socrates: Then it is not because a thing is seen that something sees it, but just the opposite—because something sees it, therefore, it is seen. Nor because it is led, that something leads it, but because something leads it, therefore it is led. Nor because it is carried that something carries it, but because something carries it, therefore, it is carried. Do you see what I wish to say, Euthyphro? It is this. Whenever an effect occurs, or something is effected, it is not the thing effected that gives rise to the effect; no, there is a cause, and then comes this effect. Nor is it because a thing is acted on that there is the effect; no, there is a cause for what it undergoes, and then comes the effect. Don't you agree?

Euthyphro: I do.

Socrates: Well then, when a thing is loved, is it not in process of becoming something, or of undergoing something, by some other thing?

Euthyphro: Yes, certainly.

Socrates: Then the same is true here as in the previous cases. It is not because a thing is loved that they who love it love it, but is loved because they love it.

Euthyphro: Necessarily.

Socrates: Then what are we to say about the holy, Euthyphro? According to your argument, is it not loved by all the gods?

Euthyphro: Yes.

Socrates: Because it is holy, or for some other reason?

Euthyphro: No, it is for that reason.

Socrates: And so it is because it is holy that it is loved; it is not holy because it is loved.

Euthyphro: So it seems.

Socrates: On the other hand, it is beloved and pleasing to the gods just because they love it?

Euthyphro: No doubt of that.

Socrates: So what is pleasing to the gods is not the same as what is holy. Euthyphro, nor, according to your statement, is the holy the same thing as what is pleasing to the gods. They are two different things (Plato and Cairns, 10a–e).

This lengthy extract may not, at first glance, appear to be of much use to teach information literacy. It deals with questions of gods and holiness, not of information, rationality, or research. However, if we can abstract from this discussion a key Socratic technique for helping students to examine their opinions, we can use this section of the Euthyphro to help our students rid themselves of several popular, yet devastating, flaws in their research processes. By replacing Euthyphro's assertion that what is holy is what is pleasing to the gods with "Research is looking for articles that support my thesis," Socrates' questions and the logic of cause and effect from the extract above can be used to help students question what they are searching for when they do research. Once they question the assertion that research is looking for articles that agree with their opinion, they can be guided to consider academic research as more about finding a thesis that conforms to the best available scholarship rather than looking for any available scholarship that conforms to their thesis. This kind of instruction not only improves the students' ability to complete research assignments but it also increases the value that completing research assignments adds to their overall educational experience.

This gets to the heart of the value the Socratic Method offers to instruction librarians. It offers a way to help students understand why they are doing research in the first place, not just how to perform an unexamined task more efficiently. As Socrates famously said in the *Republic*, "the argument concerns no casual topic, but one's whole manner of living" (Plato and Grube 1974, 352d). More than just providing students with tools to complete their existing research processes more efficiently, information literacy instruction using the Socratic Method can help students critically examine and improve their conceptions of what it means to do academic research in the first place. They are not simply completing their homework; rather, they are becoming better students.

Examine how this sort of discussion would look in the classroom. Opening with the question: "When we go to the databases to find articles, what kind of articles are we looking for?" the instructor should be able to get a student to posit "We are looking for articles that support our thesis." If no one volunteers the desired assertion, a small amount of fishing with questions such as: "Are we looking for just any articles" or "What do the articles we are looking for have in common?" may be necessary. Once the assertion has been made, the instructor can set a comfortable environment for the following dialog by taking responsibility for the assertion away from the student. Comments such as "Don't many of us approach research that way? It's a very common practice" will set the stage for effective critical discourse about the idea and make it clear that the student is being rewarded for perception and not being criticized. Follow Socrates' model from the *Euthyphro* and try to determine if sources are considered good because they support pre-existing opinions or if the quality of content in a source determines its value. Questions that can help students engage with this issue include: "What makes our opinions worth sticking to?" followed by a conversation about evidence and supporting arguments. "When is it appropriate to change one's opinion during research?" is another question that stimulates conversation and critical thinking about balancing new evidence with loyalty to existing views. These questions and conversations can all serve to stimulate critical thinking about the role that evidence and supporting arguments play in developing a thesis and lead into further instruction about tools (such as the Reference Collection) that can assist students into doing *better* research rather than just doing mediocre research more efficiently.

CONCLUSION

For librarians looking for new techniques to improve the information literacy of their students, the Socratic Method is a tool that can help encourage student learning. The Socratic Method is a pedagogy that uses guided questions, dialog, and refutation to help students critically reflect on their understanding of a particular issue. As students reflect, the instructor's questions stimulate them to reject misconceptions and gain an understanding of what they know and also what they do not know. When the students become aware of the limits of their current understanding and confront questions for which they lack answers, they become engaged in the process and motivated to improve their understanding and seek answers to the unresolved questions.

Using the Socratic dialogs to inform pedagogies, instruction librarians can avoid negative stereotypes of the Socratic Method by remembering that the focus of the Socratic Method is the student process of discovering answers to questions, not how closely they can imitate the answers of experts or the accepted wisdom of a discipline. Socratic instructors remember that their role is similar to that of a midwife with students giving birth to new knowledge. Socratic irony, or pretend ignorance, is a technique used to bracket the instructor's expertise and allow students to focus on their own understanding. Using irony to entrap students in so-called wrong answers or to humiliate students for answering incorrectly is an abuse and will have a negative effect on student learning.

Looking at Plato's Socratic dialogs can lead to a rich source of material to inform information literacy instruction sessions. The dialogs give many examples of Socrates practicing his method. Reading the dialogs can show us the methods he used to stimulate his students and help them to unlearn false knowledge. The dialogs also reveal much about how Socrates and Plato thought about issues that concern instruction librarians. They can examine Socrates' conception of pedagogy, rhetoric, and the mind, and integrate concepts from them into their teaching. Finally, studying Socrates can connect librarians to deeper motivations for teaching information literacy and critical thinking. Information literacy and critical thinking are not casual topics. They are concerned with more than successfully completing an assignment or a degree program. The Socratic Method reminds librarians that it is no idle matter we are discussing, but one's whole manner of living.

REFERENCES

Brickhouse, T. C. and N. D. Smith. 1994. *Plato's Socrates*. New York: Oxford University Press.

Copleston, F. C. 1985. *A history of philosophy*. New York: Image Books.

Edwards, P. 1967. *The encyclopedia of philosophy*. New York: Macmillan. s.v. "Socrates."

Garrett, E. The Socratic method. *University of Chicago Law School*. http://www.law.uchicago.edu/socrates/soc_article.html.

Gross, M. 2005. The impact of low-level skills on information-seeking behavior: Implications of competency theory for research and practice. *Reference & User Services Quarterly* 45: 155–162. http://www.proquest..com.

New dictionary of eponyms. 1997. Oxford: Oxford University Press. *Oxford Reference Online*. http://www.oxfordreference.com/.s.v. Socratic method.

Oxford companion to philosophy. 1995. s.v. Socratic method. http://www.oxfordreference.com/.

Phillips, C. 2001. *Socrates café: A fresh taste of philosophy*. New York: Norton.

Plato, E. H. and H. Cairns. 1989. *The collected dialogues of Plato, including the letters*. Bollingen series, 71. New York: Pantheon Books.

Plato and G.M.A. Grube. 1974. *Plato's Republic*. Indianapolis, IN: Hackett.
Vlastos, G. 1983. The Socratic Elenchus. In: Annas, J. (ed.) *Oxford studies in ancient philosophy*, Oxford: Clarendon Press, pp. 27–58.
Woodruff, P. 2006. Socrates among the Sophists. In: Ahbel-Rappe, S. and Kamtekar, R. (eds.) *A companion to Socrates*, Malden, MA: Blackwell, pp. 36–47.

Step by Step through the Scholarly Conversation: A Collaborative Library/Writing Faculty Project to Embed Information Literacy and Promote Critical Thinking in First Year Composition at Oregon State University

Anne-Marie Deitering
Sara Jameson

INTRODUCTION

"I've already written this paper. Can you help me find some articles for my bibliography?"

Any librarian who has spent time on a reference desk has heard some variation on this question, probably more than once. In fact, anyone who spends time working with student writers has had to wrestle with students who feel so strongly about a topic that they cannot open their minds to new ideas. Students who seem unlikely, or worse, unwilling to engage in critical reflection about their beliefs and opinions are a source of frustration to librarians and writing instructors alike.

Since 2001, librarians and writing faculty at Oregon State University (OSU) have collaboratively developed an information literacy curriculum for OSU's First Year Composition (FYC) course, the sole composition course all OSU students are required to complete. This four-week unit draws connections between critical thinking, writing and learning, and information literacy. In this article, OSU's composition coordinator and undergraduate services librarian describe the process of developing, implementing, and refining this collaborative curriculum. By using assignments and texts that concretely model a recursive and critical research and writing process, we help students think more deeply and critically about issues and arguments and develop new mental habits that transfer to other courses taken throughout their college careers.

DEFINITION

"Critical thinking" is a phrase everyone in academia uses, but few analyze it on a deeper level. Before digging more deeply into the particulars of our project, it is important to clarify our use of this term. To start, we do not consider critical thinking to be a checklist of skills to be acquired. Instead, it is a way of thinking our students can draw upon to deal with new information sources or new ideas.

In *How College Affects Students*, Pascarella and Terenzini (2005) synthesize several decades of research examining the social, cognitive, and other changes students go through during the college years. For most OSU students, FYC marks their first experience with academic writing. Pascarella and Terenzini remind us that these students are also new to the critical thinking processes that underlie scholarship. These processes include the abilities to: "identify central issues and assumptions in an argument, recognize important relationships, make correct references from the data, deduce conclusions from information or data provided, interpret whether conclusions are warranted based on given data, evaluate evidence or authority, make self-corrections, and solve problems" (156).

Pascarella and Terenzini highlight two additional factors of particular importance. First, they point out that not only is there a cognitive dimension to critical thinking, but there is also a motivational one. In other words, there are mental skills or processes necessary for critical thinking, but to truly understand a student's ability to think critically, we must also consider their willingness to use their brains in this way. This dimension, the "disposition to think critically," includes "the inclination to ask challenging questions and follow the reasons and evidence wherever they lead, tolerance for new ideas, willingness to use reason and evidence to solve problems, and willingness to see complexity in problems" (157). Clearly, the disposition to think critically is a necessity for students to make the shift from thinking about research as a way to find supporting quotes, to thinking about research as a way to expose themselves to new ideas so they can build new knowledge. A student with this "disposition to think critically" is willing to ask hard questions, to look beyond simple answers, to follow the evidence anywhere, and to stay open to new ideas and new information (157).

Second, there is an epistemological dimension to critical thinking. Students must be able to understand knowledge itself as something that is constructed, not something that is revealed to them. To think critically, students must be able and willing to evaluate evidence and draw conclusions. They must also be willing to consider the possibility that sometimes they will not find clear-cut answers. This tolerance for ambiguity, called "post-formal reasoning," is very difficult for many first-year students, but it is absolutely essential for students writing rhetorical argument essays. As Pascarella and Terenzini point out, the types of topics that most FYC students choose for their argument essays—gay marriage, euthanasia, global warming—are exactly the kinds of ill-structured or "wicked problems" where information is likely to be incomplete, the parameters of the problem are likely to be unclear, and the number of plausible solutions is likely to be large (160).

This ambiguity is particularly difficult for most first-year students to tolerate when the new information they find contradicts their existing belief structure. According to Swanson (2006), students arrive at college with beliefs "fairly well established" (98). Changing existing belief structures is not easy for students, as it typically results from deep learning. Perry

(1970) points to dualistic or binary thinking, or the belief that there are two (and only two) sides to every story, or two (and only two) answers to any question, as a construct that hampers students' ability to think critically.

A student who can think critically about these wicked problems recognizes that research is not a process of finding definitive answers in sources, but a process of finding the building blocks they can use to construct persuasive answers. They further understand that sometimes those building blocks may force them to reevaluate their prior constructs. This idea of research and writing as constructive learning processes is essential for our students in their first introduction to academic argument. The idea that research and writing are constructive, knowledge-building processes will be examined in more depth in our discussion of the conversation models used in both the research and writing activities in FYC.

The information literacy (IL) activities in OSU's FYC were also informed by van Gelder's (2005) work on pedagogy, critical thinking, and cognition. Van Gelder shows that critical thinking is difficult, that the mental processes that support critical thinking are not natural for most people, and that to become proficient at it, people need to practice:

> Our students will improve their critical-thinking skills most effectively just to the extent that they engage in lots of deliberate practice in critical thinking. Crucially, this is not just thinking critically about some topic (for example, being 'critical' in writing a philosophy essay). It also involves doing special exercises whose main point is to improve critical-thinking skills themselves (43).

This illustrates the need for activities that specifically ask students to think critically and to reflect upon their research and writing processes.

In summary, there are several dimensions to the term "critical thinking" that inform the way we present information literacy concepts to FYC students at OSU. On one level, the term reflects the habits of mind our students need to find, evaluate, and learn from new information sources. On another, it refers to their willingness to consider new ideas and perspectives in the first place, and to the understanding that knowledge itself is the result of a constructive process. Finally, it is something we must teach deliberately, not something we can assume students will "get" for themselves.

Our work in the FYC curriculum has been shaped by one additional assumption: our students will not become critical thinkers in one assignment, one portfolio, one library session, or even one course. Our goal is to introduce our students to a new way of thinking about research and writing. If our activities are effective, students can take the habits of mind they are introduced to in FYC and develop them in later projects and courses, but it is likely that these habits will have to be deliberately reintroduced and reinforced in later learning experiences.

CONTEXT

The partnership between the OSU libraries and the first year composition program was initiated in 2001. McMillen, Miyagishima, and Maughan (2002) describe how the library's instruction workgroup (IWG) and OSU's composition coordinator collaboratively developed information literacy activities for WR 121, OSU's first year composition course and the only composition course required for all OSU undergraduates.

In 2001, instruction librarians started teaching two class sessions in every section of FYC. Between these sessions students completed a series of IL assignments on paper, using sample topics to explore library research tools. This, obviously, represented a significant investment of time and resources by the library. Given that OSU operates on a quarter system with 10-week terms, this also represented a significant commitment to information literacy on the part of the FYC. While the particulars of the information literacy component in OSU's FYC have changed in the last five years, this level of collaboration and commitment has continued, and even grown.

There are approximately twenty-five sections of FYC offered every term, with twenty-five students enrolled in each section. These sections are taught by graduate teaching assistants (GTAs) pursuing two-year Masters' degrees in English or MFA degrees in creative writing; thus, there is significant turnover each year. Paired with GTAs are ten to fifteen faculty instruction librarians who teach between one and three sections of FYC. The remaining sections are covered by librarians working in the library's on-call reference pool. As a result, there is also a regular amount of turnover among instruction librarians in FYC courses.

Unlike GTAs in other departments, the GTAs in English are the sole instructors for their sections, under the training and supervision of the composition coordinator. GTAs follow a fairly standard syllabus and schedule, but day-to-day classroom activities are individually determined. Until 2004, the content of the library instruction sections was determined by the individual librarians and GTAs assigned to each section. As a result, the topics addressed in different sections could vary a great deal.

After three years, the IL component of the FYC was assessed and revised. In end-of-term debriefing sessions, librarians consistently reported frustration with the students' approach to research. They seemed unwilling or unable to consider multiple perspectives, or to revise their thinking based on the information they found. In the summer of 2004, the IWG and the composition coordinator identified three strategies for revising the IL curriculum. First, revise the assignments so that students could research their own paper topics, making the IL activities more relevant to class work. Second, introduce a model academic research process along with the paper assignment, instead of waiting until the library session. Finally, make the curriculum more consistent, so that students would master the same outcomes regardless of the section in which they were enrolled.

In the fall of 2004, we launched the new curriculum. One of the in-class library instruction sessions was replaced with a set of six linked information literacy assignments. These assignments are called the information literacy portfolio (ILP). Students complete the ILP in the week after the research paper portfolio is assigned. They choose their own topics, and then the ILP guides them through a model research process that emphasizes broad exploration, exposure to new ideas, and critical thinking. The ILP is graded by the librarian and counts for 10% of the students' overall course grade. After the ILP is graded, students come to the library for an instruction session.

Theoretical Model: Conversation

Exploring a topic broadly with an open mind is an essential part of successful academic research. Exploring a topic just to learn about it is time well spent. However, convincing students can be very difficult. Students tend to feel as if they are not "really" working if they are not gathering the specific sources they will quote in their papers. To help our students understand the need to research before taking a position or narrowing a focus, both the FYC faculty and the instruction librarians use the metaphor of conversation to demonstrate research and writing as recursive learning processes. Everyone has had a conversation before, and everyone can understand the importance of listening to other speakers. By comparing scholarly exploration to "listening in" on a conversation, we can shift our students' thinking by placing a new concept into a familiar context.

Information Literacy: Research as Conversation

Davidson and Crateau (2000) introduced the idea of conversation as a metaphor for the scholarly research process after developing the idea for four years in the honors writing course at OSU. They describe three levels to the scholarly conversation: eavesdropping, entering, and engaging. First, students eavesdrop on the conversation by using different research tools to tap into the scholarly conversations going on in the literature. Ideally, they will recognize that there are multiple perspectives on their topics, beyond just a "pro" and a "con," and that different speakers use different vocabularies to describe the issues.

After they have listened to the conversation for a while, students should begin to form their own ideas and opinions about their topics. At this stage, they are ready to enter the conversation. This involves defining the issues related to their topics, articulating key points of view, and, most importantly, identifying the part of the conversation where they feel they can contribute. In other words, they figure out the people they are most interested in talking to, and they begin to get a sense of what they might say.

Finally, they are ready to engage in the conversation. While most student writers do not produce original scholarship, they should still make the same moves that experienced scholars make. As Davidson and Crateau (2000) show, when students engage with their sources, write, and think, they begin to carve out their own ideas and points of view and to understand how their own argument has been influenced by the rest of the conversation. In other words, their final written product not only develops their thesis, but it also brings the reader into the broader conversation.

It is undoubtedly clear that Davidson and Crateau's conversation model was heavily influenced by Kuhlthau's (2004) information-seeking process. As such, it is worth looking a bit more closely at Kuhlthau's research on the importance of exploration before focus formation. "Prefocus exploration" is the third of seven stages in Kuhlthau's highly influential model. In this stage, learners know they have an information-seeking task, and they have selected a general topic to investigate. In prefocus exploration, their task is to "investigate information on the general topic to extend personal understanding and form a focus" (47). As difficult as it is to allow a student to explore a topic that is obviously too broad for the assignment, such as a five-page paper on terrorism, it is crucial that librarians and writing instructors allow students to explore freely, without encouraging them to narrow their focus too soon.

Kuhlthau's research is particularly important for two reasons. First, her studies repeatedly illustrate the importance of exploration to the overall success of the research process. Focus formulation is described as a "critical, pivotal point in a search" (84). If students do not reach a focus, every subsequent stage in the research process becomes harder. They cannot distinguish relevant sources from the less relevant, and they cannot effectively communicate what they learn.

Second, Kulhthau's research shows that most students have a great deal of difficulty during this stage. In the exploration stage, students reported feelings of anxiety as they found sources that contradicted each other, or that contradicted the student's previously held beliefs. Novice scholars are rarely experienced in handling this kind of uncertainty. Kuhlthau's estimate that more than half of her students never achieved any focus is not surprising. Without specific guidance through the exploratory phase of research, students will attempt to skip this phase altogether and create their argument before gathering any information at all.

Kuhlthau's model was strongly informed by constructivist pedagogy, which also informs OSU's conversation model. As Kuhlthau argues, a researcher's focus cannot be defined for them by anyone else. It is an articulation of the meaning they have constructed out of the new ideas and information they encountered in their exploratory phase, and it is influenced by the constructs and beliefs they bring with them to the research process. Kuhlthau explains how, "[t]he process of construction incorporates a cycle of acting and reflecting, feeling and formulating, predicting and choosing, and interpreting and creating" (26). Students must be taught to reflect, make adjustments, and notice how new information integrates with their prior constructs.

The conversation model of research, therefore, is very tightly linked to the description of critical thinking presented above. Students who can create meaning for themselves out of new information must be able to engage in the cognitive processes of critical thinking: evaluating sources, drawing conclusions, and finding patterns. Part of the disposition to think critically is the willingness to be reflective about their own constructs. Post-formal reasoning assumes that answers are constructed more than they are revealed and is wholly consistent with constructivist pedagogy.

They Say, I Say: Extending the Conversation Model

In the years since Davidson and Crateau introduced the metaphor of research as eavesdropping on a conversation, the writing faculty at OSU have extended it, deeply embedding the academic model of writing as conversation into the FYC. Despite the progress made in composition instruction in grades K–12, many students arrive in FYC with the idea that a scholarly argument is like a monologue. Sources, if they are there at all, stand silently behind student writers as they defeat the opposition. Too often, students do not allow their speakers to get a word in edgewise, but relegate them to supporting roles. The resulting papers give no sense of the ongoing conversation. Therefore, our first effort in introducing students to a new model of interaction about ideas or issues is to change the students' mental image from monologue to conversation and to show how ineffective it is to crash a party, shout one's opinion, and leave without hearing anyone else speak. Instead, students learn that they should find out who is already arguing on an issue before "putting in [their] oar" (Graff and Birkenstein 2006, 12). This "entering the conversation" is a concept in rhetoric called the Burkean Parlor, after the work of philosopher Kenneth Burke to describe the way intellectuals participate in an unending conversation (Graff and Birkenstein, 12).

Because of the clear way that Graff and Birkenstein use conversation to illustrate the connections between reading, writing, thinking, and researching in their text *They Say, I Say: The Moves that Matter in Academic Writing* (2006), and because of the way this text helped us extend our students' understanding of academic writing as a conversation, OSU adopted their book in the summer of 2006. Graff and Birkenstein point out that intellectual conversations, like all conversations, are not free-form affairs. We converse in particular, recognizable ways. While we can "pick up" the forms of other kinds of conversations—social small talk, professional chatter, Facebook comments, or instant messaging—just by doing it, for most people scholarly discourse is not so transparent. For FYC students, many of whom have never read scholarly writing, these forms are wholly new.

Just as the ILP structures the research process for students, *They Say, I Say* provides tools to structure thinking and writing. These tools take the form of templates that students can adapt to their own writing, on any topic. The most important and basic of these, according to Graff and Birkenstein, is the following:

They say ________, I say __________.

This template illustrates the book's central point, that all good academic writers recognize others' voices in their work.

While the "They say ___, I say ___" template reflects the most important concept for FYC students to grasp, it is far too simple to be the end of the story. In ten chapters, Graff and Birkenstein provide templates to help students make a variety of complex rhetorical moves, from quoting and summarizing to describing an ongoing debate. The templates are important because they provide the form the students need to emulate, but the blanks within the templates are even more important. The templates mean that students do not need to focus on the form of what they say, but the blanks mean that they must think about what they know and what they have learned. Thinking about how to fill those blanks, students must not only think deeply and critically about the sources they have found, but they must also think reflectively about what they still need to learn.

Graff and Birkenstein's model templates guide students toward invention and research in important ways, both showing the position of author to sources and also in pointing toward necessary sources. For example, consider such sentences:

> My feelings on the issue of ___ are mixed. I do support X's position that ___, but I find Y's argument about ___ and Z's research on ___ to be equally persuasive because ___. (Graff and Birkenstein, 169)

A model like this shows three speakers in juxtaposition and dialog, guiding students in their writing and their research. Consider another template that helps students make concessions while still holding a position:

> Proponents of X are right to argue that ___. But they exaggerate when they claim that ___. (172)

This model gets students past simplistic, binary "pro and con" thinking. While the templates themselves are deceptively simple, to synthesize their ideas into these forms requires students to really analyze their sources and their own ideas. This is another important step for our students as they become critical thinkers.

As stated above, the idea that all questions have right answers, and that research is a process by which the right choice between black-and-white options will be revealed, seriously limits students' ability to learn about complex topics. This model usually results in papers that have "three sources who support my position, plus one opponent who is obviously wrong, so I win." This way of thinking limits the kind of research a student is willing to consider. When used effectively, templates like those above push students beyond the binary way of thinking, help them construct nuanced meaning out of their sources, and open their minds to new sources and new ideas.

Implementing the Conversation Model

OSU's FYC students currently have two models that show them how to make "the moves that matter" in academic research and writing. On the research side, the information literacy portfolio (ILP) models a recursive research process that can be used in any context where the student needs to construct an answer to a complex question from a variety of information sources. On the writing side, Graff and Birkenstein's templates show students the form of a scholarly discourse that respects the voices of others.

Implementing the Conversation Model: The Online ILP

In the fall of 2004, the first version of the ILP was introduced in all of the sections of FYC. At that time, there were six linked assignments. These assignments were posted on a Web page, and the GTAs were responsible for introducing the assignments to the students. The students downloaded a workbook to fill out with their answers to all six assignments. While this paper-and-pencil format afforded the GTAs a great deal of flexibility to use some of the assignments in-class or as homework, many did not take advantage of this flexibility. Further, the logistical problems caused by students going to one Website for the instructional pieces of the ILP, another for the information resources they needed, and still another to download the workbook were so great that we almost immediately began looking for a way for students to submit the ILP online. In 2006, the OSU's Ecampus offered the first online-only versions of FYC. Converting the curriculum so it could be delivered in the course management system (Blackboard) for the Ecampus sections gave us the opportunity to implement the same online version of the ILP in all of the face-to-face sections.

The research process of the ILP models for the students has not changed dramatically in the last three years. Each of the individual assignments, however, has been revised in that time. Most significantly, we found that for our students to successfully answer the questions that required reflection and thinking, we needed to provide directions for each task that were much more specific and directive than we originally anticipated. For example, in ILP Assignment 1, we initially asked students to "write a short paragraph" about their topics, and we provided them with a few hints that we thought would spark thoughtful reflection. For the most part, that reflection did not happen. We learned to ask the questions we wanted the students to reflect upon much more explicitly. In the current version, we ask the students to "write two to three sentences each" on three specific questions which is more effective.

While every assignment has become more directive, ILP Assignment 2, which focuses on the eavesdropping stage of the research process, has been entirely reconstructed in the last year. In our initial attempt to get students to explore, we instructed them to browse through abstracts, titles, authors, and subject headings in databases and then to answer some very specific questions about the key words, speakers, and concepts they found. Despite these instructions, it was clear from the answers we were getting that most students saw no difference between the process of exploration and the process of gathering sources to quote. We realized that they did not know enough about the topics they were researching or about the research process to explore effectively using the same tools they would use for information gathering.

We agreed that our students needed to explore in reference sources, like encyclopedias, that would give them a broad overview of their topic areas. At that same time, an increasing number of our students was using Wikipedia as a source in their papers. Because many of those students chose Wikipedia articles as sources to evaluate in the ILP, we had data that proved they had no idea what kind of source Wikipedia was or how the information in that source was created. At the same time, Wikipedia's extensive hyperlinking and external resource lists made it very intriguing to us as a resource for exploration. We decided to solve two problems at once and send all of our students to Wikipedia in this assignment. We hoped that the ease with which they could explore would encourage them to do so broadly and would also help them understand Wikipedia's limitations and strengths.

The rewritten assignment is fairly lengthy, worth about one-fifth of the total points given in the ILP. Students are told to find a Wikipedia article related to their topic, to identify new keywords and potential speakers, and to identify claims in the article that they want to research further. They must also visit the Discussion pages for that article and analyze the History pages. This assignment is discussed further below.

ILP Assignment 3 simply asks the students to brainstorm three potential research questions about their topic. ILP Assignment 4 asks them to take the new knowledge they have about their topic with the potential foci suggested by their research questions, and use those things to find some potentially useful sources about their topic in online databases, the library catalog, and a search engine. After finding three types of sources, we ask them to analyze and evaluate each one and to reflect on their process. ILP Assignment 5, the final assignment, asks them to draft a working thesis that reflects their understanding of their topic and their ideas about how they might enter the conversation.

The online ILP is completed the week before students come for a face-to-face library instruction session. The librarian grades it according to a scoring rubric we created that is posted online with the assignment. For example, a student can see that to get full points for an "exemplary score" on Assignment 1, question 3 they must write two or three sentences analyzing where [they] might look for information about the topic area, with *specific* examples of types of sources [they] might use—or disciplines and/or professional groups that might be writing about [the] topic.

Blackboard also allows the librarian to write feedback on each answer in a text box to explain the grade and offer suggestions. The rubric is available to the students throughout the process. It is uploaded to their Blackboard course page, and it is also available online (http://osulibrary.oregonstate.edu/w121/ILPrubric.pdf).

In the library session, the librarian reinforces ideas presented in the ILP and helps the students develop more advanced skills. For example, if the librarian noticed several people in the same class choosing inappropriate keywords, that might be a topic for the in-class session. In addition, there are some common learning outcomes defined for the in-class session that all of the librarians address. These include using a quality source to find additional sources, troubleshooting problematic searches, and finding and using limiting features in online research tools. The librarian and writing instructor meet early in the term, so they can schedule this in-class session and talk about the content. They can agree to add additional topics of discussion to the in-class session, but they cannot eliminate topics.

Implementing the Conversation Model: They Say/I Say

Although the librarian grades the ILP and teaches a class session, the students' experience with the overall IL curriculum depends a great deal on their GTA. Course texts and the major student projects are the same across all of the FYC sections, but the day-to-day implementation of the curriculum is in the hands of the GTAs. In the standard FYC syllabus, students complete three writing portfolios, each one including multiple drafts of an essay with other supporting activities. Each of the three writing portfolios integrates the conversation model and critical thinking into the students' writing process.

In the first portfolio, "writing about ideas," students are provided with a scholarly "conversation" to analyze four to six essays on a broad theme, such as education or identity. Using this conversation, students choose two essays to juxtapose (they say) then integrate themselves into this conversation (I say). A brief overview of the research process modeled by the ILP helps them see how their tasks on the first writing portfolio relate to those steps.

In the second writing portfolio, students choose a topic for a researched argument and then find and eavesdrop on ongoing conversations so that they can assemble a panel of experts. The essay itself requires four speakers (They Say) along with the student's own position (I Say). Students must also use neutral background information. This distinction between "speaker" and "background" sources helps students distinguish between those who should be quoted—people with opinions—and material that substantiates the argument that should just be summarized or paraphrased—the background data. The ILP is assigned after the students receive the instructions for this portfolio. The GTAs explain the connection between this paper and the different ILP assignments. GTAs also show a five-minute video from Downs (2006) CD-ROM *i*cite*, a multimedia production that reinforces the idea of the conversation model.

The third writing portfolio is the rhetorical analysis, where students make a close reading of a written or visual text. Part of that analysis is to describe and analyze the extent to which the author of the text uses the "They Say, I Say" technique. As with the first portfolio, information literacy activities are informally structured through class and homework activities. This final work in the term can help reinforce and solidify the IL work that students just completed online and during the library visit with the librarian's assistance.

While all students complete these three major writing portfolios, the GTAs in their sections come up with various ways to integrate the templates into their instruction to expand and reinforce the concepts. For example, the "They Say, I Say" conversation model of thinking is reinforced by GTAs as the classes analyze required readings. When students read Martin Luther King Jr.'s "Letter from Birmingham Jail" (1963) for their rhetorical analysis essay, they can see that it is an excellent example of "You Say, I Say." King says:

> In your statement you assert that our actions, even though peaceful, must be condemned because they precipitate violence. But is this a logical assertion? Isn't this like condemning a robbed man because his possession of money precipitated the evil act of robbery? (92)

Students quickly catch on to the pattern of King's organization as he interacts with various speakers in his conversation:

> You say that I am ___, but you are wrong because ___.

This emphasis on speakers is much more common in the humanities than in the sciences, where sentences are often written with passive voice and researchers and authors are frequently relegated to parentheses. Because the FYC reflects "generic" academic writing suitable for any major, GTAs also remind students that what counts as evidence and how speakers should be presented varies greatly among academic disciplines.

Implementing the Conversation Model: Staff Development

Each fall, the incoming cohort of GTAs is given a ninety-minute orientation to the IL curriculum as part of their five-day pre-service orientation to teaching. The undergraduate services librarians provide a brief overview of the curriculum and assignments. They are taken through the ILP in detail and provided with materials to help them integrate IL into their teaching. GTAs are also introduced to general teaching techniques and the Blackboard system. With all of this intense and compact training before they start teaching two days later, it is no surprise that many of the specifics are not fully assimilated. That is why the undergraduate services librarian visits the GTAs' weekly practicum later in the term to remind GTAs about the IL program and answer questions.

On the library side, new librarians are trained to teach the FYC in two two-hour sessions. In the first session, undergraduate services librarians introduce them to the conversation model and to Kuhlthau's model, and provide an overview of the specific ILP assignments and their desired outcomes. In this session, librarians also learn the basics of teaching FYC, from using Blackboard to accessing shared lesson plans and handouts. The second session focuses more closely on teaching techniques, focusing on lesson planning, activities, assessments, and classroom technologies. New librarians observe several sessions of FYC before teaching on their own.

All librarians who teach FYC participate in a debriefing meeting at the end of each term to evaluate the curriculum and share new ideas for teaching.

RESULTS AND DISCUSSION

When we first implemented the ILP in 2004, we had concrete goals. We wanted to ensure that all of the students in FYC would do some common activities, regardless of who their class librarian or GTA was. We also expected that putting students through these common activities before the face-to-face instruction session would make that session more effective. Knowing that all of the students would arrive with a topic and some exploration of that topic done, the librarian could prepare better. These goals have been accomplished.

We also hoped to integrate the research and writing activities more closely together. While improvement is still needed in this area, particularly in terms of staff development, we have made strides here as well. On a practical level, information literacy is now reflected in the course grade. Beyond that, the ILP format means that students now learn about information literacy as they engage in their own research process, instead of doing separate activities on canned or sample topics. In addition, the adoption of the *They Say, I Say* text means that many information literacy concepts are reinforced during the students' writing process.

These concrete benefits are themselves a good argument for the value of our collaboratively developed curriculum. In the last three years, we have observed an additional benefit to the activities and curriculum. We did not anticipate the extent to which the ILP would give us glimpses into our students' thinking—about their topics and about their research processes. As the activities have been refined and improved, and the more concrete tasks within them have been standardized, more and more of our attention has turned to our students' thinking and what the ILP tells us about their skills in that area.

Modeling Critical Thinking

The ILP and Graff and Birkenstein's templates take our students step by step through a recursive research and writing process. Those steps represent ways of thinking that can be used to analyze any "wicked problem." We also want them to see the value of open-minded exploration and critical thinking, and to begin to understand that knowledge itself is the product of a constructive process. We know that students feel anxious during the exploratory phase of research because they are asked to make sense of a variety of perspectives on a topic, some of which are contradictory (and contradictory to their preconceived ideas) and many of which seem equally plausible. By requiring them to find and listen to multiple speakers, and guiding them through a model research process with built-in spaces for them to reflect on their thinking, we learn more about what they need to develop a tolerance for uncertainty.

One way our FYC helps students grasp and adapt to uncertainty is by emphasizing that most issues have more than two sides, even those issues so typically polarized as "evolution vs. creationism" or "pro-choice vs. pro-life." To show these multiple perspectives and to help students evaluate the relative validity of different perspectives, ILP Assignment 2 sends students to Wikipedia to explore their topics and visit Wikipedia's discussion and history pages, which show a large number of the behind-the-scenes debates about whether or not a particular entry reflects Wikipedia's "neutral point of view" (NPOV). Students used to the neutral style of authorities such as encyclopedias and textbooks are often unaware of the serious differences of opinion that exist under the surface of that neutrality. The transparency of Wikipedia's discussion pages makes those competing opinions visible. By requiring a visit to those pages in our model research process, we build in a spot where students must reflect on that complexity.

At the same time, Graff and Birkenstein's templates provide students with a formula for managing the complexity they find and showing how they can agree and disagree simultaneously. By giving students templates that require them to find more than two sides to the story, and to locate their own voice within those perspectives, *They Say, I Say* takes some of the anxiety out of navigating complex discourses. A fairly simple template like the one below gives students a concrete structure that shows them how to set up multiple perspectives, giving them a way to focus on what they want to say about the issues:

> In discussions of ___ one controversial issue has been ___. On the one hand, X argues ___. On the other hand, Y contends ___. Others even maintain ___. My own view is ___. (Graff and Birkenstein, 164)

Students can follow this template with another:

> I'm of two minds about X's claim that ___. On the one hand, I agree that ___. On the other hand, I'm not sure if ___. (169)

Showing students, step by step, how they can begin to juxtapose and integrate multiple perspectives helps them move beyond the comfort zone of dualistic thinking into a more critical "post-formal" reasoning stage.

Exploration and Knowledge Construction

The ultimate goal of exposing students to a variety of information sources, speakers, and perspectives is that those students will be able to construct their own meaning out of the new ideas and new information sources they encounter. To do this, they must be able to reflect upon their own beliefs. They must also have the disposition or willingness to allow new ideas and information sources to change those previously held constructs. One tiny but useful change we made to our students' ILP has helped us push our students in this direction. As mentioned above, we found that by asking our students much more directive questions in ILP Assignment 1, where they free-write about their topics, we got more thoughtful answers. One of the questions we added was a question specifically asking the students to articulate their own opinions and preconceptions about the topic and to reflect on how those preconceptions might affect their research process. This small change has had very positive results. Those students who follow the directions closely not only reflect on their preconceptions at this point but are more likely to reflect that awareness in subsequent assignments.

To help students interrogate their own beliefs and preconceptions, Graff and Birkenstein present several templates. For example, they show students how to make concessions:

> I'm of two minds about X's claim. On the one hand, I agree that ______. On the other hand, I'm not sure if ______. (169)

This example, also discussed above, reflects the central point of Graff and Birkenstein's approach, that good writing requires engaging with the ideas of others. This particular template also shows how the academic moves modeled in the *They Say, I Say* approach can push students to think reflectively about their own beliefs. More precisely, they must think about where another's ideas have influenced them and where they have not. As Graff and Birkenstein themselves say:

> The mere act of crafting a sentence that begins "Of course, someone might object that ____" may not seem like a way to change the world;

> but it does have the potential to jog us out of our comfort zones, to get us thinking critically about our own beliefs, and perhaps even to change our minds. (13)

In other words, the successful student researcher has the critical thinking skills to integrate new ideas and new information, and to integrate them into their own belief system, making new meaning out of the old and the new.

To do this well, they must also become comfortable with the idea that there is no "right answer" to the questions raised by their complex paper topics. This is another area where the transparency of Wikipedia's knowledge creation process has been invaluable. Sending students to the history pages, and requiring them to look at multiple versions of the same page has two benefits. First, it illustrates the volatility of this kind of digital information source, showing them that information that is there today might not be there tomorrow. More importantly, however, it shows them that the neutral (sometimes), polished (also sometimes) final article is actually the product of revision after revision, done by many people, representing many points of view. While many students do not dig deeply into the content of the different versions, those who do are rewarded with a deeper understanding of how knowledge is constructed.

Our initial decision to use Wikipedia in the ILP was largely practical. After using Wikipedia for a year, however, its value as a resource during the exploratory phase of student research is clear. Even more fascinating has been the opportunity to see our students' thoughts and reflections about the source as they engage with parts of it they have not seen before.

It is important to understand that these glimpses into our students' critical thinking are not tied to the specific activities and templates used in OSU's ILP and writing classrooms; any activities that model parts of a reflective critical research and writing process for students could spark this benefit. We have consistently found that the clearer we can be about the moves our students should make, the more they can and will focus on thinking about their process and their sources. This concept can be adopted at any level of instruction: the lesson, the class session, the course, or even the curriculum. It does not require teachers to change everything they do. It does, however, require us to think about models and templates a little differently. Instead of thinking of them as a way to stifle student creativity, or to control student expression, they can, in fact, allow students to be more creative. As Graff and Birkenstein state, "Creativity and originality lie not in the avoidance of established forms, but in the imaginative use of them" (11).

Challenges and Concerns

One of our main goals when the ILP was created in 2004 was to create a more coherent curriculum, where GTAs and librarians both took ownership of the content. This has had mixed results on both fronts. We are asking a lot of our GTAs, particularly in the fall term of each year, when they are brand new to teaching and to graduate school. Unfortunately, waiting for our GTAs to acclimate to OSU and to their workload as graduate students before bringing them into FYC is not an option because, unlike at some universities, our GTAs start teaching right away. This means that while they start taking classes, they must also become effective teachers of writing and critical thinking in a very short time. To do that, the GTAs must learn the conversation model of academic writing and information literacy, and learn it well enough to teach it to others. This can be challenging for several reasons.

First, like many graduate students in English, most of our GTAs tested out of FYC when they were undergraduates. Many of them learned to write intuitively, and some resist the notion of templates entirely. At the same time, the GTAs' research skills vary greatly. Having had no experience with graduate level research yet, their skills and their understanding of the research process rely wholly on their undergraduate experiences. These barriers make it difficult for some GTAs to really take ownership of the IL curriculum in the FYC. If the GTA cannot explain the ILP assignments or their connection to the students' performance on the research essay, then the students are much more likely to see the entire exercise as busy work.

For librarians, there have been some challenges as well. For many librarians, the FYC represents their only experience with non-subject-related instruction and with first-year students. This can be a very difficult transition for them. Even though Davidson and Crateau recommend teaching students to do very broad, one- or two-word keyword searches, to quickly scan results, and to browse widely, most library instructors have more experience teaching tool and skill-based search strategies for specific queries and spend less time on the concept of broad browsing for eavesdropping. This shift can be especially challenging for the new librarians who teach in the on-call pool.

Grading is an unfamiliar task for librarians who do not teach credit classes, and the responsibility of grading ILPs is stressful as well as time consuming. The grading rubric provides some guidance, but despite this tool, grading remains subjective and not perfectly consistent. More work needs to be done for norming by both GTAs and librarians.

Next Steps

As we continue to collaborate in FYC, the activities and tools that reinforce the conversation model of research and writing are constantly being evaluated and refined. The ILP itself was the result of one such revision, and the questions in the ILP have been refined after every school year based on feedback from students, librarians, and writing instructors. In addition, the writing curriculum has evolved in the last five years as the writing program faculty find new methods and tools to embed the conversation model more deeply into the curriculum. The adoption of the *They Say, I Say* text in 2006 is one example of this evolution. Another is the use of the *i*cite* video in the FYC classroom.

In the summer of 2007, the undergraduate services librarians revised and reformatted the ILP. While the content of the five modules remained the same, the goal was to improve the delivery and format of the assignments so that students can more easily understand the instructional pieces and focus their attention on the most important questions. The effects of these revisions are not yet known. One common complaint about the ILP, particularly about Assignment 4, which focuses on information gathering, is that the instructions are so text-heavy and so detailed that it is difficult for students to navigate them in the Blackboard environment. In addition, as the questions are currently formatted, it is very difficult for students to distinguish between the questions that focus on critical thinking and those that simply check that the student completed a more mechanical task. New options from Blackboard, new e-learning tools online, and resources like the *i*cite* video already in use in the FYC classes offer the opportunity to streamline the process for students, highlighting the questions and tasks that push students to think critically and reflect.

In the last year, OSU's instruction librarians and writing faculty have also been active state-wide working to establish information literacy standards across Oregon's higher education system and sharing the activities we have developed for the FYC. Sharing our strategies is particularly important because up to 40% of OSU students fulfill their FYC requirement elsewhere (Robinson 2006). To ensure that all of these students get the introduction to the conversation model of research and writing that OSU undergraduates get in FYC, continuing this level of outreach statewide is essential.

On the other side of the equation, we are working to build on the introduction to the conversation model students receive in FYC by incorporating it into subsequent writing classes. As Pascarella and Terenzini, van Gelder, and Swanson all note, critical thinking takes time and therefore needs reinforcement. At OSU we are now working to integrate activities that use the conversation model into two of the 200-level writing classes.

We are also continually working to address the issue of training and support for the librarians and GTAs who teach in OSU's FYC. In the summer of 2007, we developed a notebook of resources for all new GTAs teaching in FYC to reinforce the often overwhelming amount of information new GTAs receive in their orientation sessions. We also assessed the library instruction session to more clearly define the learning outcomes that should be addressed in that session, and identified resources to support the librarians as they help students master those outcomes.

Finally, assessment is an area where we must constantly improve our practices. To date, we have not done enough regular, formal assessment that examines the integration of IL and writing instruction in FYC. Students are assessed on the IL competency and their writing competency separately. In the 2007–2008 school year, the librarians will receive samples of student work from the argument essay portfolio to analyze. This will help them see how students actually use the materials they find and evaluate. At the same time, the GTAs will receive a rubric to help them specifically evaluate how well their students use outside resources in their argument essay. Further research is planned to evaluate the impact of these learning experiences on critical thinking, retention, and academic success.

CONCLUSION

Because the majority of traditional age undergraduates arrive at college with limited critical thinking skills, we suggest that instruction librarians and writing faculty should collaboratively introduce students to academic writing as a complex, recursive learning process based on broad and open-minded information seeking. The conversation model adopted by the library and the writing program at OSU provides an excellent way to understand such a process.

Asking students to figure out both the forms and the content of a scholarly research and writing process can impede their ability to focus on the critical thinking skills they need to effectively gather and learn from information, construct new meaning out of their sources, and communicate that meaning to others effectively. Students should be encouraged to focus on the content and on their own thinking. By providing models that show them what a scholarly research process or rhetorical move should look like, we enable them to do just that.

REFERENCES

Davidson, J. R. and C. Crateau. 2000. Intersections: Teaching research through a rhetorical lens. *Research Strategies* 16: 245–257.

Downs, D. 2006. *i*cite: Visualizing sources*. CD-Rom. Boston: Bedford.

van Gelder, T. 2005. Teaching critical thinking: Some lessons from cognitive science. *College Teaching* 53: 41–46.

Graff, G. and C. Birkenstein. 2006. *They say, I say: The moves that matter in academic writing*. New York: Norton.

King, M., Jr. 2006. Letter from Birmingham Jail. *Readings for OSU writers*. Boston: Bedford, pp. 85–99.

Kuhlthau, C. 2004. Seeking meaning: A process approach to library and information services. Westport, CT: Libraries Unlimited.

McMillen, P., B. Miyagishima, and L. Maughan. 2002. Lessons learned about developing and coordinating an instruction program with freshman composition. *Reference Services Review*. 30: 288–299.

Pascarella, E. T. and P. Terenzini. 2005. *How college affects students: A third decade of research*. Vol. 2. San Francisco, CA: Jossey-Bass.

Perry, W. 1970. *Forms of intellectual and ethical development in the college years: A scheme*. New York: Holt Rinehart.

Robinson, T. A. 2006. *Charting their own course as writers: A study of writing-intensive students' self-assessment and goal-setting at start of term*. MA thesis, Oregon State University., Oregon.

Swanson, T. 2006. Information literacy, personal epistemology, and knowledge construction: Potential and possibilities. *College & Undergraduate Libraries* 13: 93–112.

Advancing Critical Thinking and Information Literacy Skills in First Year College Students

Mark Alfino
Michele Pajer
Linda Pierce
Kelly O'Brien Jenks

INTRODUCTION

Among the most useful goals of the college curriculum is the improvement of a student's ability to think clearly and to express his or her thoughts effectively in a variety of media, especially in writing and speech. At Gonzaga University, these goals are pursued in a course block of seven credits called "thought and expression." Our approach to thought and expression involves linking the courses by putting the same twenty students in all three courses and having the faculty of those sections coordinate their teaching in various ways. While practices vary, faculty teaching-linked sections are aware of each others' course topics and assignments. They meet to discuss student progress as well as look for opportunities for curriculum integration and development. This article discusses one such set of linked classes in which library faculty have been integrated into the instructional team and have helped design several innovative assignments that support the critical thinking goals of the course block. Our working hypothesis in this collaboration has been that the critical thinking and expression goals of the thought and expression block can be enhanced by promoting information literacy skills as part of a set of sequenced assignments. While this collaboration is in its early stages, the initial results are promising. This article, then, is a case study and interim evaluation of these efforts.

As faculty focused on introductory college level instruction in critical thinking, composition, and information literacy skills, we all have a variety of educational goals. In order to see how the collaborative assignments in this case study emerged, it may help to start with some background about the critical thinking class that is linked with the English composition course. Each of these courses has a distinct disciplinary history and set of contemporary assumptions and practices. In both courses, some common themes emerge, and these are the areas of recent curriculum development. Both courses include in their aims to promote a set of values about discourse and to encourage students to consider and appropriate a variety of ideals for discussion, expression, and deliberation. Both emphasize a pragmatic approach to their fields. As we turn to the three coordinated assignments, we will see how the library faculty gave a practical design to the first and second assignments, which supported and developed some of the pedagogical themes emphasized by the teaching faculty.

CRITICAL THINKING: BACKGROUND AND THEORETICAL APPROACH OF THE COURSE

As a blend of logic and rhetoric, a modern day critical thinking course has ancient origins. Aristotle's *De Sophisticis Elenchis* gives one of the first accounts in the West of fallacies—practical errors in reasoning. The rhetorical traditions of the Hellenistic and Roman periods contain many sources of advice about practical reasoning, usually in the context of effective persuasive speech and writing. Philosophy also developed a parallel abstract field of study called "logic," again beginning with Aristotle. As is well known, the *trivium* of the medieval university included grammar, logic, and rhetoric. We could say in hindsight that literacy, competent thinking, and style were among the chief goals of this time-honored freshman studies model. In the modern university curriculum, especially from the late 19th century onward, students would typically receive an introductory course in abstract or symbolic logic which, it was assumed, would improve their practical reasoning skills. The idea that an introductory course in symbolic logic would have this "transfer effect" in practical reasoning, writing, and speaking was, arguably, an uncritical assumption of 20th century university pedagogy that was eventually challenged in the university atmosphere of the 1960s, especially in North America. The modern critical thinking course can be seen both as a recovery, though with substantial alteration, of one of the aims of the *trivium* (i.e., competent thinking) and as the rejection of the idea that training in formal logic alone is sufficient to improve one's ability to think critically about the wide variety of topics. Attention to the nature of empirical knowledge and contemporary theory of knowledge is also increasingly valued.

The modern critical thinking movement began as a subfield of logic in the western United States and Canada during the 1970s. As recently as the 1980s and 1990s one would still find markedly more familiarity with the subfield among graduates of PhD programs west of the Mississippi. In North America, the Association for Informal Logic and Critical Thinking (AILACT) is one of the major professional societies within philosophy for the theoretical discussion of critical thinking.

If there is a core theoretical consensus among philosophers in the critical thinking movement, it is that good reasoning involves both formal and informal standards of evaluation (Johnson and Blair 1997). Some practitioners focus more heavily on formalizations or quasi-formalizations of everyday arguments and on the reasoning virtues and vices that can be demonstrated clearly with some formalization. Formalization in this context typically involves distinguishing logical relationships such as "if—then," disjunction and conjunction from content, and studying the formal properties of logical relationships—especially validity. But the distinguishing mark of a critical thinking course is the attention given to the practical dimension of thought. At a practical level, most critical thinking textbooks teach some method for "reconstructing" natural language arguments into combinations of deductive and inductive arguments and explanations within the argument structure of a whole text or speech. Reconstruction is typically seen as a preparatory step toward analysis—the actual application of standards of good reasoning to a set of rationales.

After reconstructing a piece of argumentative writing, students undertake analysis. The central tasks of analysis include questioning the truth of the premises, questioning the relationship between the premises and the conclusions, and asking whether there are alternative ways of thinking about the problem under consideration (reframing). The first two forms of analysis are not difficult to teach and lead to great discussions about presupposition and the meanings of specific knowledge claims. The third involves so-called divergent or lateral thinking and some students, even some very bright ones, find that difficult.

While it helps to have some detail about current practices and theories in critical thinking, it may be more germane to the case study to focus on the theoretical commitments that are particularly relevant to curricular integration with composition and information literacy. First, like many critical thinking courses today, we focus on what is sometimes called "applied epistemology." Epistemology is the study of the grounds of human knowledge. Within a critical thinking course, applied epistemology directs us toward an awareness of the kinds of knowledge claims at work in an argument and an awareness of the standards for evaluating particular kinds of knowledge claims. Knowledge claims are made in distinctive ways by most of the typical fields of discourse found in the modern university structure, but also through personal experience and cultural practices. Since many aspects of information literacy involve assessment of knowledge claims, this course objective overlaps naturally with the work of our library colleagues.

An emphasis on applied epistemology pushes us toward a heightened awareness of "point of view." As an element in an information literacy curriculum, point of view allows library faculty to heighten a student's awareness of the various fields of knowledge at work in argumentative speech and writing and to raise questions about how the knowledge claims are evaluated within particular fields of knowledge. Along with the variety of epistemic topics, which this requires one to address, it also raises practical questions about authoritativeness in the use of sources and critical evaluation of sources. A second theoretical commitment of our approach is a general agreement with and adaptation of the "pragma-dialectic" approach of the Dutch theorists, Van Eemeren and Grootendorst. These theorists, whose work influenced North American philosophers, especially in the late 1980s and 1990s, remind us that real arguments are not abstract, disembodied linguistic structures but, rather, positions advanced by real individuals within a pragmatic speech context. In the approach of some traditional logic, a consideration of the persona, aims, and intentions of speakers might seem like a distraction from discerning the semantic content and logical structure of the "text." Critical thinking theories that emphasize pragmatics point out that context and interpretation are root and branch of inquiry and not good candidates for excision. In order to even determine that a text is argumentative, one must interpret the context and/or intentions of a writer or speaker. Next, interpretive issues arise in the process of giving a reconstruction of a text. Finally, critical responses require us to make significant assumptions about the response needed in light of our "reading" of context.

Focusing on the pragmatic speech context has a number of practical implications for our curricular collaboration in the thought and expression course block. First, it encourages us to ask about rhetorical purposes of speakers and writers. This makes it easier for students to see connections between the skills taught in critical thinking courses and some of the rhetorical skills taught in composition classes. Second, it reminds us that arguments are put forward by particular individuals working from particular points of view and with a variety of goals. Responding to an argument involves responding also to a person or group for whom that argument has a particular significance or pragmatic meaning. One of the goals of the learning community model in our work is to develop interpersonal communication skills, and, frankly, to model virtues related to discourse and communication. If you incorporate these virtues into a definition, you might say that a good critical thinker is someone who is (1) aware of his or her own perspective, commitments, and biases; (2) pursues truth methodically and relentlessly; and (3) sensitively assesses and responds to others based on an understanding of and selection among the various pragmatic goals of the speech context. As students become more reflective about how knowledge is produced and validated, they begin to see themselves as participant in academic discourse and producers of their own "local" knowledge, their own reasoned and revisable opinion.

COMPOSITION: BACKGROUND AND THEORETICAL APPROACH OF THE COURSE

The goals of English 101 are to help students express themselves effectively in writing and to teach them to compose expository and argumentative essays. To meet these goals, the English faculty follow a common syllabus that introduces students to a variety of rhetorical strategies and methods of organizing essays (Department of English, Gonzaga University). In addition, 101 teaches students how to develop unified and coherent paragraphs, to write expressive, complete grammatical sentences, and to learn and follow the grammatical, usage, spelling, and punctuation conventions of edited American English. Ideally, students at Gonzaga are registered for three thought and expression courses during either the fall or spring semesters of their freshman year. In some cases, students are registered in linked sections: a group of twenty students meets together for their sections of composition, speech, and critical thinking.

Our case study reports on the experiences of two particular linked sections of critical thinking and composition that stress intellectual self-discovery in an academic environment. An important part of becoming competent in that environment involves exploring and using the information available through technology. Developing information literacy skills helps the students see where their own ideas fit into the world of larger ideas and the arguments that relate to them.

Composition also has origins in the classical trivium. Although practices vary according to department and instructors, some treatment of logic, grammar, and rhetoric is found in most composition courses taught today. Increasingly, contemporary composition theory also makes the point that a trivium-like introduction to the academy is essential to successful higher education.

In the context of these ideas, Bartholmae's much discussed essay, "Inventing the University," reminds us that a college student must learn "to appropriate (or be appropriated by) a specialized discourse, and he has to do this as though he were easily and comfortably one with his audience, as though he were a member of the academy or an historian or an anthropologist or an economist; he has to invent the university by assembling and mimicking its language" (Bartholmae 2005, 51).

If learning how to use this "language" or at least learning how to recognize and assess it is necessary to writing an effective argument and to participating in the common language of the academy, then learning effective information literacy skills is fundamental to thought and expression. Being able to identify and reconstruct the arguments of others is essential to creating one's own argument, as well as one's own reflective voice. All are ways of learning how to participate in Bartholmae's "specialized discourse," and all provide students with a basis for developing critical thinking and academic writing skills.

Careful knowledge acquisition has always been fundamental to composing an effectively written argument; however, new technology has made sorting through the maze of information sources a challenge for even the most prepared college freshman. As students learn to participate in academic discourse, they need the skills to identify different types of academic knowledge and to recognize and appropriately question authoritativeness. They need the ability and language to assess sources. As students acquire confidence from these skills by participating in the information literacy assignments, they can also develop their academic writing voice.

Once this voice starts to mature, point of view becomes an important part of their expression. It relates directly to the question freshmen so frequently ask: What about my own opinion? They see that their backgrounds, their environments, and the beliefs of those they grew up around all have definite effects on their own views. After gaining an understanding of when and where to use their own thoughts and the thoughts of others, students begin to express themselves in a language suitable for the academy.

The combination of learning critical thinking and composition skills together lends confidence to the expression of those individual voices. The collaborative assignments under discussion in this case study help students build confidence in their writing.

THE COLLABORATIVE ASSIGNMENTS

The three collaborative assignments we focus on in this case study are (1) a Wikipedia assignment, (2) a point-of-view assignment, and (3) a researched argument essay.

Wikipedia Assignment

Having worked together in the thought and expression block over many years, the library faculty and course faculty have tried, successfully and unsuccessfully, to find ways to help freshman students gain the necessary background knowledge to even begin working on an assignment based on an argumentative issue. When asked to research an issue, most students choose a topic because of a basic interest, but that interest does not imply a base of knowledge. Those who have some knowledge of the topic may only have approached it from a single point of view and never considered opposing views or views contrary to their position. A major goal of the critical thinking course is to assist students in acquiring the necessary knowledge and background information to make rational and appropriate arguments and conclusions based on more than just their current personal knowledge or uncritical opinions. The Wikipedia assignment contributes to this course goal, but it can also be seen in the context of contemporary library practice.

For several decades, library instruction, or bibliographic instruction as it was once known, has followed a standard way to teach library research skills to students. In most cases, librarians would show students subject encyclopedias or other general works that enable students to get the background necessary to evaluate and understand the journal articles and books, which are then identified in the library research process. Prior to the evolution of the Internet, librarians teaching research skills might bring carts of subject encyclopedias to class and attempt to show the students the value of beginning with an authoritative, general introduction to their topic. Then the librarians would proceed to the next phase of research, usually involving primary or secondary research resources. Libraries are still collecting subject-specific encyclopedias that provide rich background material. But as times change, research tools change, too. As instructors, we know that students more and more turn to the Internet to provide them with background information, and, as librarians, we are seeking ways to help students understand the strengths and weaknesses of the information systems that we all use. The Wikipedia assignment was developed as a response to these changes. At a regional ACRL meeting, an Oregon State University librarian presented a Wikipedia assignment, which gave us an example from which to work (Dieterling 2006). We saw that the assignment could help us to provide students with a way of obtaining background information related to their research topics and to give us a way of demonstrating how this type of information is created and vetted.

There were several goals in Dieterling's assignment: (1) to use Wikipedia to provide background information to the student on their topic of choice, (2) to have the student read and analyze both the Wikipedia history pages and discussion pages attached to the article to help them see how knowledge is represented and vetted, and (3) to make students aware of the inherent difficulties in presenting information and knowledge in a neutral tone.

Our own adaptation embraces these same goals. However, we also wanted to encourage students to explore new and less clichéd topics before making a topic selection. With some quickly acquired information and knowledge from the Wikipedia pages, we hoped students would be able to find issues that would be particularly engaging for their research projects. Also, we wanted to encourage quick knowledge acquisition (and critical questioning of authority) as a general habit, especially in light of the development of online information.

Before deciding to use this assignment, we discussed the fact that for many academics, including librarians, Wikipedia is not considered a source that contributes to student learning. The fact that the articles are not always written by "authorities" in the field and can be edited and changed, theoretically by anyone, can cause much gnashing of teeth and rending of clothes by traditional scholars. However, despite this controversy, as a quick reference source, we decided that Wikipedia has advantages as well as deficits. In developing our version of the Dieterling Wikipedia assignment, we focused on some specific goals for the assignment, and, after collaborative discussion, we agreed that the assignment should:

1. Provide students with information about an easily accessible source for basic background material on their topic.
2. Help students develop skills in assessing authoritativeness.
3. Help students understand the value and difficulty of presenting knowledge in a "neutral" way.
4. Help students formulate efficient search strategies that lead them to other reference sources and a wide range of primary sources.

A librarian presented the Wikipedia assignment in the critical thinking classroom. Much to our surprise, many class members had not used or heard about Wikipedia. Of those who had, many were told that they should not use it, and that it was not a legitimate source of information. Our response was to put Wikipedia into the context of the larger information world. Every source needs to be evaluated and judged, not just Wikipedia, and while other more traditional sources usually are considered to have greater validity and authoritativeness, all writing is subject to bias and inaccuracy. In fact, published print reference sources can often be less current than a Wikipedia article's reference list. During this presentation we examined the history pages and discussion pages of the Wiki article on global warming. The students quickly noted that certain people were making the bulk of the comments and that the page was being edited often, though mainly with minor changes. We also noted times that the page had been closed to editing by the Wikipedia editors, and the types of changes made from small typographical errors to entire sentences or paragraphs that needed to be changed. We followed links to see if we could find out relevant information about the people suggesting changes to the article. Were the participants qualified? Could you even trust what they said about themselves? Did we have enough information to make a judgment? These were all questions we wanted our students to ask.

We then examined the list of references, discussed what we could tell about the Websites that were listed, such as explaining the .org, .gov, and .com designations, and encouraged students to make a determination of validity for each site that they might use. We also referred students back to the library Web pages to check for availability of any books or journals that might have been referenced.

One of the most interesting discoveries in presenting this assignment was that we were getting students to become aware in a very real way how knowledge is created, expressed, and edited, and that awareness might enhance their general sophistication in using other information sources, including Wikipedia. This experience also pointed out to them the difficulty that any source faces as it attempts, as does Wikipedia, to be a neutral source of information. The topics they were researching were ones that were inherently controversial, and Wikipedia contributors were quick to point out intended or unintended word usage or statements that, in their opinion, slanted the article in one direction or another. Overall, the assignment reinforced the students' skills in getting background information prior to delving more deeply into a topic, allowed them to evaluate and appropriately use a well-known Internet resource, and brought into focus the need to look for and acknowledge the kinds of bias and opinion that would be found in many of the sources they would use as they continued their research for the final assignment.

Point-of-View Assignment

In developing our second assignment, we needed to acknowledge that students who are becoming acculturated to college level academic work often have trouble making distinctions about information sources. They need to know how to identify valid and appropriate sources, a problem made more difficult by the easy availability of a wider range and greater quantity of sources. Whether their knowledge was gleaned from the Internet, a newspaper or an academic article, a time-honored volume of wisdom, or their own impressions of a topic, we wanted students to critically understand point of view and source authority. Therefore, this assignment asks students to determine the editorial stance or bias of general publications and use that information in their research. Our strategy is to engage students by having them:

1. Read an article on a topic of controversial interpretation.
2. Receive an in-class presentation by a librarian on the concept of editorial point of view in the presentation of information and the difficulty of writing without bias—also giving the students examples from well-known journals showing editorial point of view.
3. Learn to differentiate between types of information and how to locate vetted and otherwise claimed and evaluated sources.
4. Locate and post articles representing various points of view on the topic to a collaborative Wiki set-up for the class locally using a version of MediaWiki. Articles with clear articulations of the rationale for the particular viewpoint were prized.
5. Write about their perspective of the topic based on specific issues that had been addressed in the reading and reflection.

The purpose of the point-of-view assignment is to teach students source evaluation skills and to connect them through actions and reflection to a personal experience with those skills. All students in the class read a recent essay entitled, The Height of Inequality (Crook 2006), reporting some recent research in economics and income inequality. Then they were asked to find various articles that demonstrated different opinions on the topic. They were asked to reconstruct arguments that answered some of the following questions: Should we worry about income inequality? Why or why not? A librarian then visited the class to discuss the concept of point of view and perspective within the publications that students might be using in their assignment. This was done through lecture, demonstration, interactive and directed searching, handouts, and cooperative evaluation of searches by the professor, the librarian, and the students.

Our in-class session began with an introduction to the concept of point of view in sources, alerting students to its presence and relevance. This part of the lecture was a combination of giving students information about editorial bias and instilling in them the need to consider point of view as one of the criteria for selecting or eliminating a source as they searched. We also discussed other aspects of information that researchers consider when evaluating a source, including the knowledge and experience of the author, intended audience, currency, coverage or scope, and editorial oversight. We encourage our students to look at these aspects of sources as they evaluate the authority and appropriateness of any source whether it is a book, Web site, or article.

Once this general level of evaluation was explained, students were introduced to and encouraged to consider both author and editorial point of view when selecting information. A handout, "Journals of Thought and Opinion," which lists a variety of newsmagazines and non-academic journals of opinion along with a description of their editorial point of view, was distributed and discussed (Foley Library 2007). For many students, this was the first time they realized that some of the magazine titles they browse for their news have an editorial point of view. The current list ranges from general news magazines to those with a strong ideological statement and a specific readership in mind. In the context of a class on critical thought or a writing class where an argumentative paper has been assigned, students can often articulate some initial reaction to a topic or state a personal opinion on the subject. With these new skills, students can orient their ideas in relation to other points of view within the debate and begin to understand the benefit of differing types of information. During this reflection, they may also discuss whether their views are centrist or extreme. A strategy for encouraging them to become more self-reflective about this is to ask them what their usual reaction is to articles they read in *Time* or *Newsweek*. Do they find these publications balanced/liberal? Students sometimes discover their bias when they realize that publications they consider balanced and neutral are not seen that way by most informed observers.

With these initial topics and their exercise completed, students began their search for articles related to the topic they had chosen for their researched argument essay. In this class, a quick tutorial was given using Academic Search Premier and Proquest as two appropriate cross-disciplinary, general databases. The tutorial focused on how to search the databases using keywords, how to narrow the search through the addition of subject terms, and how to select from the results the most useful type of information for the assignment, which in this instance was choosing magazines and not academic/scholarly journals or newspapers. Students were asked to find a manageable number of articles to review, and they examined and sorted articles based on the editorial stance of the journal and author. Using the handout as a guide, students were encouraged to identify journals with various points of view or use contextual information, such as editorial statements online and wording of article abstracts to determine point of view.

Typically, at this juncture of their searching, students evaluate an article according to its appropriateness to their argument based on the title or abstract of the article. However, with point of view as an evaluative tool, they had an additional and possibly an even more effective way of estimating whether the information they find will be of interest and where it falls on the ideological continuum. They were able to make an informed assessment about the type of information they would obtain if they pursued various leads.

The class became highly motivated as they started to see how they could represent a more or less complete range of views and arguments on the topic, from people who thought income inequality data was irrelevant to political discourse to those who thought the level of inequality in the U.S. was alarming. They began to actively tailor the searches to fill in perspectives as they came to recognize editorial positions and their expositors. In some cases, this led them from the broader "journals of thought and opinion" to seminal journal articles and discipline specific resources. Moreover, in our setting at Gonzaga, students will often specify an interest in Catholic thought on a topic. Interestingly, some students were unaware of Catholic social teaching on this topic and found that information fascinating.

As with much instruction, students eventually took over the work and developed their search and findings. They reported their research findings on the class Wiki, which allows for quick storage of information and links, as well as interaction and discussion with other students during their research. Also, the software allowed us to follow the student's progress online.

Researched Argument Essay

The researched argument essay is the culminating activity for the linked sections. We asked students to choose topics that involved controversy (or at least reasoned difference of opinion) and had enough inherent complexity to result in an interesting and fruitful research project. After the topic and research group selection process, we had between three and five research groups per class, with an average of four to six students in each group. They shared their research using the class Wiki. In this way, we put the students in the position of Wikipedians—individuals who are contributing to an on-going body of knowledge about a topic. As students reported their research findings to the class Wiki, they also found ways to organize the research online. Often they collected findings which relate to a particular issue or question and grouped them together, using the automatic table of contents feature of the software to facilitate this process. A crucial requirement of the collaborative research process is that students are responsible for considering all posted research as they develop their own researched point of view.

After some initial research, students were ready to begin writing their synthesis essay, a requirement for their composition course. There were two basic goals for the synthesis assignment: (1) to familiarize freshmen with using sources in their writing (avoiding plagiarism, using authorities in their own prose, using proper MLA documentation style, and incorporating quotations and paraphrases effectively and smoothly into their arguments); and (2) to encourage them to start thinking about their issue in a critical way.

More specifically, the synthesis assignment asked the students to find three criteria for contrast and or comparison between the two sources. Once these were determined, their essays were organized around those three criteria. In addition to quoting and paraphrasing, they attempted to draw conclusions related to the controversy and comment on what they gained from being exposed to two different sources; however, they did not need to present their definitive thesis on the controversy. Our hope was that the synthesis essay would give students a relevant pre-writing activity before drafting their actual researched arguments essays.

The final outcome of the research project was an individual ten-page academic paper submitted for both the English composition course and the critical thinking course. The paper was expected to present supporting evidence and argue against opposing views in a coherent, well-documented argumentative essay. Although we do not prescribe a required citation format, these essays generally follow MLA style and follow the Rogerian argumentative style. They are submitted during the final week of the semester and graded by the critical thinking and composition instructors.

Given our focus on "applied epistemology" and developing the student's authorial voice as critical thinkers and junior members of the academy, our approach was to ask students to find a topic with a deliberative dimension that stimulates a genuine interest for them and to ask them to make their own critical statement about their topic in light of an in-depth process of research and reflection.

The first two assignments in our collaboration both focus on specific difficulties and limitations of the "standard unguided" research project, which invites low motivation and plagiarism. In many ways, the first two assignments in our collaboration were born of the difficulties of producing authentic work in the research project. Both of these assignments take place prior to topic selection for the research paper. The Wikipedia assignment allowed students to investigate some of their initial preferences for topics, while the point-of-view assignment helped them ask about the breadth of perspective on any topic they may eventually choose. These assignments gave students a model for academic inquiry, countering a natural tendency to simply "build a case" for one's view. They also allowed us to broach a variety of basic questions about academic life, particularly about knowledge production, authority, and the complexity of assessing competing points of view. One effect of raising these questions is to raise standards of evaluation for the research project. As technology makes retrieval and documentation less challenging for students, but trite, random, and uncritical use of sources more likely, we can respond by increasing attention on an applied version of a central philosophical problem: with reference to my topic, what do we know and does that knowledge inform action?

It must be acknowledged that the actual execution of a freshman research paper is rarely a clearly observed event. The Wikipedia pages produced and updated by the students helped make the research process a documented and transparent one showing the participation of all group members. The requirement to report research findings to the class Wiki, and for all research group members to be responsible for information posted, heightened student accountability and accounted for many office visits and library visits during the research and writing phases of the project. All of the teaching faculty, including the library faculty, were encouraged to "drop in" on the student research pages to offer advice and raise questions. Midway through the research process, we surveyed students with a questionnaire asking them about their state of knowledge of the topic, familiarity with sources that present a point of view, and their emerging perspective and influences. We asked them to identify key research questions early in the process and determine which have been answered and whether new questions have emerged. Compared to previous semesters in which we assessed these factors, students gave more convincing evidence that they chose reference and research sources with an understanding of their authority and point of view. They also did a better job of identifying deficits in their knowledge and using quick reference sources to get answers. During the drafting process, English and philosophy faculty reviewed argument outlines and noticed that students often showed that they knew the positions being developed by other research group members, had had conversations with them about their positions, and showed concern about how their position was developing in relation to their peers. We also noticed more research groups devoted to topics that had immediate relevance to the student's environment. While this is not an explicit goal of the collaboration, it could be evidence that students are following our cue and starting to see themselves as participants in an academic world that supplies resources for advocating either continuity or change in their world. For example, we initially had the typical "sex education" research topic, but several students used the topic to ask about what sex education practices Gonzaga University might engage in. This was quite a surprising reframing of the topic. Typically, this topic gives students a veiled means of reflecting on their own elementary and high school experience of sex education in relation to research literature on effective sex education programs. Equally encouraging results included a group of students who decided to study Gonzaga's student life policies related to reporting and hearing complaints of sexual harassment and rape. They acquired an understanding of legal concepts and professional knowledge in the field of student life. They found the issue so relevant and sensitive that they engaged in intense and increasingly informed discussion with many students (within the class and outside of it) as their research progressed. These examples are anecdotal and likely relate to unique features of the semester and particular students, but they do suggest one kind of authentic topic choice.

These are general positive results, which suggest that we are addressing some of the common curricular values in the collaboration: development of the student's academic writing voice, focus on applied epistemology, and acquisition of information literacy skills. We should acknowledge a number of limitations in our initial work that will shape the coming year's efforts. For instance, the Wikipedia and point-of-view assignments could be given earlier in the semester. This would allow for more time to do workshops on research group findings for the researched argument paper. We probably could spend more time looking carefully at a group's research results before the writing stage of the research paper. Also, students and faculty were just learning the MediaWiki software this semester. We may want to work more with some unique software features, such as talk and history pages in the future.

All three assignments encourage students to seek information and reliable knowledge, to understand what they need to look for to assess that information, and to understand how to craft arguments, paragraphs, and papers that show some depth of deliberation. On the whole, this semester's students, as evidenced by their researched argument papers, seemed to be performing at noticeably higher levels than in the past. They showed more awareness of the role of external authorities, conflicting evidence, and opposing views. They seemed more willing to allow their view to develop through research and more willing to respond to criticisms of their views.

CONCLUSION

As noted, the teaching faculty who read and graded the research papers reported that the quality of the papers (and student research behaviors) was higher this semester. Students seemed to fill in their knowledge deficits more quickly; they understood the need to engage a range of viewpoints, and they reflected that knowledge and understanding in their writing. While still operating within a Freshman grading rubric, the papers demonstrated more of the qualities of information literate, college level thinkers and writers—in other words, junior members of the academic community—than in previous semesters. This should allow us to raise standards for next semester's papers.

Much of the specific evidence of this improvement can be documented in more precise ways. As we refine the assignments, we will look for additional and more precise measures of the outcomes we have observed from this initial collaboration. For example, library faculty may develop a rubric that could be applied to the researched argument papers to verify teaching faculty perceptions and to assess outcomes for information literacy. Our present experience gives us considerably more confidence in our general hypothesis, that the critical thinking and expression goals of the thought and expression block can be enhanced by promoting information literacy skills as part of a set of sequenced assignments, which raise student awareness of knowledge acquisition tools, standards of evaluation for authority, and point of view.

REFERENCES

Bartholmae, D. 2005. *Writing on the margins: Essays on composition and teaching.* Boston: Bedford Publishing.

Crook, C. 2006. The height of inequality. *Atlantic,* September, pp. 36–37.

Dieterling, A. 2006. Resistance is futile: Academia meets the NeXt generation. *Panel discussion at the annual conference of ACRL, Oregon/Washington Chapter*, Corbett, Oregon, Oct. 26.

Foley Library Gonzaga University. Journals of thought and opinion. Spokane, WA. http://www.gonzaga.edu/Academics/Libraries/Foley+Library/Subject-Guides/Arts-Humanities-Subject-Guides/JournalsThoughtOpinion.doc.

Gonzaga University Department of English. English 101 Syllabus, Spokane, WA.

Johnson, R. H. and J. A. Blair. 1997. Informal logic in the twentieth century. *In:* Walton D. and Brinton, A. (eds.). *Historical Foundations of Informal Logic*, Brookfield, VT: Ashgate, pp. 158–177.

Modeling Scholarly Inquiry: One Article at a Time

Anne Marie Gruber
Mary Anne Knefel
Paul Waelchli

One of the most important responsibilities educators have is helping students learn to make defensible judgments about vexing problems.
—*King and Kitchener (1994)*

As part of an ethics initiative at the University of Dubuque, librarians, in collaboration with the writing center, created and implemented a collaborative project that incorporates critical thinking, ethical inquiry, and information literacy into a beginning composition course. ENG102, a required composition and rhetoric II course, is the equivalent of English 101 at most institutions. The assignment is designed to give ENG102 students a foundation in higher-level reasoning skills, such as analysis and synthesis, as they use scholarly articles to craft a research paper. In the assignment, a team of teaching faculty, librarians, and writing center tutors (peer and professional) model academic inquiry. In small groups led by a team member, students investigate evidence in support of a single thesis. A recent campus-wide ethics initiative frames this assignment, which encourages students to examine research on controversial social topics that may challenge existing beliefs. This article describes how the team created and implemented this collaborative assignment and analyzes the qualitative data collected during the first three semesters of its use.

LITERATURE REVIEW

Library/Writing Center Collaboration

Academic librarians have long collaborated with faculty to teach information skills, primarily focusing on a "search and find" model. More institutions have implemented or are considering a comprehensive "information literacy across the curriculum" model, including Wartburg College, Florida International University, and Bellevue Community College. The Council of Independent Colleges has endorsed the Association of College and Research Libraries (ACRL) *Information Literacy Competency Standards for Higher Education* (Association of College and Research Libraries 2000). Some accrediting agencies, including those covering the Mid-Atlantic, Midwest, New England, and West, also explicitly refer to information literacy in their standards. The traditional information literacy model concentrates on the search process itself. Increasingly, academic and school librarians, like composition faculty, are recognizing a need for a more process-based model, led by theorists such as Kuhlthau (1985), who developed the Information Search Process in the 1980s. A search of the primary information literacy list-serv, ILI-L, shows 261 posts discussing critical thinking from July 2006 through June 2007. It is clear that librarians are seeking ways to teach research as a holistic integrated process.

Writing center professionals are asking similar questions. They support research writing assignments, usually through peer tutoring and term paper counseling models. Writing-across-the-curriculum (WAC), usually located in writing centers and English departments, arose in the 1970s and 1980s in response to deficiencies in student writing skills at all educational levels (Sheridan 1995). Sheridan describes WAC as "a dramatic departure from certain long-held assumptions about the nature of writing" (xvi). Notably, WAC does not place sole responsibility of writing instruction on composition faculty; instead, it emphasizes a more interdisciplinary and process-based approach.

Within both composition and information literacy, it is becoming clearer that research and writing are two sides of the same coin, which creates the potential that "writing and information literacy can productively shape the conception of each other" (Norgaard 2004, 220). Composition instructors, writing center professionals, and librarians alike are beginning to understand research writing as a non-linear process and "a means for engaging inquiry and critical thinking" (222). As Elmborg and Hook (2005) point out, separating research and writing can undermine the success of modeling this process for students. Fister (1992) illustrates the common ground: "Because we want students to learn *how* more than *what*, we are concerned with their grasp of the process as much as with product" (154). Collaboration between writing centers and libraries, then, is a natural extension of each discipline's role.

According to Elmborg and Hook, "Writing centers and libraries have been living parallel lives, confronting many of the same problems and working out similar solutions, each in their own institutional contexts" (1). Certainly this has been the case at the University of Dubuque. The Writing Center is part of the Academic Support Center, located in the Charles C. Myers Library, and it employs both professional and peer tutors. Historically, librarians have referred students to tutors for assistance in interpreting and analyzing sources, crafting thesis statements, outlining, drafting, and proofreading. Tutors, likewise, refer students to librarians when students need assistance using sources to narrow topics or gather additional information at any stage. Consistent with the literature (Fister; Sheridan), these referrals and the physical proximity were the extent of the relationship until librarians initiated the ENG102 collaboration.

Fister offered suggestions to connect libraries and composition theory. In recent collaborations, the roles that librarians, writing center staff, and teaching faculty each takes vary by institution. In Tipton and Bender's (2006) work with under-prepared transfer students, a writing center director and librarian worked together, with the librarian presenting two to three times per semester. Huerta and McMillan (2000) collaborated to team-teach research and writing in undergraduate science courses, with shared responsibility for planning and teaching. Isbell (1995) gives another example of a team teaching model, with research writing as an intertwined, inseparable process, using composition theory as a foundation. Elmborg and Hook have collected additional examples of successful collaborations that integrate the writing center model with information literacy instruction. In successful collaborations, research and writing constitute an ongoing interconnected process. Additionally, they include more integration than a typical "one-shot" information literacy session or a basic peer tutoring model.

Peer tutoring has not traditionally been used in library instruction as it has been in writing centers (Elmborg and Hook). Deese-Roberts and Keating (2000) advocate a peer tutor model within library instruction, using existing tutoring programs as a starting point. Bruffee's (1993) social constructionist theory supports instructional design that incorporates peer group in knowledge communities, which model disciplinary discourse. Peer collaboration in the classroom has the potential to challenge students' beliefs. Bruffee posits, however, that homogenous peer groups do not have "enough articulated dissent or resistance to consensus to invigorate the conversation" (32). Diverse perspectives within peer groups develop students' critical thinking skills.

CRITICAL THINKING IN COLLEGE STUDENTS

Norris and Ennis (1989) state that critical thinking is the "reasonable and reflective thinking that is focused upon deciding what to believe or do" (1). While this definition is generally accepted by scholars (Albitz 2007; Cheung et al. 2002; Phillips 2004; Tsui 2002; Waite and Davis 2006), Norris and Ennis argue that thinking critically is more complex. They argue for a process-driven model that requires value judgments as well as supporting information and problem-solving. They expand critical thinking beyond a cognitive process and account for students' abilities and dispositions. Cheung et al. and others (Warren 1994) also include motivational, ideological, and behavioral components.

Hughes (2000) defines key traits of critical thinking: awareness of incomplete arguments, challenging conclusions and beliefs, developing intellectual worth, and developing persuasive skills-based evidence rather than feeling. These share elements with information literacy (Albitz) and create a natural connection between faculty- and librarian-led critical thinking activities (Phillips).The behavioral and emotional aspects of critical thinking are tied to students' developmental stages.

Most students enter college unable to analyze complex questions for which there is no single answer (Carroll 2002; King and Kitchener 1994; Perry 1970). They believe that all questions can be answered using the "correct facts" and so find it difficult to pose research questions, which are by definition complex. Therefore, many first-year students succeed in finding information on a topic but cannot form a research question. Thus, their papers end up as meaningless lists of data (Higgins 1993). Olwell and Delph (2004) describe the problem in history papers: "Students view history as a series of indisputable facts . . . rather than a series of problems that must be analyzed critically" (24). According to Carroll (2002), college students face a developmental challenge to move beyond the "one right answer" by considering a variety of evidence to develop a truthful reasoned answer. She states that for first-year students to succeed in writing courses, they must "abandon their 'normal' ways of writing" (47). This is often challenging for students who are confident and comfortable within their limited range of experiences and beliefs (Weiler 2005).

First-year students' dualistic mode of thinking (Perry) presents a challenge as they consider ethical questions. Based on calls "for a greater attention to the moral and civic purposes of college" (Boyer 1987, 283), an increasing number of colleges is structuring environments in which students "learn to make defensible judgments about vexing problems," especially moral ones (King and Kitchener, 1). This reflective thinking described by Dewey (1933) is closely related to critical thinking. Colby et al. called for colleges to teach students how to "offer and demand evidence and justification for their moral and political positions" (2003, 4). This call is addressed in the ACRL information literacy standards: "the information literate student determines whether the new knowledge has an impact on the individual's value system and takes steps to reconcile differences" (2000, indicator 3.5).

King and Kitchener found that most college seniors have transitioned to a state of moral relativity in which they understand that complex questions may have multiple answers. They know that facts and data can be used to support various positions, but most are unsure how to evaluate the data.

Asking first-year students to consider complex questions creates apprehension because it moves them beyond their developmental level (Weiler). Vygotsky's (1978) theory of the zone of proximal development (ZPD) suggests that students move beyond their comfort zone when assignments are structured in stages that connect their previous experiences to new knowledge. Bhavnagri and Bielat (2005) demonstrate how librarians and faculty apply scaffolding, breaking assignments into steps, to support critical thinking.

According to Higgins, first-year students need peer collaborative support to develop critical thinking skills such as synthesizing information, organizing sources, and defending a claim. Analyzing information sources with the entire class and in small groups allows them to work together to connect various data sources and find common themes. Students without this support are intimidated and less likely to learn these skills (Whitmire 1998).

INSPIRATION

The assignment grew from Knefel's fall 2005 participation in a faculty component of a campus-wide ethics initiative. The Wendt Character Initiative was established at the University of Dubuque to infuse discussions of ethics throughout the university, designating fairness, truthfulness, honesty, and the Golden Rule as key values. Each semester, selected faculty design and present an ethics component for a 100-level class. After Knefel presented her assignment at a workshop, the writing center director expressed interest in incorporating it into a spring composition class.

The assignment frames research writing as a search for a type of truth or evidence as defined by a scholarly discipline. It fills a perceived gap in students' skills in the subsequent required writing course, Introduction to Research Writing (RES104).

In RES 104, students are required to formulate and narrow their own topics, research focused questions, and write three five-page thesis papers. Librarians and faculty observed that some students were intimidated by the many tasks they were expected to perform in a short period. Librarians found many students were reluctant to use journal articles and book chapters. More problematic, however, assessment showed they did not understand the role of the research question in driving the process. They accumulated articles on a topic during library research sessions but were stymied when they had to choose information to support a thesis and craft a paper. In frustration, they would change topics and hand in a paper full of facts either with a vague or non-existent thesis.

All English composition classes are given a single research question and three journal articles that directly address the question. The class meets as a whole and in small groups led by faculty, librarians, professional writing tutors, and peer writing tutors to discuss the scope and meaning of the research question, examine the articles, and create a group thesis statement. Each student writes a four- to five-page paper using the articles to support the group thesis statement.

Modeling research as a collaborative process is key. Because many aspects of research writing are internal, first-year students can find them difficult to learn (Zimmerman and Risemberg 1997). The assignment makes this process transparent and involves students in the construction of meaning through discussion and writing. This call to conversation makes students reexamine their expectations that research writing is a lonely, isolated process.

Librarians consciously choose provocative ethical topics of interest to students. During spring 2006 and fall 2007, students examined the research question "When local television news programs report violent crime, do they reinforce negative stereotypes of African Americans?" During spring 2007, the common research question was "Does playing violent video games increase aggression in college students?" Because of the controversial nature of the topics, the librarians and tutors begin by telling students to set aside their personal opinions and engage with the evidence. Because this is most students' first experience with scholarly journals, the librarians choose clearly written, empirical studies in the social sciences and communication that support a clear and focused research question.

Objectives/Outcomes

The assignment's objectives address key skills students must learn to be successful in RES104, their subsequent writing course. These objectives are listed in the table below with the corresponding ACRL information literacy (2000) and writing program administrators (2000) outcomes.

In addition, collaborating within peer groups is an implicit objective and related to ACRL Information Literacy outcome 3.6a and the writing program administrator's objectives:

> Understand(s) the collaborative and social aspects of writing processes. Learn(s) to critique their own and others' works.

Implementation

Thirteen sections over three semesters have participated in this assignment, which typically involves eight sessions. Librarians and tutors are involved in five. On the first day, the faculty member and librarian describe the assignment and distribute a handout including activities and homework (see Appendix 1). Librarians tell students how to access three required articles using the library's electronic reserves system. Each student is responsible for reading and annotating the articles.

Initially, the whole class examines a Website to introduce the topic. Although the Website will not be used in their paper, this scaffolding reduces student anxiety by starting research with a source familiar to them. Librarians discuss using Websites to generate topics and to determine authorities and scholarly sources. Librarians transition to a scholarly article by comparing each source's audience, authority, bias, and reliability. Led by the librarian, the class then reviews the first scholarly article together, reading the abstract, finding the hypothesis, and identifying the sections relevant to the research question.

Next, students divide into four small groups, each led by a faculty member, librarian, professional writing tutor, or peer tutor. The two remaining articles are divided among the groups, who examine them to identify further evidence. Groups quote and paraphrase key points on poster paper. Each group then reports to the class. Leaders ask additional questions to clarify relevant evidence and gauge students' understanding. After this point, the faculty continues the composition process, and the librarians and writing tutors do not attend classes.

The faculty member then leads the class to a conclusion about the evidence and helps them turn the research question into a common thesis statement. This process is consistent with Bruffee's (1993) model in which the "class as a whole analyzes, compares, and synthesizes the groups' decisions, negotiating toward an acceptable consensus" (30). Together, the class constructs an outline of the research paper, and each student writes a rough draft. In class, they critique each other's papers. Each student submits a four- to five-page final paper in MLA format, which supports the common thesis with evidence from the three articles.

ANALYSIS OF PERCEPTIONS

Students

Many students respond emotionally to this assignment, consistent with Kuhlthau and Whitmire. They often have a difficult time setting aside their opinions and using only the evidence in the articles. Students complain that they "don't write this way." They criticize the assignment for forcing them to change their style; these complaints are explained in the literature (Carroll). Addressing this belief persistence (Fitzgerald 1999) is challenging, but the small group process helps students focus on evidence rather than opinion.

Throughout the assignment, students want to discuss the issues (media racism and video game violence) in order to advocate their perspectives. Trosset (1998) says the majority of first-year students do not discuss a topic to explore it, but see communication as advocacy. For example, one spring 2006 student did not agree with the thesis ("Playing violent video games increases short-term aggression in college students"), even though all three articles supported the conclusion. He attempted to disprove one article's research using his experience, but another student in the group responded with evidence from the article to support the validity of the research. As one peer tutor stated, "disagreement is part of the learning process."

Some of this frustration is expected because of the controversial nature of the topics, in keeping with the Wendt Character Initiative's purpose to challenge students' ideas and beliefs. Peer group discussion reduces student discomfort and helps them gain a sense of satisfaction and confidence, advancing their critical thinking skills (Waite and Davis).

In addition to the emotional responses, many students are challenged by the material, which clearly falls outside their zone of proximal development. Rather than try and fail, some just shut down and wait for the group leader to work through the material. The students have no experience with journal articles, so they are intimidated by the length, jargon, and data. Students often struggle to focus on the relevant data. Group leaders refocus students by asking "How does that help answer our research question?" With this support, students are able to cull out the irrelevant information. While the assignment is designed to stretch students beyond their zone of proximal development, this structure allows them to succeed.

To determine students' success and gauge perceptions, librarians piloted an assessment and evaluation in spring 2007. Ten students in one section participated, with the following results: 70% were able to determine the definition of a thesis as a specific provable claim (Objective A); 50% were able to determine that scholarly journal articles usually include a bibliography (Objective B); 80% were able to determine that scholarly journal articles usually do not include a researcher's opinion (Objective B); 60% were able to determine that scholarly journal articles usually include experiment methods and results (Objectives B and C); 70% were able to identify typical situations which require citation (Objective E); all students felt very or somewhat comfortable with the librarians who instructed their class; 70% received help from a librarian on the paper outside of class; 80% sought librarian assistance for assignments in a different class.

One student added the comment that the critical thinking unit was the "best part of the entire ENG semester." Another commented that the process was "very informative." There were also several comments relating to the librarians; it is clear that this assignment helps students think of librarians as important and helpful. This is vital as students move to the subsequent research writing course and higher-level courses in their majors.

Peer Tutors

The assignment illustrates that research and writing are inherently connected, socially constructed activities. Peer tutors, mostly juniors and seniors, work with fellow students to "engage in conversation about writing every step of the way: finding a topic; deciding what they want to say about the topic; developing material to defend or explain what they say; reading, describing, and evaluating what they have written; and rewriting" (Bruffee 1989, 218). Peer tutors are instrumental to this process.

During three semesters, six peer tutors have participated as small group facilitators. Four of the six completed an open-ended survey about the experience (see Appendix 2). One peer tutor described the benefits of the structured process: "The students were very collaborative [. . .] We would go through the article discussing and answering questions that they found important. When one issue was not understood fully, the student would further explain, and that would open up discussion from other members of the group until everyone felt they had grasped the concept."

The same peer tutor explained the importance of peer-to-peer interactions:

> I believe that working in small groups with peers instead of authority figures really brings the freshmen out of themselves and gives them

> a feeling that their learning is important. Everyone had a chance to discuss and contribute, even those who I noticed were naturally shy or who might be embarrassed about not understanding certain concepts. They were working with someone who had been through it and had used it, and could empathize with the education they were receiving, which opens up a realm that combines fun with necessity. The students really were more at ease with me in their small groups about mistakes [. . .] This opportunity allowed them to realize that the motions, although robotic, do prove to work when it comes to personal processing of information. The students really did surprise me, because at first it seemed that they might be lost or think it a joke, but in the end they proved to me and to themselves their intellectual and passionate abilities. It also made me realize that what I had learned was actually being used, and I did not even notice it because it became second nature to my educational success.

The peer tutors succeed in drawing students out of their comfort zone, as they also learn through the process. Some commented about the importance of critical reading, writing, and thinking skills in other classes. For example, when asked if the assignment would have helped them, one tutor explained: "I think seeing an older UD student working with me at that stage as freshman, no matter the major [. . .] would have made the exercise more important to me. It would have made me realize that the abilities that I was being taught would be used in all fields and at various levels and not just for that class." This is consistent with the assignment's goal to provide a foundational understanding of how to use scholarly research.

Many peer tutors also work with students following their classroom involvement. ENG102 instructors often require that students take drafts to the writing center to work with a peer tutor. Tutors involved in the classroom have a greater understanding of the assignment and how to best assist students in the writing process.

Professional Writing Tutor

To date, one professional writing tutor has participated as a small group leader. Her experience echoes that of the peer tutors: "I saw those who understood what they read talking about the important points in the article. Those who didn't comprehend it probably got a lot out of hearing the discussion. Students who don't comprehend do not usually say they don't get it." The group process clearly helps students who would otherwise be intimidated by the material. The professional tutor also noted that "students spoke about values or lack of values" when examining the articles.

Faculty

Five different English faculty members have participated. Responses from both newer and more experienced faculty have been positive. Two of the participating faculty members regularly teach RES104 and commented that this assignment is valuable in providing students a strong foundation for this class.

Three faculty members completed an informal survey in spring 2007 that gathered their perceptions about the assignment's impact on student success. All responded that:

1. Students could successfully support a thesis with evidence in the paper at the culmination of the unit;
2. Student papers were of higher quality or the same quality when compared with previous writing assignments;
3. They would like to meet with a librarian to discuss the assignment when planning their syllabi.

Some new and adjunct faculty members have expressed apprehension about the assignment because they do not know what to expect or how students would respond. Their anxiety seems to be due to the process-based model as well as using scholarly articles in a 100-level composition class. In addition, some are reluctant to introduce any research writing components. One adjunct faculty member commented, "I believe the students were energized by the discussions led by Paul and Anne Marie in the small groups. I, on the other hand, need a bit more work pulling information rather than pushing it." Librarians work with faculty to set aside the "expert" model in which an authority figure imparts knowledge, encouraging a focus on the collaborative process in which students create meaning together.

Some faculty members have also expressed concerns about the possibility of plagiarism. In this socially constructed common paper, plagiarism is reframed when students actively participate in the process. The writing center professionals and librarians believe students who learn this process are less likely to plagiarize because they know how to write from sources. The topic and articles also change regularly.

The time the assignment requires concerns some faculty. Process-based collaborative learning is effective but inherently time intensive. In some cases, as classes engage in the process, students and faculty recognize the need for and request more time. Many of the faculty who have included the assignment have shared its benefits and advocated it as a uniform requirement. Starting in fall 2007, it will be included as a common assignment, thanks to the support of the English department.

DISCUSSION

Librarians, faculty, and tutors have observed several themes throughout this assignment: Most first-year students are initially resistant to evidence-based thesis papers.

Other assignments in ENG102 are not research-based, but follow creative writing and personal essay models. Students are used to opinion- or perception-based writing assignments, and this usually is their introduction to college-level research. Librarians, tutors, and students need to be aware that the assignment was created intentionally to stretch students' zones of proximal development and is challenging at first. The facilitated process reduces intimidation and other emotion-driven responses.

Students face the challenge of realizing that their opinions are not appropriate support for this research paper. Group leaders help students understand the concept of relevant evidence. Most students gradually engage with the material and embrace the process. Scaffolding and peer group support create a structure that allows students to explore and test limits. The students' comfort and confidence increase through metered exploration of sources.

Peer collaborative learning is central to research writing and critical thinking.

Most students successfully write a research paper within the boundaries of this highly structured assignment. The collaborative experience is key to this success. Led by a team with various skills, students are invited to consider complex questions together. Peer tutors play a critical role in this conversation, providing the bridge between students and the faculty, librarians, and writing professionals. Librarians learned that the group process is equally important to student learning as the final product. It is clear from the information literacy literature, as well as our experiences in this assignment, that the peer collaboration is central to the development of critical thinking.

Ethical questions lead to critical thinking.

The assignment was intended to encourage students to consider ethical issues. These complex questions enable conversations among students with different perspectives within a scholarly research framework. In this research process model, truth is framed as a type of evidence. Group leaders shift students' thinking from their opinions to a concept that truth is more than personal conviction.

Librarians and writing center professionals are well-positioned to lead in teaching critical thinking.

Because librarians and writing center staff work in multidisciplinary, process-based models, they are uniquely positioned to partner with faculty to teach critical thinking throughout the curriculum. Faculty sees the value of teaching scholarly discourse and critical thinking, particularly those who observe students struggling in courses requiring research writing. The faculty recognizes that assignments such as this prepare students for success in future classes. Librarians and writing center staff can provide leadership, expertise, and structure to make this possible.

Limitations

The limitations of this assignment are lack of student engagement with the topic, attendance concerns, and librarian and writing center time commitments.

First, by definition, a single-topic assignment does not engage all students immediately. The librarians discuss the scope and social relevance of the topic to address some students' expressed lack of interest. This assignment models the process of writing from sources. Therefore, when students are able to choose their own topics, they are familiar and comfortable with the process of scholarly inquiry. Because this is a process-based model, students who do not consistently attend class or are unprepared do not learn the targeted critical thinking skills, even if they complete the paper. Further, they slow down the class's progress.

Although librarians and writing center staff are concerned with the time the assignment takes, they recognize the value and are committed to it. It is challenging to schedule all the staff necessary for each of seven to ten sections per semester. In 2006/2007, the five librarians taught 375 information literacy sessions, eighty six of which were for this assignment. Because peer tutors are often campus leaders and students themselves, they are always available.

Initially, only some sections participated in the assignment. Some of the university's adjuncts taught a composition model that did not include information literacy and were reluctant to commit to the assignment. Although the librarians have strong institutional support for information literacy, like most collaborations, this assignment started with personal relationships which developed into departmental support.

Future Directions

Faculty have requested a descriptive introduction to the assignment to better understand the objectives and components. The library's marketing committee designed a brochure for this purpose (see Appendix 3). There are also collaborative meetings planned to discuss the assignment, answer questions, and clearly lay out responsibilities for librarians, faculty, and tutors.

Librarians are working closely with the writing center director to ensure consistent integration and training of peer tutors. Of the four tutors responding to the survey about their experiences, two felt "very comfortable" working as small group leaders, but one each responded "somewhat comfortable" and "somewhat uncomfortable." Potential training could include working through a sample article in a mock group process. Tutors recommend allowing more time to discuss paper organization, MLA format, and effective peer review. These are the instructors' responsibility rather than the librarians' and will be discussed in future semesters.

The librarians, faculty, and writing center staff plan to undertake several assessment measures, among them statistically analyzing the assignment's impact on persistence and grades in RES104. Another potential assessment is a student reflection about the research writing process.

Instructors have informally shared assignment sheets, peer review forms, and grading rubrics, and there have been preliminary conversations about creating a common rubric. This would ensure grading consistency, allow information literacy in course-wide authentic assessment, and enable comparison of student success across sections and semesters.

There are preliminary plans to incorporate a similar unit in introductory courses in other departments, such as Introduction to Sociology. Several instructors of ENG100, Composition and Rhetoric I, have requested a modified version of the assignment for fall 2007. An adaptation of this unit would also be applicable in upper-level and graduate courses. This assignment lays the groundwork for students' critical thinking skills, which develop throughout their specific disciplines and majors.

CONCLUSION

Students cannot be research writers if they do not use valid evidence in thesis-driven writing. Most first-year students do not understand the need for a thesis because they see knowledge as a series of indisputable facts or opinions. They view the research process as any method that quickly unearths these facts. They approach ethical issues in a similar manner and thus do not see that there are problematic questions for which there are no absolute answers. The research question is by nature a problematic question. Scholars attempt to define and answer these questions based on disciplinary methods, acknowledging that their evidence and conclusions are not final.

Research writing, especially on ethical issues, takes students outside their comfort zones. For them to learn the many tasks involved, they need to have the process scaffolded. They must see it modeled, because research writing is in part communal. When an assignment is structured as an invitation to community, students construct arguments based on evidence and commit to answering problematic questions. Peer group interactions challenge belief persistence and help students create meaning together.

Students develop critical thinking skills by investigating ethical questions in evidence-based research writing assignments. Academic librarians should partner with faculty and writing center professionals to engage students in critical thinking using this integrated process.

REFERENCES

Association of College and Research Libraries. 2000. *Information literacy competency standards for higher education*. Chicago: Association of College and Research Libraries.

Albitz, R. S. 2007. The what and who of information literacy and critical thinking in higher education. *Portal: Libraries & the Academy* 7: 97–109.

Bhavnagri, N. P. and V. Bielat. 2005. Faculty-librarian collaboration to teach research skills: Electronic symbiosis. *Reference Librarian* 89/90: 121–138.

Boyer, E. L. 1987. *College: The undergraduate experience in America*. New York: Harper & Row.

Bruffee, K. A. 1989. Thinking and writing as social acts. *In:* E. P. Maimon, B. F. Nodine, and F. W. O'Connor (eds.) *Thinking, reasoning, and writing*. New York: Longman, pp. 213–222.

Bruffee, K. A. 1993. *Collaborative learning: Higher education, interdependence, and the authority of knowledge*. Baltimore: Johns Hopkins University Press.

Carroll, L. A. 2002. *Rehearsing new roles: How college students develop as writers*. Carbondale, IL: Southern Illinois University Press.

Cheung, C., E. Rudowicz, A. S. F. Kwan, and X. Dong Yue. 2002. Assessing university students' general and specific critical thinking. *College Student Journal* 36: 504–525.

Colby, A., T. Ehrlich, E. Beaumont, and J. Stephens. 2003. *Educating citizens: Preparing America's undergraduates for lives of moral and civic responsibility*. San Francisco: Jossey-Bass.

Council of Writing Program Administrators. 2000. *WPA*. Outcomes statement for first-year composition. http://www.wpacouncil.org/positions/outcomes.html.

Deese-Roberts, S. and K. Keating. 2000. *Library instruction: A peer tutoring model*. Englewood, CO: Libraries Unlimited.

Dewey, J. 1933. *How we think: A restatement of the relation of reflective thinking to the educative process*. Boston: D. C. Heath.

Elmborg, J. K. and S. Hook. 2005. *Centers for learning: Writing centers and libraries in collaboration*. Chicago: Association of College and Research Libraries.

Fister, B. 1992. Common ground: The composition/bibliographic instruction connection. *In:* T. G. Kirk (ed.) *Academic libraries: Achieving excellence in higher education*. Chicago: Association of College and Research Libraries, pp. 154–158.

Fitzgerald, M. A. 1999. Evaluating information: An information literacy challenge. *School Library Media Research* 2. http://www.pla.org/ala/aasl/aaslpubsandjournals/slmrb/slmrcontents/volume21999/vol2fitzgerald.cfm.

Higgins, L. 1993. Reading to argue: Helping students transform source text. *In:* A. M. Penrose and B. M. Sitko (eds.) *Hearing ourselves think: Cognitive research in the college writing classroom*. New York: Oxford University Press, pp. 70–101.

Huerta, D. and V. E. McMillan. 2000. Collaborative instruction by writing and library faculty: A two-tiered approach to the teaching of scientific writing. *Issues in Science and Technology Librarianship* 28. http://www.istl.org/00-fall/article1.html.

Hughes, W. 2000. *Critical thinking: An introduction to basic skills*. 3rd ed. Peterborough, Ont.: Broadview Press.

Isbell, D. 1995. Teaching writing and research as inseparable: A faculty-librarian teaching team. *Reference Services Review* 23: 51–62.

King, P. M. and K. S. Kitchener. 1994. *Developing reflective judgment: Understanding and promoting intellectual growth and critical thinking in adolescents and adults*. San Francisco: Jossey-Bass.

Kroll, B. M. 1992. *Teaching hearts and minds: College students reflect on the Vietnam War in literature*. Carbondale, IL: Southern Illinois University Press.

Kuhlthau, C. 1985. Teaching the information search process: A step-by-step program for secondary students. West Nyack, NY: Center for Applied Research in Education.

Norgaard, R. 2004. Writing information literacy in the classroom. *Reference & User Services Quarterly* 43: 220–226.

Norris, S. P. and R. H. Ennis. 1989. *Evaluating critical thinking*. Pacific Grove, CA: Midwest Publications.

Olwell, R. and R. Delph. 2004. Implementing assessment and improving undergraduate writing: One department's experience. *History Teacher* 38: 21–34.

Perry, W. G. 1970. *Forms of intellectual and ethical development in the college years: A scheme*. New York: Holt, Rinehart, and Winston.

Phillips, R. 2004. Information literacy, critical thinking, and theological education. *Journal of Religious & Theological Information* 6: 5–12.

Sheridan, J. 1995. *Writing-across-the-curriculum and the academic library: A guide for librarians, instructors, and writing program directors*. Westport, CN: Greenwood Press.

Tipton, R. L. and P. Bender. 2006. From failure to success: Working with under-prepared transfer students. *Reference Services Review* 34: 389–404.

Trosset, C. 1998. Obstacles to open discussion and critical thinking. *Change* 30: 44–50.

Tsui, L. 2002. Fostering critical thinking through effective pedagogy: Evidence from four institutional case studies. *The Journal of Higher Education* 73: 740–763.

Vygotsky, L. S. 1978. *Mind in society: The development of higher psychological processes*. M. Cole (ed.). Cambridge, MA: Harvard University Press.

Waite, S. and B. Davis. 2006. Collaboration as a catalyst for critical thinking in undergraduate research. *Journal of Further and Higher Education* 30: 405.

Warren, T. H. 1994. Critical thinking beyond reasoning: Restoring virtue to thought. *In: Re-thinking reason: New perspectives in critical thinking*, K. S. Walters (ed.). Albany, NY: State University of New York Press, pp. 221–231.

Weiler, A. 2005. Information-seeking behavior in Generation Y students: Motivation, critical thinking, and learning theory. *Journal of Academic Librarianship* 31: 46–53.

Whitmire, E. 1998. Development of critical thinking skills: An analysis of academic library experiences and other measures. *College & Research Libraries* 59: 266.

Zimmerman, B. J. and R. Risemberg. 1997. Becoming a self-regulated writer: A social cognitive perspective. *Contemporary Educational Psychology* 22: 73–102.

APPENDIX 1: Student Handout

Charles C. Myers Library University of Dubuque

Wendt Character Initiative: A Joint Project with Librarians, ENG 102 Faculty, and Writing Tutors

Facts are stupid things.—Ronald Reagan

Any trend to produce programmes and products—including animated films and video games—which in the name of entertainment exalt violence and portray anti-social behavior . . . is a perversion . . .

—Pope Benedict XVI, January 24, 2007

In this unit, the English faculty, librarians, and writing tutors will combine the objectives of teaching the Wendt principles with teaching information literacy skills. Specifically, we will address the Wendt principles of fairness and truth by examining how scholars test the "truth" of a thesis—that is, how they gather evidence in support of a thesis—how to craft a thesis that can be supported by evidence, and how to summarize and evaluate sources in support of a thesis.

In this unit, students will examine the research question, "Does playing violent video games increase aggression in college students?" Students will break into groups and examine a scholarly article with the help of a facilitator (faculty member, librarian, or writing tutor). They will evaluate the authority of the author and periodical, determine the article's thesis, and find evidence that answers the class research question. After activities in which the students work individually, as a group, and as a class, each student will write a 4- to 5-page research paper (of text) answering and perhaps refining the research question using the articles examined in class cited in MLA citation style.

As a result of this unit, students will be able to:

1. Identify a valid thesis for a short research paper.
2. Identify a credible source (author, journal, etc.).
3. Identify evidence from three journal articles that supports or refutes research question.
4. Write a short paper based on credible sources.
5. Cite the sources used in a paper in correct form.

Day 1

A librarian will be in class the last 15 minutes to give instructions for the unit. Each student will write a 4- to 5-page paper based on the research question, "Does playing violent video games increase aggression in college students?" using sources that will be provided through the class E-Reserve page.

Homework DUE Day 2:

1. Copy the Website and three other articles on the class's E-Reserve web page.

Instructions: All articles are available through the library's e-reserves system. To access e-reserves, go to the library Webpage at www.dbq.edu/library. Click on E-Reserves. Log in with your university ID and password. You may search for ENG102 by department, instructor, or course number. When prompted for the course password, type in *eng102*. Click on the PDF for each article to print it out. Contact a librarian at reference@dbq.edu if you have any questions or problems. Read the introductory Website and the first page of the class article. Bring all articles to class every day during this assignment.

Day 2

Presentation

A librarian will briefly present:

1. How social science scholars formulate and test a thesis.
2. What constitutes evidence (or a certain kind of "truth") and why this matters.
3. How journal articles are used to form and support a thesis for a paper.

In-Class Activity: Review the introductory readings and the class article to analyze each source's credibility and value to your topic. Faculty will divide the class into groups and assign/introduce a facilitator (faculty member, librarian, or writing tutor).

Homework DUE Day 3

Read the following parts of the article assigned to your group:

1. For the small group article 1, carefully read the abstract, introduction, and discussion sections. *Highlight information that is relevant to the research question and make notes in the margin.*
2. For the small group article 2, carefully read the abstract and introduction sections. *Highlight information that is relevant to the research question and make notes in the margin.*
3. All students: Review the class article. *Highlight information that is relevant to the research question and make notes in the margin.*

Day 3

In-Class Activity: Continue to review the class article to determine what information is relevant to the research question. Groups meet with the facilitator to begin examining the article assigned to them. Groups decide what information is relevant to answering the research question.

Each student will highlight and make notes on the article based on the discussion.

Homework DUE Day 4

1. Review your small group's article.

Day 4

In-Class Activity: Each group continues to review their article for relevant information pertaining to the research question. Members of each group work together to record on newsprint the following items: (a) article citation in MLA format; (b) relevant evidence from the article, quoted directly or paraphrased; and (c) proper MLA in-text citation for each bullet point.

Homework DUE Day 5

1. Read the article that was not assigned to your group, annotating and highlighting relevant evidence.

Day 5

In-Class Activity: Each group presents to the class the information that is relevant to the research question. The class determines that they have all relevant information from the articles. The class turns the research question into a thesis statement. The class discusses the arrangement of the paper.

Homework DUE Day 6

1. Review all articles and evidence related to the research question.

Day 6 (ASC tutors/librarians not present)
In-Class Activity: Discuss drafting process. Create class outline for paper. Review MLA format. Each will student write a 4- to 5-page paper (of text) in MLA format in support of the class thesis using the articles provided.

Homework DUE Day 7

1. *Prepare paper draft for Day 7.*

Day 7 (ASC tutors/librarians not present)
In-Class Activity: Peer review first draft of paper.

Homework DUE Day 8

1. *Final paper is due during finals week.*

Day 8 (ASC tutors/librarians not present)
In-Class Activity: Discuss/reflect upon process.

APPENDIX 2: Peer Tutor Survey

Instructions

The librarians are collecting information from peer tutors who have participated in the ENG102 classes over the past three semesters. These classes required peer tutors to meet with small groups as they focused on two common research questions: "When local television news programs report violent crime, do they reinforce negative stereotypes of African Americans?" and "Does playing violent video games increase aggression in college students?"

We will use the feedback we collect to adjust the unit for future semesters. Information collected may also be used in an article to be submitted to a peer-reviewed library science journal. If you have any questions, contact Anne Marie Gruber at amgruber@dbq.edu. Thank you for taking the time to respond!

The survey will take approximately 10–15 minutes, and responses will be collected until Friday, June 15.

Name

1. In how many ENG 102 sections have you participated as a peer tutor?

   – One Section
   – Two Sections
   – Three Sections

2. What was the research question during the section(s) in which you participated?

   – When local television news programs report violent crime, do they reinforce negative stereotypes of African Americans?
   – Does playing violent video games increase aggression in college students?
   – I participated in sections focusing on each of the above research questions.

3. The ENG102 unit usually lasts for about two weeks and includes several parts. How comfortable did you feel in each part of the unit?

	Very comfortable 1	Somewhat comfortable 2	Somewhat uncomfortable 3	Very uncomfortable 4	Did not attend this part of the class 5
Unit introduction/e-reserves instructions	1	2	3	4	5
Introductory articles (magaz/ine/newspaper)	1	2	3	4	5
Scholarly article with whole class	1	2	3	4	5
Scholarly articles with small groups	1	2	3	4	5
Small group presentations	1	2	3	4	5
Creating a class thesis	1	2	3	4	5
Drafting process	1	2	3	4	5
Peer-review of paper drafts	1	2	3	4	5

4. Within your small group, how did you deal with students who disagreed with the class thesis?
5. How did you see students helping each other understand the articles and determine evidence to support the thesis? Please provide any anecdotal situations to illustrate how students worked collaboratively.
6. Which of the following were you required to do in UD classes you have taken FOLLOWING ENG102 (not counting RES104)?

   – Choose a focused topic
   – Determine a research question
   – Read and interpret scholarly articles independently
   – Read and interpret scholarly articles for class discussion
   – Cite sources in a specified format (MLA, APA, etc.)
   – Turn in multiple drafts of a paper
   – Peer review papers

7. Would this unit have been helpful when you took ENG102? Please explain.
8. Please share any positive aspects of your participation leading a small group in the ENG102 classes.
9. Please share any aspects of the class unit that you think should change.

Council of Writing Program Admistrator s Outcomes (2000)

Unit Outcomes	ACRL Outcomes	WPA Outcomes
A. Identies a valid thesis for a short research paper	Recognizes interrelationships among concepts and combines them into potentially useful pnmary statements with supporting evidence (3.3a) Extends initial synthesis, when possible, at a higher level of abstraction to construct new hypotheses that may require additional information (3.3b)	Focuses on a purpose
B. Identies a credible source (author, journal, etc.)	Examines and compares information from various sources in order to evaluate reliability, validity, accuracy, authority, timeliness, and point of view or bias (3.2a) Analyzes ihe structure and logic of supporting arguments or methods (3.2b)	N/A
C. Identies evidence from 3 journal articles to support or refute a thesis	Reads lhe text and selects main ideas (3. la) Restates textual concepts In his/her own words and selects data accurately (3.1 b) Identies verbatim rtialerial that can be then appropriately quoted (3.1c) Recognizes interrelationships among concepts and combines them into potentially useful primary statements with supporting evidence (3.3a) Uses consciously selected criteria to determine whether lhe information contradicts or veries information used from oihe sources (3.4b)	Understands a writing assignment as a series of tasks, including nding, evaluating, analyzing, and synthesizing appropriate primary and secondary sources.
D. Writes a short paper based on credible sources.	Organizes he contenl in a manner lhal supports the purposes and format of the product or performance (e.g. outlines, drafts) (4.1a) Integrates the new and prior information, including quotations and paraphrasings. In a manner that supports the purposes of the product or performance (4.1C) Communicates clearly and with astyie lhat supports the purposes of the intended audience (4.3d)	Is aware that it usually takes multiple drafts to create and complete a successful text. Develop e xible strategies for generating, revising, editing, and proof-reading.
E. Cites the sources used in a paper in correct form.	Differentiates between the types of sources cited and understands the elements and correct syntax of citation fora wide range of resources (2.5c) Records all pertinent citation information for future reference (2.5d) Selects an appropriate documenlation style and uses it consistently to cite sources (5.3a)	Learns comrnenl formats for different kinds of texts. Practices appropriate means of documenting lheir work.

APPENDIX 3

Appendix C: Faculty Brochure

ENG102
Wendt unit:
Truth

Modeling scholarly inquiry, one article at a time

Charles C. Myers Library

UNIT OUTCOMES:

This unit encourages students to investigate the meaning of "truth" as students work as a class, in small groups, and individually to gather evidence from scholarly articles in support of a thesis. After working together to understand 3 articles, students each write a paper in MLA format proving a thesis the class determines. Past research questions have included:

- *When local television news programs report violent crime, do they reinforce negative stereotypes of African-Americans?*
- *Does playing violent video games increase aggression in college students?*

Outcomes for this unit are based on the Association of College & Research Libraries Information Literacy Competency Standards for Higher Education[1] and the Writing Program Administrators Outcomes for First-Year Composition[2]. In summary, objectives are as follows.

As a result of this unit, students will be able to:

A. Identify a valid thesis for a short research paper.
B. Identify a credible source (author, journal, etc.).
C. Identify evidence from 3 journal articles that supports or refutes research question.
D. Write a short paper based on credible sources.
E. Cite the sources used in a paper in MLA format.

1. Association of College and Research Libraries (ACRL). Information Literacy Competency Standards for Higher Education. (Chicago: American Library Association, 2000). Accessed May 30, 2006, from http://www.ala.org/ala/acrl/acrlstandards/standards.pdf
2. Writing Program Administrators (WPA). Outcomes Statement for First-Year Composition. Accessed June 11, 2007, from http://www.wpacouncil.org/positions/outcomes.html

TYPICAL SCHEDULE:

Day 1: Librarian meets with the class for the last 15 minutes of the period to explain the unit, discuss the common research question, and provide instructions for accessing the library's electronic reserves, where all articles may be accessed.

Day 2: Librarian introduces social science research and leads class in discussion about 1-2 websites to introduce the topic. Librarian begins class discussion of 1 scholarly article, modeling how to read, interpret, and find evidence relating to the common research question. Librarian works with instructor to assign students into 3-4 groups.

Day 3: Librarian concludes class discussion about first scholarly article. Small groups each meet with a facilitator (instructor, librarian, or writing tutor) to begin dissecting scholarly articles assigned to each group.

Day 4: Small groups continue to meet, determining evidence that helps answer the common research question. Group members work together to note evidence on easel paper.

Day 5: Small groups each present evidence to the whole class. Instructor leads class in determining a common thesis statement.

Day 6: Instructor reviews MLA format and drafting process with class, and leads class in creating outline.

Day 7: First draft due. Instructor leads students in peer review process.

Day 8: Final paper due.

The schedule is somewhat flexible based upon instructor preferences and class needs. Eight class days is the minimum needed for the unit. Usually this unit is done at the end of ENG102 because it provides foundational skills in academic inquiry that benefit students in the following course, RES104.

Who does what?

ENG102 students:

-Print all articles from e-reserves

-Come to class each day having read & annotated the assigned articles/sections

-Participate in all class & group discussions

-Write individual thesis paper in MLA format using 3 scholarly articles provided

Librarians:

-Provide guide for accessing e-reserves

-Provide schedule & handouts for students, instructor, and tutors

-Lead discussion about social science research

-Lead discussion of large group articles

-Facilitate small group discussion process

ENG102 instructor:

-Explain importance of assignment in composition & expectations of participation

-Facilitate one small group

- Lead class in thesis & outline creation, and peer review process

Peer or professional tutors:

-Facilitate one small group

-Share applicable experiences

Next steps:

Contact an instruction librarian as you are putting together your syllabus to talk more about this common assignment unit. We will go through a more detailed timeline, schedule the sessions for your section(s) and answer any questions you may have.

Contact:

Charles C. Myers Library
Questions about the unit?

Contact Anne Marie Gruber or Paul Waelchli

amgruber@dbq.edu / 589-3849

pwaelchl@dbq.edu / 589-3649

FEEDBACK:

From students:

"Best part of the entire ENG semester"

"very informative"

From peer tutors:

"...the student would further explain and that would open up discussion from other members of the group on the topic until everyone felt they had grasped the concept."

From ENG102 faculty:

"Kudos to Paul and Anne Marie who labored tirelessly with students (and me) to develop this component. I believe the students were energized by the discussions led by Paul and Anne Marie in the small groups."

Critical Thinking is a Life Relevancy: A Hospitality Management Student Case Study

Monica Berger

INTRODUCTION

A focus on developing critical thinking skills and information literacy competency is emerging in the profession. When the author's hospitality management freshmen workshop transitioned from traditional bibliographic instruction to instruction that integrated information literacy, critical thinking about information became a primary learning objective.

Critical thinking about information is specifically "determining the reliability of a source," (Goad 2002, 73) and otherwise evaluating information. Rather than using a checklist or purely analytical approach, critical thinking about information is infused throughout the session.

Early in the session, after students participate in an active-learning approach to research, the author creates a specific moment that for some students results in a moment of self-awareness that may encourage students to develop critical thinking skills. Through this exercise, which involves an element of surprise, students may be affected on an emotional as well as intellectual level, where they can begin to see the relationship between their personal welfare and their ability to think critically. Specifically, students need to learn that there is a connection between how they evaluate information and life-relevancy issues such as finding and keeping a good job.

After several years of teaching one-shot library skills workshops to hospitality management freshmen at New York City College of Technology, the author needed to change teaching style, and, more importantly, incorporate classroom experiences that were fresh and exciting. Google reigned triumphant and students were increasingly unenthusiastic about the library workshop. Hospitality management students can be challenging because many have come to college with very clear professional goals that preclude learning how to use a library and do research. Many of the hospitality freshmen have never used any library whatsoever.

At New York City College of Technology, City University of New York, also known as City Tech, there is often a disconnect between the library and the reality of student life, which often includes a full-time job and family responsibilities (although students are increasingly traditional college age and full-time students). City Tech, with a student population of over 12,000, is a comprehensive four-year college that offers two-year degrees predominantly. Institutional research identified 51% of students born outside of the United States, 63% are the first in their families to attend college, and 60% report speaking a language other than English at home. Nearly 80% of first-year students receive need-based financial aid.

THE LIBRARY WORKSHOP

Library sessions for the freshmen hospitality students are sixty and seventy-five minutes long and begin with student-oriented active learning. Students are asked to explore how they would solve a "real life" problem: preparing for an interview and choosing an employer. This exercise closely matches the assigned research project—a three-page research paper comprised of a company profile (referred to as an industry profile in the syllabus). The assignment reflects how the entire course is oriented toward career exploration. Although one of the assigned companies could be selected for the library workshop, the focus is on a well-known company that is undergoing bankruptcy. Companies have included the Trump Taj Mahal and airlines such as United Airlines and Delta Air Lines. Students are almost universally ignorant of the financial status of these companies.

The class begins with a discussion of how the students will prepare for the job interview. Some students offer the suggestion of contacting someone within the company. The class discusses the limitations as well as the pros and cons of personal contacts, but students agree that they need more objective information. With the occasional exception, students always choose to use the company's Website. Students spend considerable time exploring the company's Website and we discuss at length the audience for the Website, its currency, if the Website is promoting a product or a service, and where to go to learn more about a company, typically the "about" area of the Website. We discuss the function of an annual report and consider how the financial data can be somewhat incomprehensible except for those with business training. At this point, the difference between public and private companies is presented and linked to how company type affects access to information about the company. If time permits, students examine copies of the two respective versions (for public and private companies) of *Hoover's Handbook*. We discuss how public companies are required to disclose their financial situation to the Securities and Exchange Commission on a quarterly basis. We also discuss why the annual report of a public company is important to potential investors. The class becomes aware of the connection between access to information and legal requirements to disclose information. They relate this in turn to their projects (many of the companies that the students need to research for their assignment are private). Students also begin to consider why some information is transparent and easily available or why it is hidden.

Time is also spent looking at the news section of the company Website, which some students, usually with the instructor's prompting, recognize as public relations fodder. The class spends some time discussing how too much honesty about negative news would not be in the interest of the company, and how, in general, the company's Website functions to make the company look its best.

The corporate Website reflects reality in that it is ambiguous,authentic, and biased. Goad refers to "unbounded thinking," which removes traditional boundaries such as "using established formulas, addressing multiple realities, and using conflict as the basis of thought" (69). This indeterminate aspect is echoed by Collins who refers to the need for open-ended assignments because they reflect the reality of the workplace (1988, 61). The author's experience using only bogus Websites in a Website evaluation workshop was not very satisfying. In the literature on teaching students how to evaluate Websites, Harley co-taught a semester-long freshmen seminar focused on critical thinking entirely around evaluating information, and used both bogus and non-bogus Websites (2001, 303). Meola takes issue with the traditional checklist approach to evaluating Websites. He also feels librarians are excessively critical of the open Web lacking in standards (2004, 333). Wathen and Burkell examined how users consider Websites credible. First, users consider if the Website looks professional and if the information is easy to get. Then they consider if the source of the Website is trustworthy or has credentials. Finally, they will evaluate content (2002, 141). Wathen and Burkell also note that the issue of likeability is also at play and goodwill of the source as well as familiarity with the source (136). Hospitality students at City Tech are fairly influenced by the cutting-edge, professional look of the company Website as well as the cheery, civic-minded programs offered by the company.

Most students tend to be satisfied with the information they find on the company Website and generally feel that their research is done. Meola argues that although students will use poor-quality Websites, this does not mean that they use *only* poor-quality Websites and/or lack the ability to evaluate sources/Websites (334). At issue is the assignment itself, as well as the expectations of depth and quality on both the part of the student and the teaching faculty member. Students should be explicitly required to compare related, published sources to the Website and to evaluate it in terms of audience, currency, authorship, bias, and other qualities.

The instructor tells the students that two key elements are missing in their research: sources external to the company Website and highly current sources. When asked how to find current information on a company, some students suggest newspapers. At this stage, students locate any available external information about the company, such as recent news. In Lexis-Nexis, a simple search is performed on the company's name. Articles detailing the company's bankruptcy and other business crises constitute most of the news retrieved. Some students are aghast, and the entire library session is reframed. The energy in the classroom palpably shifts. We talk at length about what it means when a company is in Chapter 11: how the company is still operating and needs to continue to project a positive image via its Website. When a company is bankrupt, workers may not get their paychecks or pensions, a new worker might be hired to replace multiple positions or to replace a more experienced worker, or the new employee might face layoffs (first hired, first fired) in the near future. Our hospitality students are strongly driven by vocational aspirations, and the scenario of taking a position at a company in crisis can evoke strong reactions. Everyone knows someone who has been let go due to corporate downsizing.

The class then goes on to talk more generally about point of view and bias in information sources. Examples tend to come from the popular media as students are familiar with the idea of political bias in broadcast journalism. The conversation extends to how industry trade associations like the National Restaurant Association exist to further a very specific agenda and how that affects their research and how they represent the restaurant industry in their publications and Website specifically.

Students are asked to explain how Google works. No student has ever successfully explained the underlying mechanism, although increasingly students are aware that Websites can and do pay to get ranked higher. For the students who are not aware that companies can pay to be ranked higher, this information provokes indignant reactions and further advances critical thinking about the so-called objectivity of search engines.

After the Lexis-Nexis section of the workshop, different types of periodicals are covered in a show-and-tell style that includes passing around the periodicals. Scholarly peer-reviewed journals are also covered, with an emphasis on how the peer review process is a way of vetting information. Students seem to have limited interest in this topic, and their waning attention is not improved by more lecture and less hands-on during this part of the session. However, peer review clearly reinforces the idea that not all information possesses the same quality. Publishing and the editorial process are described as well and further connected to vetting and quality control. Copyright is briefly explained, with some clarification of the limitations of access to materials. For example, students need to know that most published articles are not available on the World Wide Web and are available only through the library via paid subscriptions to periodicals and databases. Differentiating between published and non-published materials seems to be difficult for students.

Next, the class searches a business database to find Datamonitor company profiles and a SWOT analysis (strengths, weaknesses, opportunities, and threats) of the company and compare how much easier these sources are to work with compared to the annual report on the company Website. SWOT analyses are interesting tools for critical thinking because they are relatively simple to parse while not being value neutral. Online catalog searches for books and other materials on the company conclude the session. Students are asked if they notice an issue with the search results that includes at least one very out-of-date book. The class always correctly identifies the issue of currency.

By staying with the same subject of research, the students are able to compare sources. Goad, in defining critical thinking, stresses comparison as well as comparing and contrasting. Even if students are limited in critical thinking about the content of different information sources, tracing a specific topic through different sources gives us opportunities to discuss how the sources and the related content vary. Meola refers to looking at data via different sources leading to comparative thinking that helps identify bias.

Some students consider, for the first time in their life, how different information sources have a point of view and an agenda, and how these sources need to be questioned and critiqued. It is this awareness that is the one condition needed for lifelong learning: the willingness to be receptive to learning and recognizing that learning happens all the time, everywhere, and throughout life. Jacobson and Xu talk about how students need to take their existing knowledge set and compare it to what is taught in the library workshop in order to create a new knowledge set (2004, 65). This library workshop gives students a good beginning on their path towards becoming aware of the need to learn and the need to find what is needed in order to learn.

ASSESSMENT

Assessment is a way to improve teaching methods and student learning when it does not function simply as a method of evaluation. Identifying clear student learning outcomes and developing a rubric to measure student learning is an assessment goal for the near future for this class. Another assessment goal is direct involvement with the post-workshop student work, including a review of students' company profiles and, in particular, a review of the sources students used in their list of references.

In the first few years of this workshop, the teaching faculty member created a post-library session quiz. The quiz had one very simple yes/no question which was insufficient to determine if the students learned the bibliographic vocabulary that was such a major focus of the workshop. A revised quiz has been administered for four semesters, and student results are consistently very good for the multiple-choice questions relating to the bibliographic instruction vocabulary and concepts. To get a better sense of how students experienced these modifications in teaching, and to get a sense of student perceptions of the session, an open-ended, reflective question was added. Students are now asked to: "Reflect on what you learned in today's library session and where you need to go next to become a more efficient and more sophisticated researcher." Their responses vary tremendously, from no response at all to responses showing that students recognize their own need to engage with the library and research.

PROBLEMS AND OBSTACLES TO LEARNING

Many students cannot evaluate sources because they lack critical thinking skills as well as reading comprehension skills (Sterngold and Hurlbert 1998, 248). However, other factors are at play as well. The main culprit seems to be Google. For students, the physical library has become irrelevant and library electronic resources require too much work to learn. Students, as well as their professors, often conceive of research as using Google. According to the De Rosa and Online Computer Library Center's (OCLC) 2005 *Perceptions of Libraries and Information Resources*, 89% of college students start their search via a search engine. Only 1% start their research via a library Website or a library database (1–17). Just under 50% of college students completely agree that the library Website is a source of worthwhile information, as the college students surveyed do not generally trust purchased information more than free information. Today's "Net Generation" students obtain information on a "need-to-know" basis: most are not interested in research in and of itself. Students grossly overestimate their research skills, but they will readily admit that they get more irrelevant results than not and waste too much time searching and not finding. Google creates a false perception of mastery and completeness of content. Mastering use of the library Website for research, unlike searching Google, takes time and effort to learn.

In addition to issues of basic literacy, many students may experience some kind of library anxiety. Kwon, Onwuegbuzie, and Alexander (2007) found a clear connection between library anxiety and weak critical thinking. Although they investigated graduate students of education, they learned that a majority of students are uncomfortable negotiating library resources, which, by their complexity and quantity, offer too many choices and decisions. New York City College of Technology offers over 100 electronic resources and databases.

Motivating students is very challenging, and the threat of a quiz does not motivate some students. Even when the workshop is tied into their assignment, which is always a best practice, it is not a given that students are attentive. Jacobson and Xu note that the two most important factors in student motivation are that the library session is tied into an assignment that the students have already done some work on and the instructor's attitude toward the library workshop (12–13). Unfortunately, City Tech hospitality students usually have not started their research before their library session, which is typically very early in the semester. Also, how the instructor communicates about the value of the library workshop makes all the difference. Unless the instructor is enthusiastic about the library, students tend to interpret the library session as a low-priority add-on.

Life relevancy is extremely important for students on career tracks: Jacobson and Xu connect information literacy classes and student careers (40). However, if the teaching technique is traditional, as it was the first year or two of this workshop, all exhortations to pay attention because "you need to know how to research in order to get an interview, perform well enough on the interview to get the job and thrive on the job" often fell on deaf ears. In a far more in-depth, six-week group research project in a seminar co-taught by a classroom faculty member and a librarian, Sterngold and Hurlbert did find that many students do connect their industry profile to their career (248).

CHANGES IN TEACHING TECHNIQUES AND CONTENT

Before using active learning techniques in the current class, the library workshop was primarily a lecture with some discussion. The universe of information sources available to students was covered as well as the difference between published and non-published sources. Peer-reviewed journals were also covered along with the show-and-tell of periodicals and reference books. The class searched the same databases and catalog. Essentially, the library resources covered were identical. Classes went fairly well if the classroom instructor was highly engaged and the students were relatively mature. However, the style of instruction created passive learning, and the students digested what they could without any major shift in their understanding. The active learning teaching style, based on personal observation and feedback from the classroom instructor, really connects students. It connects them to the librarian as an instructor, connects them to the information literacy piece, and connects their experience to their professional aspirations. Another minor improvement is staying on the same topic; it provides more continuity and removes the barrier of revising the search strategy.

CRITICAL INFORMATION LITERACY

A call for critical information literacy is increasingly found in the library literature and noteworthy are Harley (2001) and Swanson (2004). Albitz's 2007 article provides a good overview of the literature, and she notes that there is some confusion about the meaning of critical thinking in library literature (99–100). Some authors, including Doherty and Ketchner (2005), focus on the profound political aspects of self-determination in learning what ensues when students become critical thinkers about information. Influenced by educator and political theorist Paulo Freire's "goal of social transformation through education," Doherty and Ketchner call for a radical revision of information literacy instruction that empowers the learner by "engaging students in the terms of students' own experiences." Swanson, on a more pragmatic level, states: Before we train students to use search tools, before we send them to books, periodicals, or Web sites, we need to teach them *about* information. What is it? How is it created? Where is it stored? (260).

Breivik, an influential thinker on information literacy, also considers information literacy a type of critical thinking and not as a skills-based entity (Albitz, 99). The problem, however, is that the expectation of a one-hour one-shot library workshop is to provide some basic search skills and familiarity with resources. This is a prime example of the need for information literacy to be more extensive and pervasive in the curriculum. It is problematic that teaching faculty and librarians use different terminology, and information literacy is not necessarily a part of the teaching faculty's language of pedagogy (Albitz, 98). On the one hand, critical thinking is understood as higher-level reasoning and does not necessarily involve information retrieval. Albitz articulates this disconnect:

> The disconnect between the definitions of information literacy and critical thinking, which tends to fall along librarian, teaching faculty/administrative lines, foreshadows the differing opinions

> concerning which group should be responsible for teaching these overlapping skill sets. (101)

Grafstein also notes that the ideas of critical thinking and lifelong learning, both heavily present in the library literature, are historically always placed within the "purview" of classroom faculty (2002, 199).

THE SOCIAL CONSTRUCTION OF KNOWLEDGE AND GROWING AWARE

Latour (1987) and other social constructivist philosophers have advanced the idea that knowledge is socially constructed, fluid, and complex. Bruckman (2005) feels that students cannot navigate the online environment and begin to grow information literate without understanding the social construction of "truth": how an insight is asserted by an individual or small group and then becomes socially accepted. Understanding the social construction of truth requires higher-level thinking than what occurs in the bankrupt company exercise. However, the exercise is on the beginning end of the continuum of self-questioning and metacognition that engenders critical thinking.

ACTIVE LEARNING

The Arizona Faculties Council (2000) defines learner-centered education as one that

> . . . places the student at the center of education. It begins with understanding the educational contexts from which a student comes. It continues with the instructor evaluating the student's progress toward learning objectives. By helping the student acquire the basic skills to learn, it ultimately provides a basis for learning throughout life.

To reiterate, active learning and learner-centered education teach students how to learn. Bruce's (1997) idea of relational information literacy focuses on the student's perspective. Doherty and Ketchner acknowledge that it is difficult to work with freshmen, as their prior educational experiences may not have prepared them for active learning. Their previous learning experiences often were centered around listening to classroom lectures. However, students' first experiences with active learning are all the more powerful because they feel empowered in their learning experience for the first time. Active learning techniques are challenging to use because so much depends on student response and dynamics. Issues of control of the classroom in active learning are often at play: teaching faculty do not have total control when they invite students to participate actively (Gradowski, Snavely, and Dempsey 1998, viii). In the case of this workshop, the teaching librarian maintains overall control of the classroom, but student responses vary greatly and are unpredictable. There are other ways to intensify the active learning aspects of the workshop. Since many students may be reticent to volunteer their comments or opinions, students could be placed in small work groups to analyze the corporate Website. The librarian provides guidelines to the students who then report back their responses to the entire class for a discussion of their findings.

HOSPITALITY MANAGEMENT PEDAGOGY AND THE LIBRARY

Critical thinking, and, to a much lesser degree, information literacy have both been identified as skills and modes of thinking which have been essential to the hospitality management workforce since the 1980s. It is telling, however, that the Accreditation Commission for Programs in Hospitality Administration, in their *Handbook for Accreditation* (2004) views the library largely as a facility of resources and has no mention of information literacy or library instruction in their accreditation process. In the literature of hospitality management pedagogy, Sivan et al. (2000) describe student responses to a series of active learning exercises. "Activities that had no direct link with industry were rated much lower: examples included life cycles and library exercises" (387). The author does not specify exactly what kind of library exercises occurred. The library literature has a good number of articles on discipline-specific information literacy instruction but lacks discussion of the needs of hospitality management students as well as other trade and vocational areas. The closest body of literature is on information literacy for business and marketing.

HOSPITALITY MANAGEMENT INDUSTRY NEEDS

Sigala and Baum characterize the current hospitality industry as "information intensive" (2003, 368). Traditionally, hospitality management was considered a craft enterprise and/or a service-oriented field. Today, the field requires managerial abilities together with information handling skills. In hospitality management education, there is a tension between the traditional focus and new orientations. However, Sigala and Baum believe that hospitality management education provides too great a focus on traditional technical skills (369).

Employers who hire hospitality graduates want employees with problem-solving skills, not skills or knowledge per se (Collins, 59). Many people problem-solve with a solution in mind, thus not fully exploring all aspects of the problem and not asking enough questions (Haywood 1987, 53). Students often are taught with a case-methodology that supplies the information needed. Alternatively, students already have the knowledge base from their education to basically solve the problem. In reality, however, every problem is unique and often requires investigation and research. Because some students have poorly developed critical thinking skills, they may be weak in recognizing when they need information and when they need to do research (Haywood, 54).

Guests and travelers (and other customers and clients) are increasingly sophisticated and have more complex needs. The hospitality workplace is highly mutable, and employment is no longer fixed or stable. Employees need to be engaged learners who can recognize trends and other forms of change in order to respond to a constantly evolving profession (Sigala and Baum, 369–370). Globalization has created multicultural and multinational workplaces and customers. As a result, employees require more sophisticated collaborative and communication skills.

CONCLUSION

This workshop will always be a work in progress. If more than one hour was available to teach students about library research, the possibilities for more extensive student evaluation of sources and critical thinking exercises would greatly increase. However, this scenario is highly unlikely, and the most likely way to reinforce and expand student critical thinking about information would be to collaborate with faculty in creating an assignment.

A postscript: The author recently completed teaching workshops for all sections of the introductory hospitality management course. Fall 2007 freshmen students are markedly more sophisticated about information and participate in classroom discussion in much greater numbers. The students continue to be satisfied with the company Website as their only source, but, increasingly, classes are conscious of the importance of other sources and aware of bias. The recent increase in student enthusiasm for the library workshop is highly rewarding.

Parts of this article were originally presented at the 2nd Annual CUNY General Education Conference, "General Education in the Disciplines and Professions: New Approaches to Old Debates," Queensborough Community College, Bayside, NY, May 5, 2006.

REFERENCES

Accreditation Commission for Programs in Hospitality Administration. 2004. *Handbook of accreditation*. Oxford, MD. *http://www.acpha/cahm.org/forms/acpha/ acphahandbook04.pdf*.

Albitz, R. S. 2007. The what and who of information literacy and critical thinking in higher education. *Portal: Libraries in the Academy* 7: 97–109.

Arizona Faculties Council. 2000 Arizona Faculties Council (AFC) definition of learner-centered education. *http://www.abor.asu.edu/4_special_programs/lce/afc-defined_lce.htm*.

Bruce, C. 1997. Seven faces of information literacy in higher education. *http://sky.fit.qut.edu.au /~bruce/inflit/faces/ faces1.htm*.

Bruckman, A. S. 2005. Student research and the Internet. *Communications of the ACM* 48: 35–37.

Collins, J. 1988. The library: Learning lab for managers. *Cornell Hotel and Restaurant Administration Quarterly* 29: 59–61.

De Rosa, C. and Online Computer Library Center (OCLC). 2005. *Perceptions of libraries and information resources*. Dublin, OH: OCLC. *http://www.oclc.org/reports/2005perceptions.htm*.

Doherty, J. J. and K. Ketchner. 2005. Empowering the intentional learner: A critical theory for information literacy instruction. *Library Philosophy and Practice* 8: 1–10. *http://libr.unl.edu:2000/LPP/doherty-ketchner.htm*.

Goad, T. W. 2002. *Information literacy and workplace performance*. Westport, CT: Quorum Books.

Gradowski, G., L. Snavely, and P. Dempsey. 1998. *Designs for active learning: A sourcebook of classroom strategies for information education*. Chicago: The Association of College and Research Libraries.

Grafstein, A. 2002. A discipline-based approach to information literacy. *Journal of Academic Librarianship* 28: 197–204.

Harley, B. L. 2001. Freshmen, information literacy, critical thinking, and values. *Reference Services Review* 29: 301–306.

Haywood, K. M. 1987. Thoughts on thinking: A critical human-resource skill. *Cornell Hotel and Restaurant Administration Quarterly* 28: 50–55.

Jacobson, T. and L. Xu. 2004. *Motivating students in information literacy classes*. New York: Neal-Schuman Publishers.

Kwon, N., A. J. Onwuegbuzie, and L. Alexander. 2007. Critical thinking disposition and library anxiety: Affective domains on the space of information seeking and use in academic libraries. *College & Research Libraries* 68: 268–278.

Latour, B. 1987. *Science in action: How to follow scientists and engineers through society.* Cambridge, MA: Harvard University Press.

Meola, M. 2004. Chucking the checklist: A contextual approach to teaching undergraduates Web-site evaluation. *Portal: Libraries in the Academy* 4: 331–344.

Sigala, M. and T. Baum. 2003. Trends and issues in tourism and hospitality higher education: Visioning the future. *Tourism & Hospitality Research* 4: 367–376.

Sivan, A. et al. 2000. An implementation of active learning and its effect on the quality of student learning. *Innovations in Education & Training International* 37: 381–389.

Sterngold, A. H. and J. M. Hurlbert. 1998. Information literacy and the marketing curriculum: A multidimensional definition and practical application. *Journal of Marketing Education* 20: 244–249.

Swanson, T. A. 2004. A radical step: Implementing a critical information literacy model. *Portal: Libraries in the Academy* 4: 259–273.

Wathen, C. N. and J. Burkell. 2002. Believe it or not: Factors influencing credibility on the Web. *Journal of the American Society for Information Science and Technology* 53: 134–144. *http://dx.doi.org/10.1002/asi.10016.*

Information Literacy in Subject-Specific Vocabularies: A Path to Critical Thinking

Linda Heichman Taylor

INTRODUCTION

The teaching of specific information-seeking skills, or information literacy, can complement and reinforce methodologies and pedagogy associated with developing and encouraging critical thinking in the college classroom. This article discusses the formation of a vocabulary skill-building workshop created to increase understanding of key business concepts, teach information-seeking skills, and provide an opportunity for students to advance further along the academic continuum toward sophisticated development of critical thinking skills. Simply stated, this learning opportunity attempts to help students understand rudimentary business concepts so that they can spend more time thinking creatively, analytically, and strategically, and less time deciphering and digesting the topics and ideas presented in the classroom. The workshop presents a successful collaboration between business librarian and business writing faculty to increase awareness of key business vocabulary among business students and to reinforce business communication skill-building learned as part of the business writing curriculum.

The development of the business vocabulary workshop grew out of a need identified by students and faculty in the College of Business and Economics at California State University, Fullerton. Students exhibited a lack of understanding of basic business vocabulary and were demonstrating difficulty in utilizing proper research techniques. Faculty observed that many of their students did not read with purpose, lacked the ability to summarize reading material effectively, and did not possess the ability to think critically about specific business issues presented to them via class discussion, assigned readings, or research assignments.

This article will discuss the theoretical, ideological, and pedagogical frameworks of the workshop within the context of curriculum development and learning objectives. Student behaviors observed during the workshop will be interpreted qualitatively to show that the vocabulary skill-building learning opportunity has produced positive indications that critical thinking has taken place. Implications for further research will also be discussed.

THEORETICAL AND IDEOLOGICAL FRAMEWORK

The theoretical framework of the workshop relied heavily on Perry's research on cognitive development of college students (1970). His research supports a schema of positions that demarcate learning at the onset, midst, and conclusion of a four-year academic period. These positions represent a linear progression of intellectual and ethical development. He found that students at the beginning of their academic career exhibited qualities of thinking associated with the lower tier of the positions. According to Perry, many freshmen begin their college careers with total acceptance of authority (Position 1), and, as they proceed through their coursework, interaction with faculty, and general life experience, begin to rebel against authority (Position 2). After one year or more of college study, students express uncertainty about learning and question authority (Position 3), and they begin to function as independent learners (Position 4) before developing a sense of restructuring their reality (Position 5). It is this crucial Position 5 which serves as the genesis of the critical thinking process.

Once students recognize that thinking critically is a choice open to them, they then advance to a stage of commitment toward seeking knowledge as an ongoing, lifelong pursuit (Position 6). Perry found that most often this stage appeared during the latter part of a student's academic career. Once students progress to Position 6, they then could choose to deepen commitment to critical thinking and discovery by taking personal responsibility for decision making (Position 7), expressing individuality (Position 8), or creating self-awareness and identity (Position 9).

Key elements of the workshop curriculum were designed to align with one or more of Perry's positions, with the goal of cultivating the ability to utilize complex reasoning and thinking required in the more advanced positions. Objectives and activities were structured to engage several types of learners to recognize the importance of business vocabulary, provide task-based exercises with defined goals, and to work both collaboratively and individually through the vocabulary skill-building process.

The workshop was developed to utilize both a faculty-centered learning approach (see Figure 1) and a student-centered learning approach (see Figure 2). The faculty-centered approach stems from the faculty observation that students lack adequate written or oral skills. Once this characteristic is observed, students can exhibit one or more behaviors such as incomplete knowledge of subject, failure to think creatively, or reliance on non-objective sources for analytical research. Student behaviors can develop into poor learning outcomes such as lack of understanding, inability to formulate a thesis statement, or substandard research techniques. Actions that can be taken to correct these behaviors include skill-building learning

FIGURE 1. Faculty-Centered Model

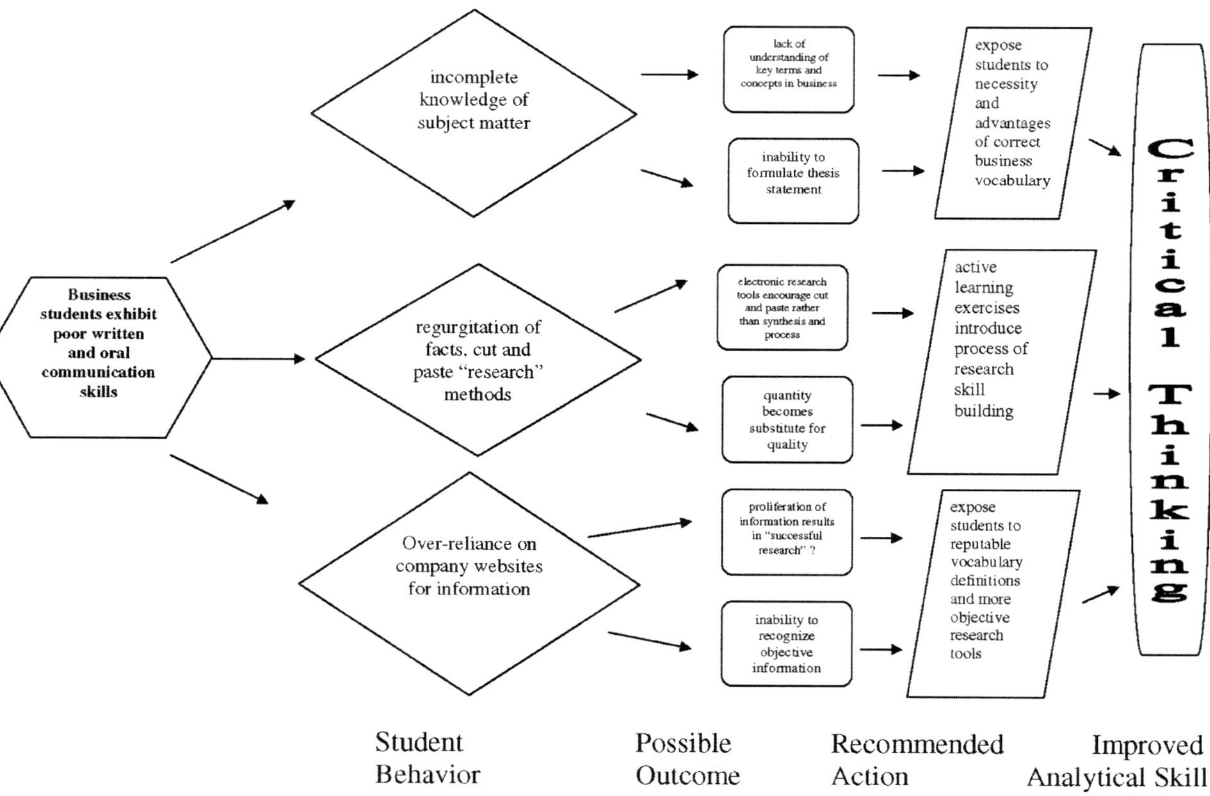

Business students exhibit poor written and oral communication skills
incomplete knowledge of subject matter
regurgitation of facts, cut and paste "research" methods
Over-reliance on company websites for information
lack of understanding of key terms and concepts in business
inability to formulate thesis statement
electronic research tools encourage cut and paste rather than synthesis and process
quantity becomes substitute for quality
proliferation of information results in "successful research" ?
inability to recognize objective information
expose students to necessity and advantages of correct business vocabulary
active learning exercises introduce process of research skill building
expose students to reputable vocabulary definitions and more objective research tools
Critical Thinking
Student Behavior
Possible Outcome
Recommended Action
Improved Analytical Skill

FIGURE 2. Student-Centered Model

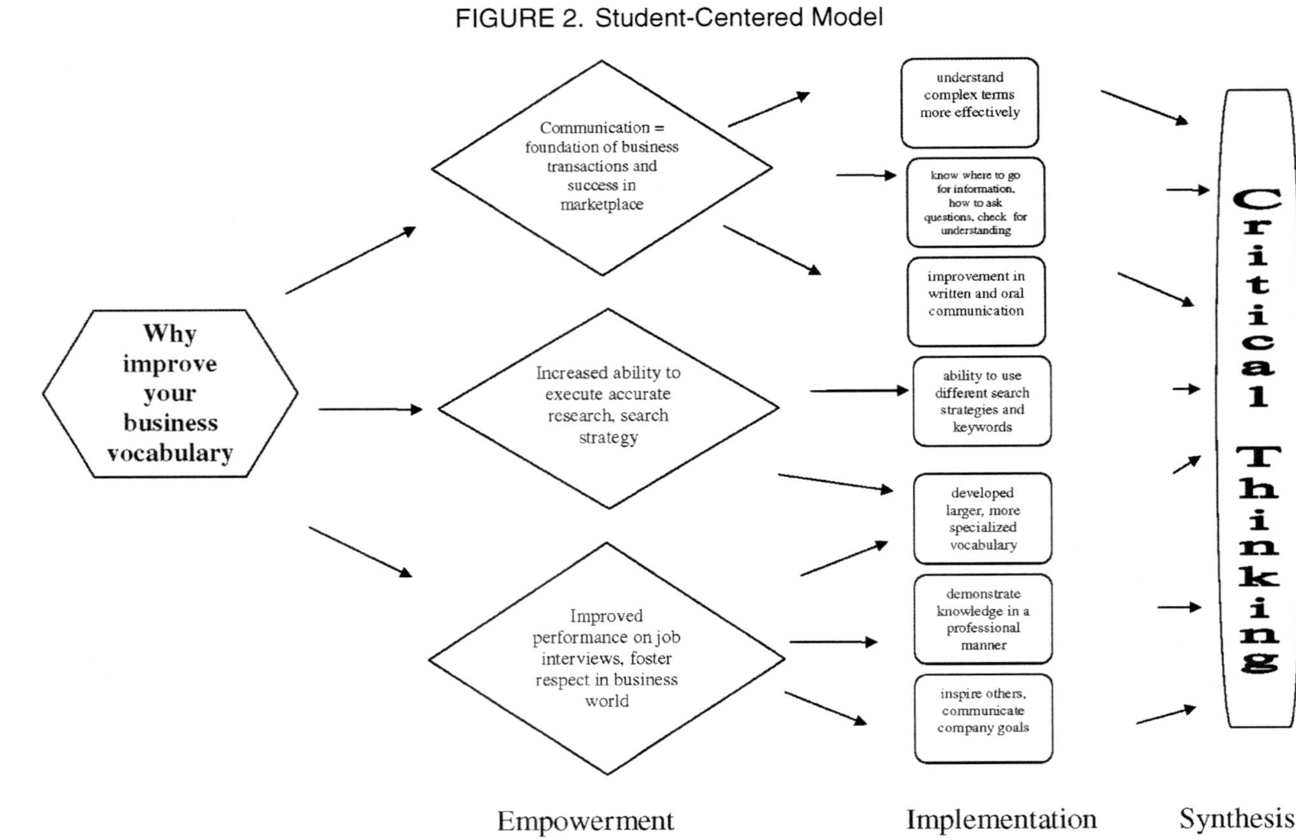
Why improve your business vocabulary
Communication = foundation of business transactions and success in marketplace
Increased ability to execute accurate research, search strategy
Improved performance on job interviews, foster respect in business world
understand complex terms more effectively
know where to go for information, how to ask questions, check for understanding
improvement in written and oral communication
ability to use different search strategies and keywords
developed larger, more specialized vocabulary
demonstrate knowledge in a professional manner
inspire others, communicate company goals
Critical Thinking
Empowerment
Implementation
Synthesis

opportunities, active learning, and identification of reputable research tools. Once these actions are taken, critical thinking can be observed.

Beginning from the student perspective, the student-centered model begins with student inquiry (Position 3). Once students are curious to learn, they can discover empowerment opportunities by partaking in vocabulary skill-building (Position 4). Students can then implement one or more learning outcomes (Position 6) in order to reach the final goal of thinking critically (Position 7).

LITERATURE REVIEW

Critical thinking in business education and in library instruction has been a prevalent field of study in recent years (Bodi 1992; Herro 2000). A significant impetus to foster critical thinking is the increasing need for business schools to tailor their curricula to the demands of the workplace (Braun 2004). One of the specific demands acknowledged is the need for information retrieval and analysis. In response to this need, Henninger and McNeil Hurlbert devised a learning experience designed to introduce information literacy concepts at the beginning of the undergraduate business curriculum (1996). They explain the modern business curriculum as one that has largely focused on quantitative methods as the foundation for business decision-making. Additionally, they discuss the recognition by practitioners and accreditation agencies that quantitative skill has been identified as an important learning outcome for business students. Henninger and Hurlbert also point out that qualitative approaches to teaching often mirror managerial decision-making in a more realistic, pragmatic fashion. It is this qualitative approach they utilize to create an active learning exercise that helps students distinguish information as an important tool in problem solving. Their efforts have been successful in moving students beyond Perry's first stage of critical thinking (acceptance of information as omnipotent) to the second stage of development (learning to select relevant sources).

Business faculty have also incorporated critical thinking objectives into the business school curriculum. Ladyshewsky (2006) presents an overview of the concept of coaching to promote managerial skill, emphasizing peer coaching as a successful method to improve managerial communication and decision-making. The author advocates a non-traditional teaching approach that emphasizes peer-to-peer, interactive, non-evaluative discussion and feedback, which, in turn, build partnerships based on trust. These partnerships promote more equitable communication among participants, which results in maximal learning outcomes. Students evaluated in Ladyshewsky's research reported enhanced critical thinking and heightening of meta-cognition as a result of the peer coaching experience. Specific critical thinking skills exhibited by participants include perspective sharing, verification of knowledge, and appreciation of alternate perspectives.

Quinton and Smallbone (2005) focus upon the learning outcome of reading with purpose in their research. They study business students in their second year of the business school curriculum, a time in which students should "begin to engage with a more critical approach to business concepts" as part of "becoming critical independent learners" (299). They express concern that, as a result of conducting research using computers, information is collected in an ad-hoc fashion. This haphazard information-gathering presents problems for students when attempting to evaluate information and collate it with concepts taught in the classroom. The authors analyze several teaching approaches designed to encourage students to critically reflect on what they are reading, foster the ability to discern meaning, and show evidence of learning as a means to interpret reality in a different way (Perry Position 5). Their research describes a successful attempt at designing learning experiences that assist in developing the critical perspective needed to arrive at a deeper stage of learning (Perry Position 6).

Although sparse research exists to document the importance of information literacy and critical thinking skills in the workplace, Klusek and Bornstein (2006) and Braun each utilized U.S. Department of Labor information to underscore the workplace expectation that students will have the ability to analyze information and think creatively as they enter the professional milieu. Braun cites the U.S. Department of Labor Commission on Achieving Necessary Skills as an agency that was one of the first bodies to recognize critical thinking as an essential skill needed to compete in the global economy. Klusek and Bornstein examined business and financial operations job profiles provided in the Department of Labor occupational database O*Net, and found that ten of the skills identified in O*Net demonstrate activities facilitating knowing, accessing, evaluating, and using information—basic skills which translate into the workplace as a worker's ability to "acquire information and use it when working with others" (11). Additionally, these skills were found to be rated as "important" or "very important" in a majority of the jobs. All jobs analyzed rated information gathering and analysis as "important" to "extremely important" for decision making.

PEDAGOGY

Although little knowledge on effective pedagogy has been derived to date from research on critical thinking (Tsui 2002), this workshop is structured using techniques which are designed to stimulate critical thinking while enlisting a variety of learning styles. Tsui employs a traditional business school teaching method, the case study, to research pedagogical methods that enhance students' ability to think critically. One of the strongest factors which the author found to enhance critical thinking is class discussion. Class discussion is utilized several times during the workshop, and the author similarly has observed improved critical thinking as a result of these discussions.

Other methods utilized during the vocabulary workshop are lecture and individual and group exercises. Henninger and Hurlbert found that in-class exercises provide tangible evidence to students that behaviors associated with enhancing critical thinking are successful and have a purpose (35–36). Another successful technique shown to improve critical thinking is interactive learning (Braun). Two types of active learning exercises are employed during the workshop—a group exercise and an individual exercise. The group exercise, in particular, supports the ideas that peer interaction stimulates cognitive development and peer coaching enhances critical thinking skill development (Ladyshewsky).

A variety of activities was offered during the workshop not only to recognize the needs of auditory, visual, and kinesthetic learners, but also to satisfy the AACSB expectation of providing "interaction opportunities that are available to meet the unique needs of individual students" (AACSB 2007, 39). Activities are deliberately designed using active learning techniques so as to developmentally shape critical thinking and to further stimulate lifelong habits of thinking.

Curriculum Development

Impetus for integrating vocabulary workshops into the business curriculum arose through discussions with business faculty about the dearth of writing, reading, and research skills among their students. Additionally, the author observed that business students coming to the library for research help were unable to conduct effective search strategies due to the fact that they could not effectively articulate the concepts they were charged with researching. As a result, the author developed a workshop designed to improve business vocabulary skills among students in the College of Business and Economics.

Business writing faculty were consulted frequently during curriculum development to ensure that the objectives and learning outcomes presented in the workshop complemented and enhanced objectives and goals within business communication coursework. Workshop components were crafted to cultivate primarily oral but also written communications skills in a business context—one of the key outcomes in the business communication curriculum. An added benefit of this close collaboration with faculty was the invitation to include the workshop as a component in the recurring business writing workshop series taught at the College of Business each semester.

The workshop curriculum was designed to incorporate tenets of existing core competencies in business communication developed by business writing faculty (Brzovic et al. 2002). The individual exercise was developed to facilitate improvement in written communication, while the introductory interactive discussion and elements of the group exercise were developed to facilitate improvement in oral communication, teamwork/group dynamics (AACSB), and the ability to solve complex issues. Competency in articulating information needs, evaluating information sources, and using information to accomplish a specific purpose (ACRL 2000) were also addressed when designing the curriculum.

The comprehension of business vocabulary provides an opportunity to foster higher-order thinking skills among business students because students will engage sooner in understanding those concepts which may be either foreign or lack clarity. Scholarly research in the field of secondary education (Thompson 2002) indicates that critical thinking skills depend on mastery of vocabulary. This mastery of vocabulary has the effect of expanding global consciousness to provide the ability to recognize phenomena once terms are learned for them. Another aspect of the interdependence of vocabulary comprehension and critical thinking is the use of critical thinking education in management as one way to reduce vague or ambiguous information conveyed to managers in their roles as evaluators, problem solvers, and strategists. Improved comprehension of concepts communicated is advocated as a method to improve clarity in decision-making (Smith 2003). Business communication research correlates knowledge of vocabulary terms related to ethics as one way students can exercise critical thinking toward development of awareness of ethical approaches to conducting business (Kienzler and David 2003).

Instructional Tools

The author created an original business terminology workbook to serve as an interactive instructional tool to facilitate and reinforce learning of the concepts presented. This tool was designed to provide college-level business students with ample resources to develop an improved business vocabulary. The workbook includes discussion of the importance of a polished business vocabulary, lists of relevant vocabulary words broken down by business discipline, strategies for defining terms, an in-class exercise, resources for more information, and bibliography. Students are encouraged to utilize the vocabulary words to develop effective search strategies and to communicate ideas presented in research papers or term projects.

OBJECTIVES

The workshop itself is designed to inform students about the importance of a sound business vocabulary, provide practical applications for success in the classroom and in the professions, discuss strategies for improved communication, expose students to the benefit of two-way exchanges of information, and address the commonality necessary to succeed in a global business environment. Students are introduced to the possibility of enriched business communication in a dynamic business atmosphere as a direct result of improved business vocabulary and enhanced critical thinking.

Each component of the workshop curriculum addresses one or more of the theoretical or pedagogical concepts presented, reinforces documented, researched teaching methods that encourage and promote critical thinking, and incorporates learning goals stated in AACSB accreditation and ACRL information competence standards. Each individual element of the curriculum as well as the curriculum as a whole has the objective of enhancing awareness and execution of critical thinking.

The first element of the workshop curriculum involves a short participatory dialogue between students and instructor, which introduces the concept of business vocabulary and its correlation to success in the classroom and workplace. Students and instructor discuss the potential learning outcomes of the workshop and the importance of a sound business vocabulary as a tool to facilitate successful outcomes in academic and professional pursuits. Specific learning outcomes presented by students include improved communication skills, better comprehension of material presented in class, mastery of business language by non-native English speakers, and a desire to gain advantage during professional interviews. Additional learning outcomes for the workshop as a whole are the impetus to gain a vast knowledge of the language of business, ability to identify and locate resources to define business terminology, enhancement of search strategies using relevant keywords, and knowledge of a variety of terms related to a student's subject concentration.

This discussion is designed to align with Perry's first stage of critical thinking, in that most students who begin the workshop will accept the authority figure's (instructor's) mastery of the subject material in lieu of their own independent mastery of subject. Students should progress to Perry's second stage after they have exchanged ideas about the merits of increased understanding of business vocabulary and have begun to reconcile these statements in readiness to question and reject simple acceptance of an authority figure's presentation of subject matter (see Figure 3). Additionally, the discussion produces outcomes consistent with the definition and articulation of an information need—one of the foundations of information competency in higher education (ACRL, 8).

Students then take part in a group exercise designed to involve peer groups in collaborative problem solving. The students are divided into small groups. One person in each group randomly selects a basic business vocabulary term to define from a finite list of terms created by the instructor. Groups are tasked with discussing the word, its context, and meaning without consulting any dictionaries, books, or other sources to aid in comprehension of the term selected. Each group appoints a representative to report their discussions and definitions back to the entire class. As each group presents its definition and cites examples of how the term is used in the business world, the instructor reinforces learning by enriching the discussion with additional illustrative scenarios. This activity provides the opportunity for students to "use information effectively to accomplish a specific purpose" (ACRL, 13) and to learn from their peers. It also encourages students to perceive understanding independent from that presented by the instructor, and may begin to foster the desire to restructure understanding as a whole (see Figure 4).

At the conclusion of the group exercise, the students move on to undertake an individual exercise (see Appendix 1). This activity is designed to advance students deeper into Perry's scheme by engaging them in independent learning, self-discovery, and commitment to lifelong learning. Students are instructed to select a word from one of the specialized discipline lists that corresponds to a field of business study in which they are interested (accounting, economics, finance, information systems

FIGURE 3. Progression from Position 1 to Position 2 as a Result of Participation in Interactive Dialogue

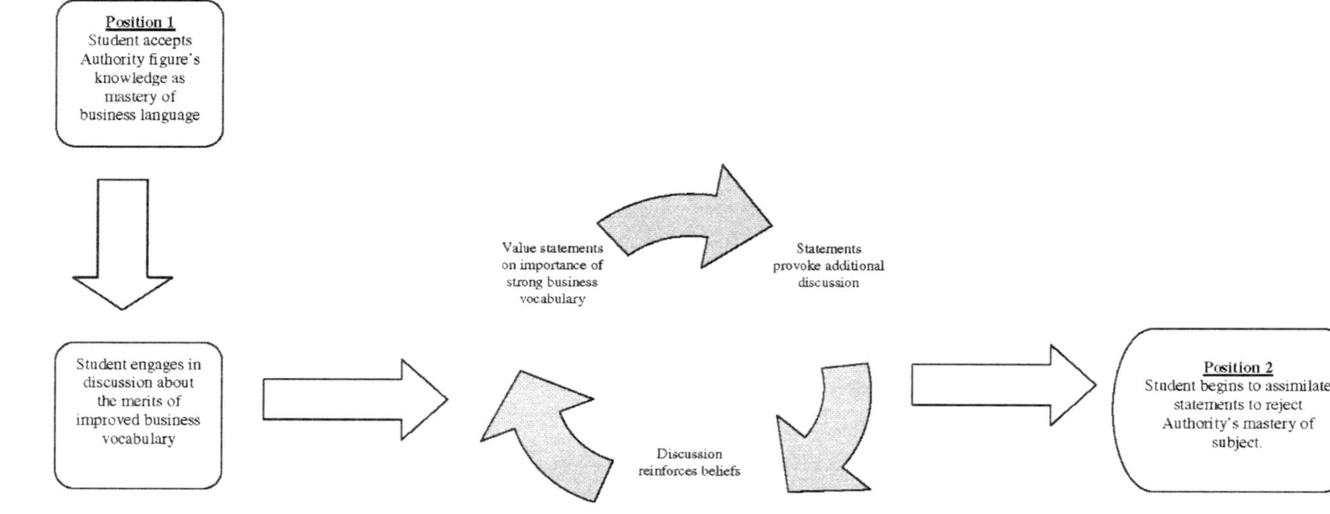

FIGURE 4. Progression from Position 2 to Position 3 and/or 4 as a Result of Completing Group Exercise

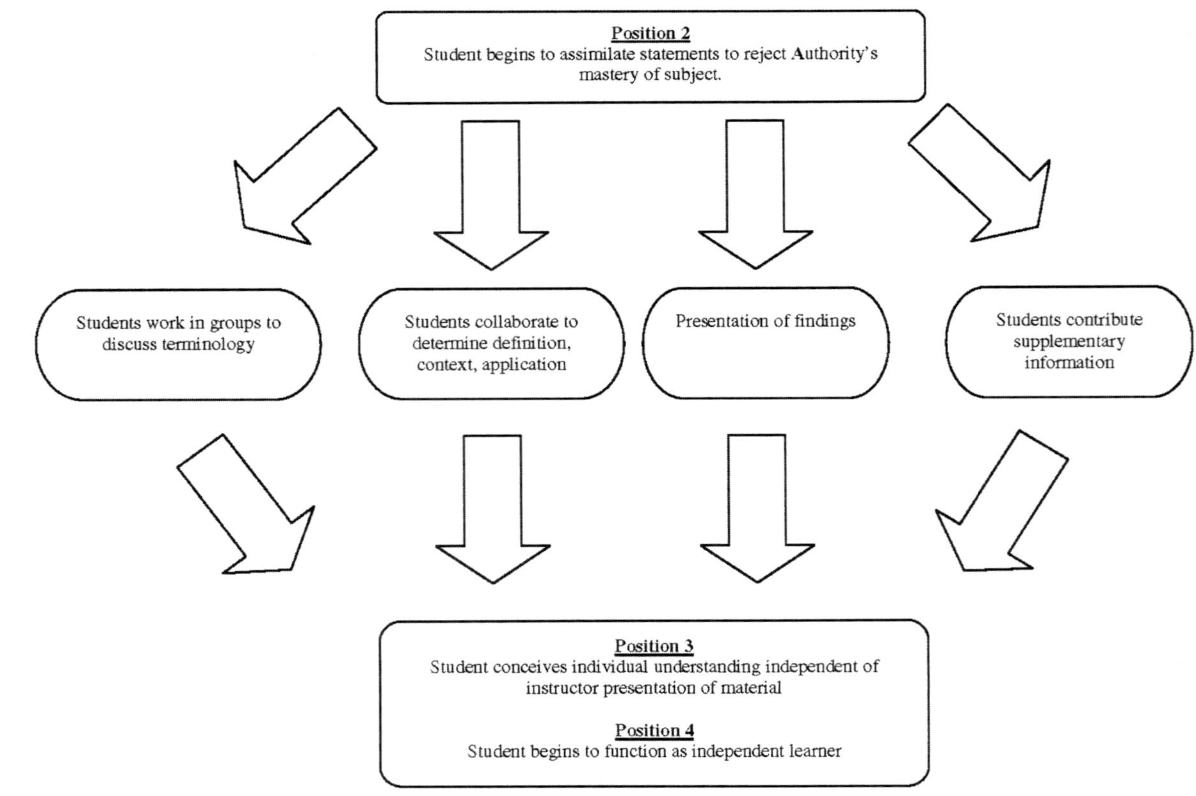

and decision science, international business, management, marketing) and which is unfamiliar to them. The student utilizes two resources to aid in discerning the meaning of the term selected. Students may use online resources, print resources, or a combination of the two. The student must write the definitions on the in-class exercise sheet provided, identify the sources consulted, and explain why they would utilize one or both sources as a tool for locating and defining information. This exercise is designed to achieve the following: cultivate curiosity toward learning something unfamiliar; accomplish information competence through identification and evaluation of appropriate information resources (ACRL); demonstrate clear, written communication of business concepts or ideas; enhance problem solving ability and decision-making; and deepen interest in a specific business discipline (see Figure 5).

RESULTS

Although no quantitative measures were used to verify that critical thinking has indeed taken place as a result of participation in this workshop, several qualitative observations can be made to verify that learning outcomes have been achieved and critical thinking development has occurred. In many cases, students were observed as having met or exceeded the intended learning outcomes embedded into the curriculum. During the introductory lecture, students exchanged ideas with the instructor and peers to take an active role in the justification for a sound business vocabulary, in effect defining their own information need and discovering the necessity of learning for their own edification as opposed to complying with a one-way educational experience by an authority figure. This constitutes students' evidence of their progression from the first stage to the second and third stages of Perry's schema of intellectual development. Several students commented on the effectiveness of the learning experience, noting that they did not realize exactly how much they had to learn and how important business vocabulary can be to success in the workplace. Students demonstrated progression through the middle stages of Perry's scheme by conversing with their peers about specific context and application of the terminology, stating individual opinions, and working together to accomplish the task at hand. Students were observed as successfully interacting together as peers and genuinely building upon their knowledge by working collaboratively. Students who initially were reticent to participate in the open discussion at the beginning of the workshop were shown to exhibit

FIGURE 5. Progression to More Advanced Stages of Critical Thinking as a Result of Completing Individual Exercise

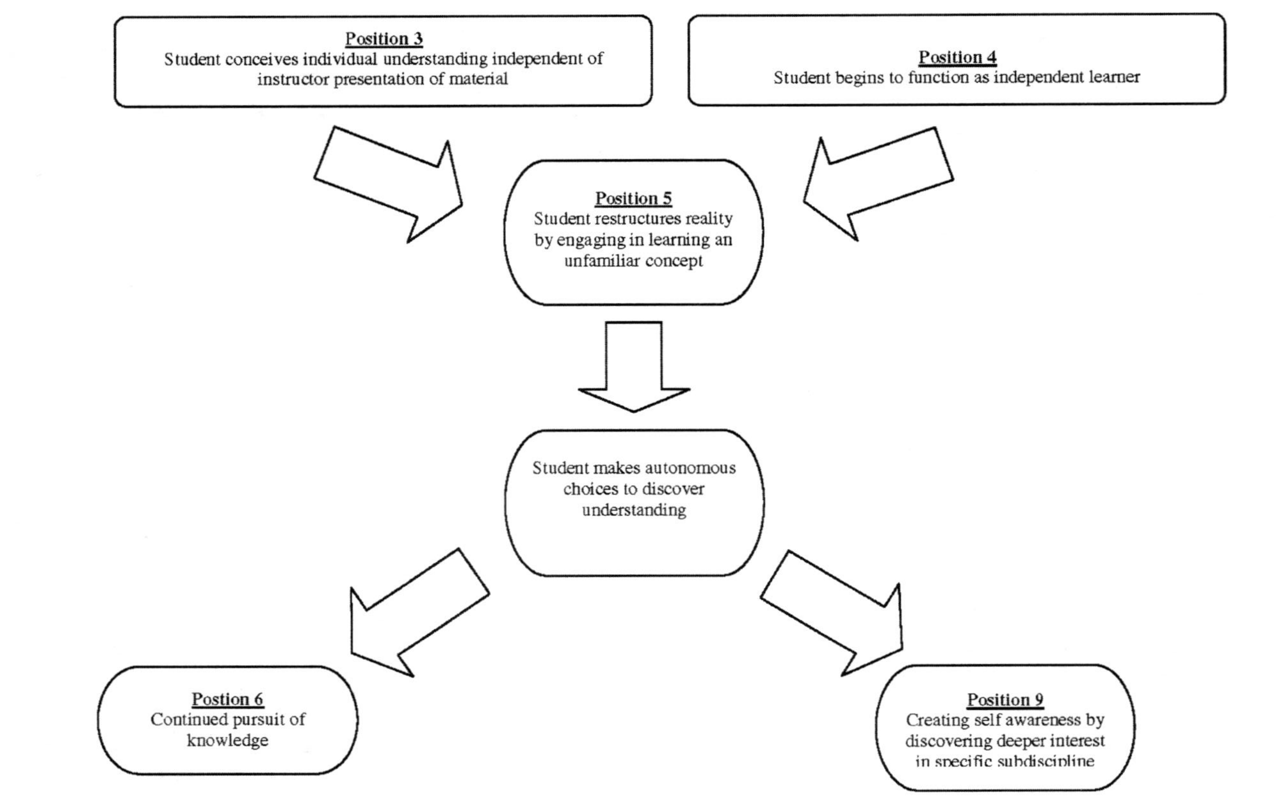

more active behavior and involvement in critical dialogue when in the group environment.

During the individual exercise, students were observed achieving a more personalized, individual discovery of information indicative of characteristics of Perry's latter stages of development. Students were observed effectively choosing terminology of personal interest, successfully evaluating information resources, and working independently to pursue a goal. As with the group exercise, reticent, reserved students gained more from this facet of the workshop than the introductory phase, immersing themselves in the tasks at hand and communicating knowledge gain as well as appreciation for the learning experience.

IMPLICATIONS FOR FURTHER RESEARCH

Quantitative methods for assessment of acquisition of critical thinking skills should be investigated to measure effectiveness of this type of skill-building workshop. A number of research methods could be employed, including administering one or more pre- and post-test pairings to determine knowledge or understanding of business vocabulary, reading comprehension, or case study analysis, interactive vocabulary testing for control and test groups, business communication development exercises, or post-graduation workplace interviews. Continued research should be undertaken with the goal of providing insight into effective teaching methods, which encourage, empower, and inspire students to develop enhanced critical thinking skills, not only for academic gain but also as an integral component of success in the marketplace.

REFERENCES

American Association for the Advancement of Collegiate Schools of Business (AACSB). 2007. Eligibility procedures and accreditation standards for business accreditation. http://www.aacsb.edu/accreditation/standards.asp.

Association of College and Research Libraries (ACRL). 2000. Information literacy competency standards for higher education. http://www.ala.org/ala/acrl/acrlstandards/informationliteracycompetency.htm.

Bodi, S. 1992. Collaborating with faculty in teaching critical thinking: The role of librarians. *Research Strategies* 10: 69–76.

Braun, N. M. 2004. Critical thinking in the business curriculum. *Journal of Education for Business* 79: 232–236.

Brzovic, K., L. Fraser, D. Loewy, and G. Vogt. 2002. Core competencies and assessment in business writing. *BUAD* 201, 301, 501. http://business.fullerton.edu/buswriting/CoreCompetencies.pdf.

Henninger, E. A. and J. M. Hurlbert. 1996. Critical thinking and information across the undergraduate business curriculum. *Journal of Business and Finance Librarianship* 2: 29–40.

Herro, S. 2000. Bibliographic instruction and critical thinking. *Journal of Adolescent & Adult Literacy* 43: 554–558.

Kienzler, D. and C. David. 2003. After Enron: Integrating ethics into the professional communication curriculum. *Journal of Business and Technical Communication* 17: 474–489.

Klusek, L. and J. Bornstein. 2006. Information literacy skills for business careers: Matching skills to the workplace. *Journal of Business & Finance Librarianship* 11: 3–19.

Ladyshewsky, R. K. 2006. Peer coaching: A constructivist methodology for enhancing critical thinking in postgraduate business education. *Higher Education Research & Development* 25: 67–84.

Perry, W. G. 1970. *Forms of intellectual and ethical development in the college years.* New York: Holt, Rinehart, and Winston.

Quinton, S. and T. Smallbone. 2005. The troublesome triplets: Issues in teaching reliability, validity, and generalization to business students. *Teaching in Higher Education* 10: 299–311.

Smith, G. F. 2003. Beyond critical thinking and decision making: Teaching business students how to think. *Journal of Management Education* 27: 24–51.

Thompson, M. C. 2002. Vocabulary and grammar: Critical content for critical thinking. *Journal of Secondary Gifted Education* 13: 60–66.

Tsui, L. 2002. Fostering critical thinking through effective pedagogy: Evidence from four institutional case studies. *Journal of Higher Education* 73: 740–763.

APPENDIX 1

Business Terminology Exercise

Name: ______________________________

Class Year: Fr So Jr Sr Grad Student

Major: ______________________________

E-mail: ______________________________

1. Highlight, underline, or circle all words on the preceding lists that are the same.
2. Look up each duplicated word in its specific subject context.
3. Choose one word from these lists to define.
4. Once you verify the context of the word, use TWO resources (electronic or print or a combination of the two) to look up the word (see Recommended Resources to Define Business Vocabulary on page).
5. What is the definition of the word?

Source 1 ____

____

Source 2 ____

____

Electronic Source ____

____

Which sources did you use?

Source 1 ____

Source 2 ____

Which of these sources would you use again? Why?

____

____

____

____

____

Using Bloom's Taxonomy to Teach Critical Thinking Skills to Business Students

Nancy Nentl
Ruth Zietlow

INTRODUCTION

Critical thinking skills are vitally important for business students as they prepare for strategic analysis and decision making in organizational settings. While the need for infusing sophisticated analysis and thought into a business curriculum is clear (Roy and Macchiette 2005), engaging students in critical thinking can be complex and challenging. Furthermore, determining evidence that critical thinking has actually occurred is problematic. This article suggests that Bloom's Taxonomy of Educational Objectives, a classic learning objective and evaluation model in the U.S. since its publication in 1956, is an important framework both for developing course assignments and for serving as a yardstick against which to measure evidence that critical thinking has occurred.

BLOOM'S TAXONOMY

Benjamin Bloom's Taxonomy of Educational Objectives, herein referred to as Bloom's Taxonomy, was developed at the University of Chicago by a group of cognitive psychologists and spearheaded by educational psychologist, Benjamin Bloom (Bloom 1956). Bloom's original purpose for enlisting this group of measurement specialists from across the United States was to reduce the labor of preparing annual comprehensive examinations and to bring about some standardization of learning objectives in academia (Krathwohl 2002). The group's intent to identify and standardize learning objectives for student achievement led to the collaboration of banks of test items, each measuring the same educational objective.

Bloom's Taxonomy rose to significant prominence in the 1960s with the increased emphasis on education during the period of Lyndon Baines Johnson's Great Society, and today the model is well known to many educators. Although Bloom's taxonomical theory addresses three domains of learning (the cognitive, psychomotor, and affective), the primary interest of this article is the cognitive domain with its six successive stages of learning: the lower-order learning of knowledge, comprehension, and application; and the higher-order learning of analysis, synthesis, and evaluation.

The appeal of Bloom's learning model is its elegance, simplicity, and versatility. Its elegance and simplicity emanate from the notion that learning presumes to occur in this linear and hierarchical fashion. That is, relatively simplistic learning such as concrete knowledge, comprehension, and application must necessarily occur before learners can engage in more sophisticated and creative learning such as analysis, synthesis, and evaluation (see Figure 1). The versatility of the model is seen in its application for all levels of education, from kindergarten through higher education, as well as its cross-disciplinary use in business, the social sciences, and other applied sciences (Athanassiou, Mcnett, and Harvey 2003; Bissell and Lemons 2006; Blazelton 2000; Buxkemper and Hartfiel 2003; Granello 2001).

FIGURE 1. Bloom s Taxonomy

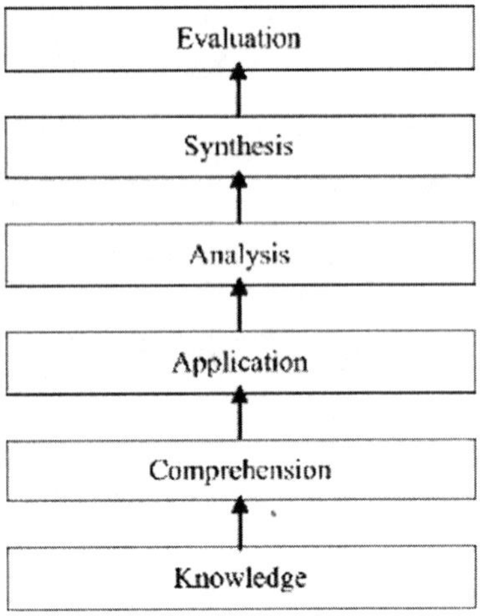

Evaluation

↑

Synthesis

↑

Analysis

↑

Application

↑

Comprehension

↑

Knowledge

While learning is arguably linear and hierarchical, it is also iterative and dynamic, particularly in the higher learning stages as critical thinking is engaged (Zohar and Dori 2003). In other words, the cognitive action of analyzing new information, synthesizing new information with other information, and then evaluating the parts of the whole and creating new knowledge is ongoing and interrelated, rather than strictly hierarchical, as presented in Figure 2.

APPLYING THE TAXONOMY

To operationalize these learning stages and objectives in a business course, we first look to Moore, Winograd, and Lange (2001) who provide a representative lexicon of definitions and related action verbs that characterize each successive stage. We also add how successful achievement of each stage might be demonstrated and provide specific examples of business course activities.

Knowledge:

Definition: To define, memorize, and remember previously learned material such as common terms, specific facts, and basic concepts.

Related verbs: List, describe, identify, show, label, and quote.

Demonstration of achievement: A student can define and recall terms, dates, events, and places or describe subject matter.

FIGURE 2. Interrelated Stages of Bloom s Taxonomy

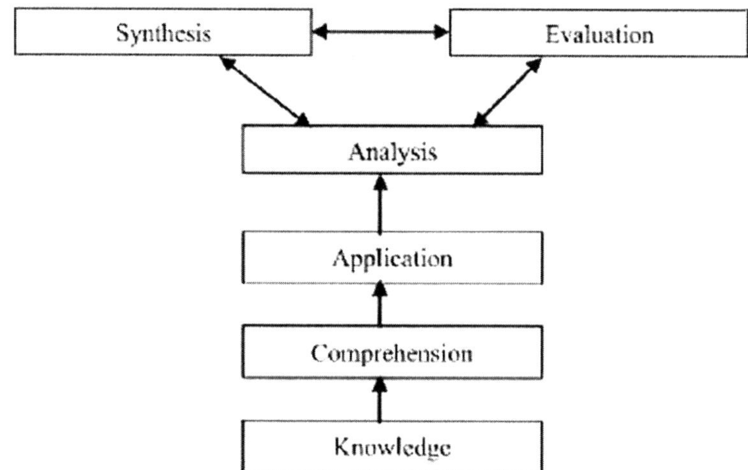

Examples of course activities: Define the GDP (gross domestic product); list the four Ps of marketing (product, price, place, promotion); identify the purpose of a balance sheet and label its components.

Comprehension:

Definition: The ability to grasp conceptual meaning.

Related verbs: Understand, discuss, estimate, compare, contrast, rank, recognize, and report, or explain facts and principles.

Demonstration of achievement: A student can correctly explain the history of an event, report on the status of an organization, or differentiate phenomena.

Examples of course activities: Summarize the most important social factors that led to the formation of the Securities and Exchange Commission; rank in order of risk the various investment vehicles such as mutual funds, treasury bonds, and individual stocks; compare and contrast qualitative research methods versus quantitative research methods.

Application:

Definition: The ability to use learned material in new and concrete situations or to demonstrate the accurate use of a concept or theory in a different context.

Related verbs: Apply, relate, demonstrate, illustrate, interpret, solve.

Demonstration of achievement: A student can apply a theory in a practical context or recognize and then use the correct methods to solve problems.

Examples of course activities: Calculate a break-even point for manufacturing a new product; utilize Porter's Five Forces (supplier power, barriers to entry, buyer power, threat of substitutes, exit) as a framework for understanding the challenges of starting a new business.

Analysis:

Definition: The ability to break down a complex problem into different parts and to determine the relationships between those parts.

Related verbs: Analyze, appraise, criticize, differentiate, discriminate, distinguish, examine, experiment.

Demonstration of achievement: A student can explain why a particular solution process works to resolve a problem. A student is able to see patterns underlying content or deconstruct the critical components of a framework.

Examples of course activities: Discuss what customer lifetime value is and why it is a potent measure of profitability. Design a segmentation strategy for the U.S. Hispanic market. Write a paper on how the current tax structure in the U.S. impacts taxpayers at various income levels. Analyze the implications of corporate authorship when used as a secondary source.

Synthesis:

Definition: The ability to put parts together to form a new whole.

Related verbs: Arrange, assemble, collect, compose, construct, create, design, develop, formulate, manage, organize.

Demonstration of achievement: A student can rearrange, reconstruct, or combine parts of a process to form and utilize a new whole.

Examples of course activities: Write a five-year plan for an IT department at a state university whose budget is constrained by the legislature. Design a prototype of a new consumer product and conduct a beta test. Formulate a problem statement that reflects a variety of industry data from different secondary sources.

Evaluation:

Definition: The ability to judge the value of material for a given purpose based on a definite set of criteria.

Related verbs: Persuade, appraise, judge, recommend, conclude.

Demonstration of achievement: A student can create a variety of ways to solve the problem and then, based on established criteria, select the solution method best suited for the problem. A student is able to judge an argument's veracity or evaluate another person's work.

Examples of course activities: Evaluate another student's stock portfolios in a global industry. Assess the market value and profitability of a technological innovation. Write a case where ethical violations have occurred between two businesses and persuade the stakeholders to maintain the relationships in spite of the breach.

Developing course activities and deliverables that reflect the lower learning stages of Bloom's is relatively easy to accomplish for most instructors. In many curricula, in fact, there are courses whose primary learning objectives are acquiring the knowledge and comprehension of business fundamentals necessary for successive courses. For example, a typical accounting course is called Financial Accounting, in which the focus is largely on learning and recognizing relevant accounting vocabulary. This is also found in many other principles courses that familiarize students with business terms and the application of those terms. For example, a description of a typical Principles of Marketing course from the Carlson School of Management, University of Minnesota, reads: "Introduction to terms, concepts, and skills for analyzing marketing problems and factors outside the organization affecting its product, pricing, promotion, and distribution decisions" (University of Minnesota Curtis L. Carlson School of Management 2007). These types of courses are essential and important because they provide the necessary foundation for students to advance to more substantive business courses. However, even more advanced courses inadvertently may have what amounts to lower-order learning requisites, placing few demands on the students to dissect, add to, and evaluate existing knowledge structures. Failing to engage analytical thinking beyond knowing, understanding, and applying a concept presents a barrier to the learning process (see Figure 3).

BREAKING THROUGH THE LEARNING BARRIER

A dilemma many instructors face is how to move students from the foundational stages of learning into more dynamic interrelationship learning. Many types of course activities such as publisher test banks and end-of-chapter exercises, etc., that are commonly used as course activities

FIGURE 3. The Learing Barrier and Bloom s Taxonomy

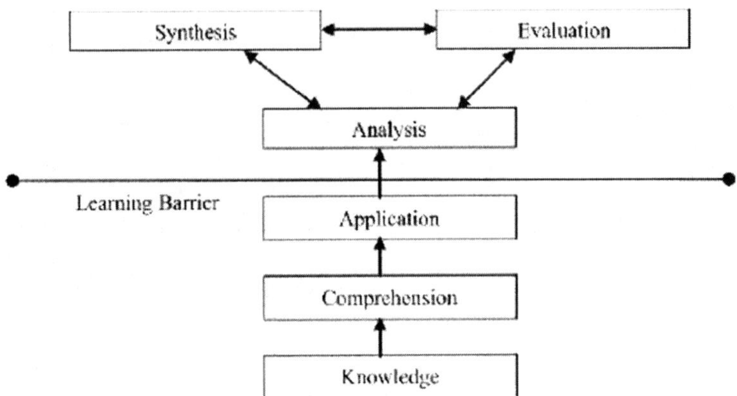

and evaluation, have a limited ability to compel business students to break through the learning barrier and engage in greater analytical thinking (Simkin and Kuechler 2005; Davidson and Baldwin 2005). The possible exception to this is the integration of simulations into the course curriculum. The use of simulations can be effective since quality simulations have the potential to move students through increasing complexity, motivating students to assimilate, build on, and evaluate "chunks" of prior, stored information (Miller and Nentl 2002).

Another effective way to break through this learning barrier and advance analytical thinking is to teach students how to do quality secondary research, which is becoming increasingly important in professional life (Fallows 2005). Integrating serious secondary research methods into the course curriculum can teach students how to analyze rather than simply replicate information, how to combine that information with other information to create a new understanding, and how to evaluate that new understanding for its veracity and authenticity.

SECONDARY RESEARCH

The sheer volume of secondary research available to students today is vast when the massive amount of information found on the Internet is combined with the extensive resources that reside in physical and electronic libraries. Yet, studies have consistently shown that when asked to investigate an issue or an organization, students rely almost exclusively on an organization's Website or search engines like Google and Yahoo (Van Soyoc and Cason 2006; Rainie 2005; Jones 2002). Moreover, this is often where the investigatory process stops (Fallows). Students can recognize concepts and even demonstrate applications of concepts of data using such limited sources, but almost certainly this capture of information is insufficient to compare, consolidate, validate, verify, and evaluate. Furthermore, students are at a loss when asked to critique, defend, or integrate their various sources. While this "grab it and go" style of research is often deemed acceptable by students and instructors alike, the reliance on this shallow research activity hampers students' ability to analyze, synthesize, and evaluate the quality of the information they cite. Critical thinking is inhibited, context is often lost, and reliability and validation of sources are tenuous.

Therefore, how does one teach students how to gather, analyze, and validate secondary research? First, students must learn that their school's library has a wealth of information that is available to them beyond Google and Yahoo, and typically at no additional direct cost other than that built into the student fees. Students are often surprised to learn that there is an information market and that accessing and using secondary reports and articles have both direct and indirect costs. Then, students must learn how to find and pinpoint relevant information, analyze and consolidate their sources, and how to judge source veracity and authenticity. One excellent approach for teaching these skills, and one that serves as a catalyst for breaking through the learning barrier and compelling higher-order thinking, is that of Communications Professor, James Herrick, and his discourse on building and critiquing arguments.

HERRICK'S FIVE CRITERIA

Herrick (2004) describes five criteria that should be used to evaluate the evidential validity of information supporting a logical argument: accessibility, consistency, relevancy, recency, and adequacy. These criteria can also be used by business students as they seek to validate information gathered from their secondary resources.

Accessibility

Much of the media coverage and the business success of Google, Yahoo, and other search engines have raised our expectations about information accessibility. The unasked question, however, is accessibility to what information? Many Websites represent an organization's promotions or opinion threads masquerading as valid evidence and facts. Because of the seduction of the convenience and abundance of this type of information, it often doesn't occur to students and sometimes even instructors to ask questions about institutional and authorial objectives. Moreover, this so-called evidence often forms the sum and substance of an entire student paper or project. When students extract data from an organization's Website, it has been our experience that they often are confused and frustrated about who is ultimately responsible for the content they are citing, and how to properly cite that content.

Consistency

For evidence to be valid, it must be consistent, both internally and externally. To be internally consistent, evidence must not contradict itself; to be externally consistent, there needs to be a consensus around its validity from outside sources. Students often find contradicting facts from different sources, and one indicator of whether a student is critically engaged is when the student questions which one of the competing facts is the correct one. An interesting approach to the problem of establishing external consistency is the idea of triangulation (Brown and Duguid 2000), finding at least three different and unrelated entities that confirm the facts or analysis. Requiring students to establish the validity of the evidence they gather is more work for both the student and the instructor, but it is important work. This substantiation process enables students to engage in breaking apart arguments and constructing and rebuilding new conceptual frameworks, the very definition of Bloom's stages of analysis and synthesis.

Relevancy

Relevancy questions whether the evidence has any bearing on the argument's claim. While this seems to be intuitive, it is often surprising to us that students frequently cite information that is unrelated to their topical area. Examples of problems with business students include using a cost/benefit analysis of a training program in a very labor-intensive industry to argue for a training program in a less labor-intensive industry. Another is using a current newspaper article from one state to argue that real estate values are on the rise in another state. Questioning students about the relevance of their citations and source selections forces students to defend their choices and thus evaluate their own research.

Recency

Like relevancy, the dimension of time has a compelling effect on information quality and use. Knowing the date of document creation is helpful in judging the current usefulness of an article. For example, articles on innovation written in the 1990s obviously have little value and importance compared to articles published in the last six months unless the student is conducting historical research. A "grab it and go" mentality may overlook or marginalize publication dates. However, chronology can significantly affect the context and meaning of those sources dealing with technological advances as well as in areas such as accounting regulations, tax law, supply chain management logistics, marketing, etc.

Adequacy

This criterion asks if the amount of evidence is sufficient to support the claim for which it is used. Adequacy determines if enough research has been gathered to support the argument. "Grab it and go research" activity, of course, would rarely meet this criterion for any substantive topic. Often a student's bibliography can serve as an indicator of adequacy and thus deserves close attention. If the bibliography is comprised of a particular organization's Website, blogs, and Wikipedia, there is not only questionable authenticity, but it is also apparent that the research activity has been superficial and the information gathering inadequate.

Clearly, none of Herrick's criteria can be effective in isolation. That is, research can be relevant but not recent and accessible but not consistent. Thus, an instructor should require good quality information that satisfies all five criteria. The best way to assure this level of quality is for students (and instructors) to first learn how to use their library, and, in particular, their online library. Many faculty and students are surprised by the convenience, the quality, and the volume of proprietary, vetted, third-party information available for no direct cost to the students. For example, if a student wants to know how to analyze an industry, its trends, its financials, and key ratios and statistics, a library subscription database such as S&P NetAdvantage readily supplies that information. Or, if a student is required to understand a company's history and watershed events over the last decades in addition to its financials, a database such as the InfoTrac Business and Company Resource Center can provide detailed information that is not readily available or as well-organized through popular search engines. The ValueLine database provides investment analysis of over 1,700 companies, including stock price data and performance, business description, and detailed operating information that is helpful in portfolio management. Many online libraries also carry numerous article databases such as Lexis Nexis and ProQuest that allow users to tap into the world's publications. These and many other important databases contained in online libraries allow for seamless triangulation that facilitates the gathering of secondary sources and satisfy Herrick's criteria for evidential validation.

EXAMPLE OF AN ASSIGNMENT REQUIRING SECONDARY RESEARCH

The following is an actual assignment that has been effective in using secondary research methods as a tool to advance students to more complex stages of learning. The assignment is required for a course, Practical Research Methods for Managers, which is a two-credit gateway course for incoming MBA students at Metropolitan State University.

Mgmt 600 Assignment 1

This assignment represents the first component of your final research proposal and requires you to use secondary data sources to learn about the organization and the marketplace. You must first think of an organization that is of interest to you and one that is facing some type of researchable issue. For example, *XYZ Computers* has lost significant revenue over the last two years and management wants to know why. Management suspects that customers are no longer satisfied with their product offerings since the company has been plagued by customer service issues. They also suspect there are industry changes going on that affect their business.

You should include a background discussion of the organization, including a brief history, the market it serves, plus some important recent/relevant events or accomplishments. You should also discuss the organization's leadership, its mission, its resources, its size, etc. Then you should provide an analysis of important characteristics of the market or industry, the firm, and its competition. When discussing the industry or market, you should describe the product or services (retail gasoline, gaming, printing services, etc.), the number of firms in the industry, how easy or difficult it might be for new firms to enter the industry, where the firms are located, and how firms compete with each other. Please provide a thorough analysis of the organization's main competitors in the sector, its resources relative to competitors, and how it is differentiated from other firms.

Gathering this information from a variety of reliable resources, you will then be able to identify the organization's primary and most relevant strengths, weaknesses, opportunities, and threats, the so-called SWOT analysis. For example, referring to our example of *XYZ Computers*, some of the points in a SWOT analysis may be high expertise on its board of directors (strength), managerial marketplace myopia (weakness), nano technology advancements in the marketplace (an opportunity for XYZ since one of its board members is a leading nano scientist), major competitors who are quick to respond to technology advancements in the marketplace (threat).

In order to demonstrate a sufficient exploration of your topic, you must cite at least six different sources from three proprietary library databases. Please use APA format. You are not allowed to use Wikipedia or blogs. Information gathered from an organization's Website will count for only one of the six sources. Furthermore, in order to earn full credit, your sources should be relevant, timely, and logically consistent. If you find two views that significantly disagree with each other, please find other verifiable sources that support one of the views. These additional sources should be independent from either of the conflicting views.

You will be graded on your accurate application of secondary research and your ability to analyze your information for its veracity and significance for your topic. You will also be judged on your ability to synthesize the information into a logical and comprehensive picture of your organization's current situation.

A comprehensive situation analysis should reveal a variety of issues that are potential areas for primary research inquiry. Therefore, the accurate evaluation of all your information is expected to lead to a logical, researchable question that will form the foundation of your final proposal.

CONCLUSION

As Fornaciari and Loffredo Roca (1999, 735) stated: "Internet research needs to become, in Langer's terms, a 'mindful endeavor.' More than how to use search engines, how to narrow searches, and how to locate masses of information, we need to teach our students about "mindfulness."

Bloom's Taxonomy is the ideal framework for teaching "mindfulness" using secondary research methods. Our experience as co-instructors of the Mgmt 600 gateway course using this framework is that students move beyond Google and learn to refine their secondary research skills. They gain a greater appreciation for valid and reliable information and demonstrate a fresh interest in the quality resources that are readily available through the online library. Moreover, they become less enchanted with ubiquitous Internet searches and more reliant on and fascinated with proprietary data. Students begin to recognize the strengths and weaknesses of their own sources, as well as to evaluate those of others. They better understand the value and purpose of quality information and its integration into business content. Most importantly, they begin to think more critically and move beyond the learning barrier. We are encouraged that instructors who have our students in succeeding courses frequently remark that the Mgmt 600 students exhibit substantial research and analysis skills and sophistication of thought in their written work. Our successes have, in fact, led to recent faculty discussions about integrating these teaching approaches across the business curricula.

In spite of, or perhaps because of, the volume of information that students have at their fingertips, many are cavalier about the research and analysis processes. However, when students are challenged to move to the higher planes of thinking as described in Bloom's Taxonomy, analytical sophistication grows quickly. As business students transcend the learning barrier, they are well on their way to becoming strategic decision makers and mindful thinkers.

REFERENCES

Anderson, L. W. and L. A. Sosniak. 1994. *Bloom's Taxonomy: A forty-year retrospective*. Chicago: NSSE. Distributed by the University of Chicago Press.

Athanassiou, N., J. M. McNett, and C. Harvey. 2003. Critical thinking in the management classroom: Bloom's Taxonomy as a learning tool. *Journal of Management Education* 27: 533–555.

Barnet, S. and H. Bedau. 2005. *Critical thinking, reading and writing: A brief guide to argument*. 5th ed. Boston: Bedford/St. Martin's.

Bissell, A. N. and P. P. Lemons. 2006. A new method for assessing critical thinking in the classroom. *Bioscience* 56: 66–72.

Blazelton, J. K. 2000. Students may blossom using Bloom's Taxonomy in the accounting curriculum. *In:* B. N. Schwartz and E. Ketz (eds.) *Advances in accounting education: Teaching and curriculum innovations*. Stamford, CT: JAI Press.

Bloom, B. 1956. *Taxonomy of educational objectives: The classification of educational goals*. New York: McKay.

Braun, N. 2004. Critical thinking in the business curriculum. *Journal of Education for Business* 79: 232–236.

Bray, P. and J. Rogers. 1995. *Ideas in Bloom: Taxonomy-based activities for U.S. studies*. Portland, ME: J. Weston Walch.

Brown, J. S. and P. Duguid. 2000. *Social life of information*. Boston, MA: Harvard Business School Press.

Buxkemper, A. and D. J. Hartfiel. 2003. Understanding. *International Journal of Mathematical Education in Science and Technology* 34: 801–812.

Castleberry, S. B. 2001. Using secondary data in marketing research: A project that melds Web and Off-Web sources. *Journal of Marketing Education* 23: 195–203.

Davidson, R. and B. Baldwin. 2005. Cognitive skills objectives in intermediate accounting textbooks: Evidence from end-of-chapter material. *Journal of Accounting Education* 23: 79–95.

Fallows, D. 2005. Search engine users: Internet searchers are confident, satisfied, and trustingflbut they are also unaware and naïve. *Pew Internet & American Life Project.* http://www.pewinternet.org/pdfs/PIP_Searchengine_users.pdf

Fornaciari, C. J. and M. F. Loffredo Roca. 1999. The age of clutter: Conducting effective research using the Internet. *Journal of Management Education* 23: 732–742.

Granello, D. H. 2001. Promoting cognitive complexity in graduate written work: Using Bloom's Taxonomy as a pedagogical tool to improve literature reviews. *Counselor Education & Supervision* 40: 292–307.

Herrick, J. 2004. *Argumentation: Understanding and shaping arguments.* Updated edition. State College, PA: Strata Publishing.

Krathwohl, D. R. 2002. A revision of Bloom's Taxonomy: An overview. *Theory Into Practice* 41: 212–218.

Jones, S. 2002. The Internet goes to college. *Pew Internet & American Life Project.* http://www.pewinternet.org/pdfs/PIP_SearchData_1105.pdf.

Miller, C. and N. Nentl. 2002, October 24. Learning by playing: Teaching business learners with computer simulations. *Conference Proceedings Emerging Issues in Business and Technology,* Myrtle Beach, NC.

Moore, G. S., K. Winograd, and D. Lange. 2001. You can teach online: Building a relative learning environment. Boston: McGraw-Hill.

Rainie, L. 2005. Data memo: Search engine use November 2005. *Pew Internet & American Life Project.* http://www.pewinternet.org/pdfs/PIP_SearchData_1105.pdf.

Roy, A. and B. Macchiette. 2005. Debating the issues: A tool for augmenting critical thinking skills of marketing students. *Journal of Marketing Education* 27: 264–276.

Simkin, M. G. and W. L. Kuechler. 2005. Multiple-choice tests and student understanding: What is the connection? *Decision Sciences Journal of Innovative Education* 3: 73–97.

University of Minnesota Curtis L. Carlson School of Management. 2007. MKTG 3001 Principles of Marketing. University of Minnesota University Catalog. http://onestop2.umn.edu/courses/courses.jsp?designator=MKTG&submit=Show+the+courses&institution=UMNTC.

Van Scoyoc, A. M. and C. Cason. 2006. The electronic academic library: Undergraduate research behavior in a library without books. *Portal: Libraries and the Academy* 6: 47–58.

Zohar, A. and Y. Dori. 2003. Higher-order thinking skills and low-achieving students: Are they mutually exclusive? *Journal of Learning Sciences* 12: 145–181.

You Can Lead Students to Sources, but Can You Make Them Think?

Pamela Hayes-Bohanan
Elizabeth Spievak

INTRODUCTION

What happens when a librarian and a psychology professor create a course designed to incorporate what psychology knows about thinking into an information literacy class? Not much, at least at first. The authors (instructors) ensured that the course, entitled the "Psychology of Academic Success," would include appropriate content and require the use of information literacy skills. However, teaching the students to do the kind of thoughtful reflection required to apply psychological research and theory to their own lives and scholarship turned out to be much more difficult. In this article, the authors demonstrate how students' difficulties in critical thinking were identified, illustrate how targeted intervention methods and materials were developed, and present evidence of student improvement in both critical thinking and information literacy. These findings are presented so that the course and associated documents can be used as a prototype for classroom faculty and librarians in their efforts to infuse information literacy into the college curriculum.

In teaching this course, we did everything right and still got a great deal of it wrong. We regularly incorporate active and cooperative education techniques that are engaging, outcome based, and learner centered. However, particularly at the college level, many of the critical thinking tasks we expect students to perform are difficult to describe explicitly. As teachers, we "know" what needs to be done; however, we do not have explicit access to task performance details. By crafting assignments that require critical thinking, we assume that students will incidentally learn to use those skills to negotiate the library, perform source analysis, or synthesize materials without plagiarism. Even when educators discuss what it is we expect students to learn from an assignment, that discussion is usually focused on content, while the critical thinking aspects are left unspoken and remain implicit. Implicit learning, "learning complex information without complete verbalizable knowledge of what is learned" (Seger 1994, 163) may be sufficient, but why take the chance? More explicit teaching may help students understand assignments in a way that will afford access to the knowledge and principles underlying task performance. This is particularly important when teaching information literacy and library skills, which we expect students to take with them into other classes as well as other aspects of their life and work.

NEGOTIATING THE LABYRINTH

To be information literate, one must be able to gather and use information regardless of setting or format. In order to be truly information literate, people have to have "learned how to learn" (American Library Association 1989). Without the proper skills, users can become more overwhelmed and lost in the labyrinth of information available, today more than ever before. The task can be thought of as a maze. In the unlikely event that the typical college student user has a clear understanding of his or her initial state (standing outside the maze) and the goal state (the center of the maze), there is still an infinite number of intermediate states, and each operation generates numerous alternative states, many of which might be viable paths through the maze.

To more clearly define the critical thinking behind negotiating the library, librarians in the CONNECT consortium, a six-campus consortium of which Bridgewater State College (BSC) is a part, developed a rubric (see Appendix 1) that defines skills associated with each of several levels. As a novice, users are not equipped with the knowledge or resource management skills to do purposeful planning for information gathering, reflect on the validity of information or their methods of attaining it, or understand the importance of documentation. As they become practitioners, users plan their investigation and begin to discriminate among sources and search techniques. Practitioners demonstrate some understanding of plagiarism and recognize that opinion and fact are not equivalent, although they may not always be able to put their understanding into practice. At the expert level, users identify research as a learning process, attempt to develop new perspectives that contribute to the knowledge base, and are respectful of intellectual property. Sources are critically analyzed and synthesized, bias is identified, and library resources are used methodologically.

The progression from novice to expert in the rubric reflects advances in critical thinking, from unreflective thinking (novice) to challenged thinking (practitioner) to advanced or master thinking (expert), as explained by Elder and Paul (1996). In addition to demonstrating purposeful research planning and exploration, an expert is practicing Paul's (1995) elements of reasoning by assessing point of view; performing assumption, problem, evidence, and conceptual analyses; and being mindful of inferences and implications. In terms of information literacy, this involves first knowing when information is needed, being able to gather and evaluate it, and ultimately using it ethically and legally (American Library Association). It is important for scholars to understand that the ethical use of information goes beyond simply citing other's work appropriately. Ethical use requires the acknowledgement of bias when applicable and the ability to know when to broaden one's own ideas and change viewpoints, rather than manipulating information only to advance an agenda. Realistically, we did not expect our first-year students to attain the final (expert) stage, but did hope that we would see some firm evidence of "challenged" thinking (the practitioner level) in the majority of our students by the end of the semester.

LIKE RIDING A BIKE

To understand this case study, it is useful to review what psychologists understand about learning. In psychology, we often use the terms "procedural knowledge," or experience-based organization processes and task performance, and "declarative knowledge," or knowledge explicitly stored and retrieved upon demand (Cohen 1984). These terms describe the learning and memory systems that allow us to "know" something without "remembering" it, or to perform a task, such as riding a bike, without conscious awareness of our thought processes. Countless studies have supported the existence of separate systems. Evidence suggests that a great deal of information that cannot be accessed on direct tests of explicit memory is available on indirect tests of implicit memory (Gardiner and Java 1993; Schacter 1987). The notion that memory and task performance always depend on conscious awareness has been convincingly refuted. However, there is also much evidence that conscious processes are quite valuable in the type of problem solving students are expected to perform in developing information literacy. Effective use of the library skills used in the process of finding sources for a freshman English composition paper on James Baldwin's *Go Tell It on the Mountain*, or for a sophomore history paper on Longstreet's military strategy during the Civil War, requires analogical thinking. Such transfer of coherent and integrated knowledge from one domain to another is often the basis of what we commonly call "insight" and what gestalt psychologists call productive processing. Reproductive processes involve the re-use of previous experience (which may be both useful and undermining), while productive processes involve information restructuring (Ohlsson 1984, 1992), often through the use of analogies that facilitate a new understanding or perspective of the "problem space" or the abstract structure of a problem (Newell and Simon 1972). While great thinkers like Rutherford, Einstein, and Kekulé have reportedly developed solutions to unfamiliar problems based on deep analogical thinking (Koestler 1964), the usefulness of analogies often goes unnoticed.

A long history of research suggests that the impasses reached when the thinker has the required knowledge, but for some reason cannot use it, are often overcome by flexing or combining information, recategorizing or deleting (distracting) information, and, perhaps most important, through hints. Even when people have successfully used analogies, they often have to be given a hint to use it to solve a new problem. In a classic study by Gick and Holyoak (1980), solution rates were improved by the memorization of an analogous story; however, without a specific hint to use the analogy, participants did not tend to notice it, and over 20% were never able to use the analog. Other research has revealed that unless there are superficial and semantic similarities between the base and target domain, there is little hope of analog use (Keane 1987; Holyoak and Koh 1987). In fact, people tend to retrieve analogs that share superficial features, more readily than deep analogs that may be more useful (Gentner, Rattermann, and Forbus 1992), unless they are made distinct from competing analogs stored in memory (Wharton et al. 1994). This is not to suggest that people cannot become better problem solvers. If a solution depends on applying one rule, and then another repeatedly, then the regular pattern is generally noticed, and a verbally encoded rule or declarative knowledge results. According to Anderson (1993), "proceduralization," the process that transforms declarative knowledge into production knowledge, and "composition," the development of a parsimonious set of production rules, explain the move from novice to expert. The shift involves a replacement of weaker methods of problem solving (such as means-end analysis) with domain-specific rules that help problem solvers work forward. Experts spend more time analyzing a problem and less time solving it. They use their analysis to apply selected principles that help them generate the unknowns needed to solve the problem. This "working forward" is efficient and powerful. Novices tend to focus on the surface features of a problem, particularly key words or goals, then search for a principle that will help them generate an unknown (and usually no more than one unknown), and, hence, work backward to the givens in the problem (Larkin, McDermott, Simon, and Simon 1980).

The above research suggests why problems, particularly puzzles requiring information literacy, are sometimes difficult to solve. When people (in this case college students) have to search through a large, ill-defined or unfamiliar problem space (a library and cyber world filled with information of various levels of usefulness and no clear method of navigation), identifying what the problem is about or how it might be solved is hampered by both resource and knowledge limitations. Resource limitations involve the ability to manage and make use of available information, and knowledge limitations may be the lack of facts or rules relevant to the domain. There is an interaction effect in that increased knowledge improves resource use. Undergraduate students rarely have strong content knowledge, so conscious, declarative understanding of conventions relevant to information literacy is vital. In knowledge-poor situations, the only useful strategies available, such as working backward, attacking sub-problems, or applying a superficially matched analogy, are weak (Carbonell 1986). Students will likely be unable to see the entire landscape, focusing instead on readily identifiable key words or superficial aspects of the problem, and thus produce ill-conceived notions of the problem space they should be negotiating. They will, by default, address the problem in a limited fashion and fail to integrate and synthesize resources, thus producing a crude, incomplete, biased or completely off-target solution.

More knowledgeable problem solvers can use their domain-specific production rules to fill in the blanks, effectively narrowing and clarifying the problem space as well as recognizing the most valuable information and useful analogies (Carbonell). Information literate students are more likely to see the entire maze, more accurately identify their initial and goal states, and manage their resources more effectively, thus making effective use of content area knowledge and analogies to produce an on-target insightful solution.

This brief review of what the psychologist member of our team knew about thinking and problem solving may seem like a bit of a digression, but what is relevant is how much of what she did know was not put to effective use until midway into this course. Teaching was, after all, like riding a bike. We assumed that we "knew" what had to be done. The problem was that neither of us had taught a class that was not content driven, so the problem space was ill defined, analogous information was superficially generated, and a mean end strategy was adopted in planning the course. We became novice teachers, focusing on our declarative knowledge of class material and skills, creating assignments that reflected reproductive processes regarding explicitly defined subject matter. We unwittingly relegated the critical thinking skills to incidental learning. It took productive problem solving and insight provided by a hint (the critical thinking articles referred to later in this article) to realize that we should be teaching the class quite differently.

BACKGROUND

Bridgewater State College is a four-year liberal arts college with approximately 10,000 (FTE) students in southeastern Massachusetts. Originally established as a State Normal School in 1840, the college now houses a School of Education and Allied Studies, a School of Arts and Sciences, and a School of Business, with over thirty major areas of study, as well as graduate programs in education, psychology, english, management, social work, and public administration. The Clement C. Maxwell Library has a staff of eight full-time librarians, four part-time librarians, and fifteen support staff. The library houses over 300,000 volumes and subscribes to over seventy online databases.

The impetus for creating the course, "The Psychology of Academic Success," was two-fold. At the time that BSC was about to launch its new core curriculum to replace the old general education requirements (GERs), it was also investing in developing an undergraduate research initiative. Under the GER, all students were required to take a course called Library Media Studies 102, a one-credit course in library skills. The course was eliminated under the outcomes-based core curriculum, and no specific course replaced it, although information literacy was identified as one of the outcomes in the core curriculum document. Recognizing that integrated assignments were the best way to teach information literacy (Lindstrom and Shonrock 2006), the BSC librarians began to look for ways to do more collaborative work with classroom faculty.

The core curriculum includes a requirement that all students complete a first-year seminar. These new writing-intensive courses, on topics of the instructors' choosing, are based less on content than on student introduction to academic thought and discourse. They also are designed to prepare students for their college careers, while focusing on achieving some of the outcomes in the core curriculum. Recognizing that a first-year seminar would be an excellent venue to begin teaching information literacy skills and realizing that students need library skills to conduct research effectively, the authors designed the course to address both the information literacy outcome and introduction of students to the undergraduate research program at the college.

DEVELOPMENT OF THE SYLLABUS

Since the course was team taught by a psychologist and a librarian, the syllabus was designed to address both information literacy skills and topics in psychology. Information literacy skills were developed using the aforementioned rubric created by the CONNECT consortium. During the spring of 2006, librarians from each of the campuses had been charged with creating a rubric to identify information literacy outcomes for first-year students across campuses, in part to make transfer between institutions easier. The rubric was approved by the chief academic officers of the institutions in the summer of that year, and was in place in time to be used to identify areas of concentration in our course.

In addition to the information literacy agenda, the syllabus was designed to introduce psychology topics related to academic achievement. Students were to progress through a series of assignments on psychology topics by applying their information literacy skills and disseminate information to the class in a series of individual and group presentations. All topics were to be explored as they pertained to academic achievement, thus providing presenters and peers with many opportunities to critically analyze and apply research and theory. This was designed to serve several purposes: to encourage metacognition (thinking about thinking); to serve as a basis for writing assignments, presentations, and discussions that would be sufficiently personal, relevant, and practical to engage students in the application of theory to their own lives and work; to introduce students to the nature of scientific inquiry in the social sciences; and to provide a theme that would serve as a foundation for purposeful and reasoned habits of thinking regarding the evaluation of information.

Broad topical areas included developmental psychology (the influence of family, peers, early experiences, personality), biological psychology (neurological and genetic influences), cognitive psychology (memory, problem solving, metacognition), clinical psychology (behavior modification, coping strategies), and social psychology (including attributions, conformity, stereotype threat). We did not choose specific materials, opting instead to require students to find academic sources that were interesting to them and relevant to their daily lives as college students. We did try to guide them toward materials we thought would be more understandable and straightforward, explaining the logic and reasoning of our recommendations, but ultimately leaving the choice up to them.

The instructors worked quite hard to prepare a course that would require the execution of library assignments and a series of writing and speaking assignments that would encourage thoughtful reflection and analysis of topics known to be relevant to student achievement. In essence, critical thinking was "built-in" to the syllabus as an implicit learning goal. Students were expected to progress through information literacy and source analysis assignments with increased sophistication, eventually learning to apply and synthesize psychological research. However, it did not happen quite that way. While we gave specific assignment instructions, including detailed step-by-step procedures, we found that students were so preoccupied with the superficial aspects of their work that they often missed the central purpose of the assignment, which was not explicitly described.

Initial Assignments

During the first week of class, we took the students to the library, where a classroom is reserved for library instruction, and gave the students a lesson on finding peer-reviewed articles in psychology journals. We explained the difference between a peer-reviewed article and what they would find in the popular press, explaining that it was based on original research. The psychologist related her own story about the process of having an article peer reviewed. Students were surprised to learn that *they* would be presenting the psychology topics the instructors had identified, but they quickly learned to find a peer-reviewed article for dissemination to the class. What we failed to appreciate was the need to discuss more purposefully the assignment's goals *beyond* dissemination, perhaps because we did not have an explicit understanding of this ourselves. While we did describe the process of peer review and its importance relative to psychological research, we did not discuss how the information literacy skills (use, understanding, and value of an online subscription database) we were teaching were integral to task performance. Although the course was to be skill driven, we defaulted (likely by habit and by working backwards) to having them practice critical thinking in the content area (psychology), relegating the critical thinking skills required for information literacy to incidental learning.

After an introduction to our first content area, developmental psychology, the instructors asked students to "brainstorm" some topics with us. With a list of possible topics, we asked students to identify which were most interesting to them, in order to begin our search strategy using those topics. We walked the students through the steps of finding the databases from the library Web-page, and limiting their choices to peer-reviewed journals. Students were shown how to track down useful search terms related to the developmental psychology topics of interest and to further refine their search by adding "college" to the search string and changing the term "academic success" to "academic achievement" as was the preferred term in that database. We purposefully did not "try out" the search terms in advance in order to go through the process of refining the search naturally with the students. This traditional active learning experience appeared to be a successful strategy; the students were engaged, asking targeted questions and using the database themselves in short order.

Students identified two articles concerning developmental psychology factors related to academic achievement that were of particular interest to them. They assigned one to each of us so that we could model the presentation process during the following class meeting time. The librarian included in her presentation a discussion of her own critical thinking process. She shared how she explored the information in a reasoned and goal-directed way. She helped students see how she kept the purpose of the activity in mind, determined the general concept of the article, and identified the evidence on which conclusions were drawn. She also demonstrated how important it is to consider the point of view of the authors and the implications of the assumptions they made. All of these are steps in Paul's critical thinking guide, but were not discussed as such.

Students were given a "pre-write" journal assignment each day in order to generate thoughts relevant to the daily class topic. On the first day, it was a letter to their parents (and other family members) concerning their classes, friends, and scholarly and extra-curricular activities thus far. While listening to the presentations, students took notes. After class discussion, which included questions and applications, students completed a "post-write" entry in which they were expected to show how they would integrate what they learned from the presentation into their own learning. On that first day, they were to write about the ways in which the family upbringing issues presented and discussed might help them, or make it more difficult for them to be a high achiever. Each post-write included a reminder that their work should demonstrate to their audience (their professors) that they had been attentive, could apply the day's material, and could use psychological evidence to back up thoughts and comments. The writing was intended as a path to deep analogy, as elaborate and deep memory encodings are triggered when information is self-relevant (Rogers, Kuiper, and Kirker 1977) and the self is the preferred reference for organizing information (Klein and Kihlstrom 1994). In addition, writing about thoughts, emotions, and behavior plans (such as changes in study habits) has been linked to a variety of favorable academic outcomes (Brooke and Ruthven 1984; Goldman 1978; King 2001; Rooke and Malouff 2006). Unfortunately, we did not discuss the multipurpose nature of the writing assignments with students, and there was little evidence that the concepts and connections were acquired incidentally. They satisfied the surface requirements of the three-part (pre-write, class notes, and post-write) journal entries throughout the first half of the course, but only the occasional paper was insightful.

Most of the writing was quite superficial and revealed little or no evidence of self-reflection.

Student Criteria

Students were presenting psychological research related to academic achievement by the third week of the course, and we saw mixed results in their first attempts. Most did find peer-reviewed articles (although some did not, and, in fact, in at least one case, the use of "Google" was all too evident). We noticed, however, that while most students did manage to technically meet our requirements, their presentations lacked anything resembling source analysis, and the presenters were largely unable to answer questions about the articles. We realized that students had their own criteria in addition to those which we designated: articles needed to be short (five pages maximum) and available online. On numerous occasions, students engaged instructors in a meticulous and vigorous search for an appropriate source, only to reject all articles for length. Even when students were physically in the library and could have easily previewed or acquired hard copies, they refused to consider a print journal. The goal, as they saw it, was to find an article. Since one was likely the same as another (in their estimation), why read a longer one and why spend the time finding a hard copy when they could simply "click" on another and print it off at a printer within arm's reach? The instructors, of course, felt frustrated. We reasoned that if the students would just go and find the articles we helped them to select, they would learn the value therein.

What the instructors realized too late was that we had, in fact, modeled the novice form of problem solving. We taught them how to work backwards to solve for one unknown: a peer-reviewed article. We assumed students had implicit knowledge of the problem space and would recognize that this was but one leg of the trip through the maze. But by not explicitly discussing how and why the reproductive strategy we were teaching them would become the template for solving many types of problems, we succeeded only in creating declarative knowledge for the mechanics of negotiating the subscription database. They did not identify the problem space and were not transforming the article-finding algorithm into what Anderson called production knowledge. During their own searches, the deep analogy was never identified, and the students focused instead on surface features of two sub-problems: finding an article and producing a PowerPoint presentation that contained keywords or phrases related to the day's topic. We had modeled conceptual and inference analyses in our sample presentations, but we did not explicitly discuss their importance or relevance to article or presentation content selection. Perhaps if we had engaged students further in an explicit discussion of why an article might be appropriate, why we wanted them to find it, what we thought they would learn, and why that learning mattered, we may have had a better understanding of their critical thinking process as well as our own.

Student search criteria resulted almost exclusively in brief reports. By design, brief reports are usually of highly specialized interest, of limited importance, often single studies that cannot be accepted as regular articles, replications or null result studies of previously published works, and, in some journals, include articles that are speculative, controversial, or intended as commentary. Brief reports lack the background information, clarifying details, examples, and applications important for novice readers. Thus, student standards for choosing articles left them unable to identify the author's larger purpose or understand the evidence or assumptions on which conclusions were drawn. In other words, their ability to practice critical thinking was impaired, which, in turn, prevented them from effectively disseminating information in a way that would allow their peers to practice the critical thinking skills we were requiring of listeners. The application of theory was to be part of the presentations, discussions, and regular writing assignments, but students quickly grew frustrated and all but gave up. Presentations often consisted of reading directly from text-dense PowerPoint slides of unanalyzed information with no synthesis or evaluation of content. When asked to clarify information or define terms or acronyms used in their reports, the response was usually that "the article didn't say" or that the information was not included. In many cases, this may have been true. Since the students had selected brief reports, rather than full-length articles, much of the background information was indeed missing. Their peers also gave up trying to take effective notes, engaging in meaningful discussions or writing personal applications in their "post-write" assignments. The students and instructors were discouraged. Presentations and written work were repetitive, tedious, and ineffectual. As Tufte points out "PowerPoint is *presenter-oriented, not content-oriented, not audience-oriented*" (2006, 158). Students believed they had created a presentation, but as Tufte further states, "PowerPoint's convenience for some presenters is costly to the content and the audience" (158).

While students at the midpoint of the semester seemed to have the "mechanics" of finding articles in the library databases, it became evident that we needed to revise the course in order to focus on teaching critical thinking. It was not enough to model it, make conceptual references to it, ask them to think about it, and remind them to do it. The instructors realized that we actually had to consciously teach critical thinking skills and make them consciously aware that they were learning them. We took the opportunity during spring break to revise the course, considering how we could teach critical thinking in psychology and information literacy skills.

COURSE REVISION—LEARNING ABOUT CRITICAL THINKING

Instructors spent the spring break researching critical thinking skills and teaching methods. In order to formally introduce the topic and teach students how to read journal articles, students were provided with research articles *about* critical thinking at the college level. Each student read either two short (Williams et al. 2003; Foos 1989) or one longer article (Reed and Kromrey 2001), and was given 20 questions to answer from their readings (see Appendix 2). They were instructed to annotate the article(s) based on the questions provided. In this way, the instructors were able to guide students through the articles in a way that would ensure some degree of success and at least a minimum level of understanding. During the following class periods, students worked in groups to complete a series of assignments that required them to review the reading about critical thinking and apply the skills they had read about. First, they met with others who had read the same material and completed a worksheet (see Appendix 3) designed to encourage conversation about the background that supported the hypotheses, the experimental manipulation (or correlation variables), and results. They were to contemplate author assumptions, biases, discrepancies, and their implications, as well as summarize the meaning of the research and consider their own interpretations. Next, students worked with a peer who had not read the same material and were guided through a series of questions to synthesize all of the articles and draw conclusions (see Appendix 4). They were provided with sentence fragments to complete, an exercise that was to help them compare and contrast the authors' assumptions, methods, and inferences, as well as consider alternative hypotheses and ideas for further study.

Aside from a review and practice of critical thinking, these exercises (some of which were developed from Bean's *Engaging Ideas*, 2001) were created to require active reading and the evaluation and integration of source materials. These skills would be practiced again in preparation for the next assignments: a group presentation combining several sources and later revised for a group poster presentation on the same topic.

Learning to Evaluate

As students had already learned to effectively navigate the library databases, the instructors prepared a list of library holdings (without call numbers) specific to social psychology topics (the final unit of content instruction) implicated in college achievement in three categories: books, reference resources, and journal articles. Topics included alcohol, aggression, risky behaviors, gender differences, and stereotypes. Students were assigned to groups by the instructors, but were randomly assigned to a topic by lottery drawing. They were advised that their group would be expected to choose and synthesize material from at least two journal articles, one book, and one reference work from the provided list. By removing the focus on the sub-goal of finding peer-reviewed articles and explicitly describing the end goal, the instructors essentially worked to more clearly define the problem space. It was expected that, while they would be revising their group presentation for the campus poster session, their knowledge of the problem space and the content would increase, thus allowing them to manage their resources more effectively. However, the aspects of critical thinking involved in the expected progression from novice to expert were not explicitly discussed. The instructors again focused on means-end problem solving in their instruction on using the library catalog (few students had used it before) to do a title search in order to find call numbers, as well as during another lesson in going to the stacks to find the print journals, which are arranged alphabetically by title. At this point, we did explicitly state what specific library skills we wanted them to learn (finding and using the online catalog, see CONNECT rubric under "use of online catalog").

When students made their group presentations, there was some evidence of critical thinking in that they did present a broad overview first, briefly identifying the purpose of their presentation, providing an introduction to the general concepts involved in the topic and describing why it was of interest. However, only one group followed the guidance implicitly provided by the previous critical thinking assignments (and explicitly described on the group presentation checklist) to perform evidence analysis, clarify assumptions, integrate the information from their sources, and draw conclusions at the end. In most cases, it was obvious that each student in the group was presenting just one of the resources used, without drawing any information from the other sources or making conclusions based on all of the information. Still, the presentations were more engaging to their peers, and students seemed to have a better understanding of "their part" of the presentation. This may have been attributable to better quality sources, formal instruction on critical thinking while reading research materials, or discussions of materials in group meetings, and the increased confidence that grows out of planning and negotiation.

As instructed, all groups came prepared with an audience participation exercise or included application questions to encourage discussion, and these tactics worked. Audience members, both peers and instructors, completed a feedback worksheet (see Appendix 5) while listening to the presentations. The peer feedback did indicate an ability to evaluate evidence and critically analyze conclusions, in that they tended to elaborate on questions concerning a need for more information and possible applications. The worksheets were returned to presenting groups for use in refining presentations for the poster sessions at the annual Undergraduate Research Symposium at the end of the semester.

Poster Presentations

Participation in the symposium required students to submit an abstract of their work and demanded a new type of critical thinking: the persuasive and parsimonious communication of "essence." Initially, students completed another worksheet (see Appendix 6), on which they were to answer a series of questions and then complete sentence fragments to help them draft language useful for writing their abstract. They did an excellent job of completing the worksheet, demonstrating that they could integrate their knowledge of the material and communicate their fundamental purpose. However, when asked to write their own abstract, all but one group failed to use any of the language they had so nicely crafted earlier in the exercise. It was not clear to us why students did not effectively use the exercise. It may be that they failed to see the analogous usefulness of the exercise, they were too concerned with creating their own version, did not believe that the sentences reflected what they had done, or perhaps were hesitant to promote themselves and their work as strongly as the exercise recommended. Instructors reviewed the worksheets and helped students combine all sample wording and examples to construct a final draft before they completed the on-line submission form. As the students had no understanding of what a poster presentation entailed, we also helped students to lay out their poster by explicitly directing them to use several analogs:

their earlier group presentations to the class; an example poster from a professional conference; and an instructor provided crude mock-up of how their group's poster might look.

There was evidence in most of the posters that the students had worked to integrate the information from their sources, but they made egregious errors indicating reproductive rather than productive knowledge; all used wording that implied they had accomplished original experimental or correlational research, and all failed to properly synthesize their literature research with one clear, coherent theme. While this was a great disappointment to us, it was a valuable learning experience for the students. Repeatedly, students were forced to explain to session attendees that their posters were, in fact, a bit confusing and lacked some crucial facts.

Although it was not reflected in the language on the posters, students were able to verbally articulate a unified theme and how the literature supported their conclusions. The true indication that the students had learned to synthesize and analyze the information came when they were asked questions about and were forced to clarify their work. They elaborated on their poster materials and were able to clear up misunderstandings. For example, on several occasions students described to attendees how BSC students might respond or behave differently, indicated bias in author perspective, or discussed what they believed to be flawed assumptions or interpretations. For the first time, we heard students answering thoughtfully and demonstrating an understanding of the material in a way that illustrated their critical thinking skills.

PULLING IT TOGETHER—LITERATURE REVIEW

Students were also required to write a literature review on a psychology topic of their choice as an end-of-semester project. They were told to use the opportunity to do an in-depth exploration of a topic that we had discussed earlier in the semester, or to pick something that we had not covered but about which they were curious. We tried a "scaffolding" approach to this assignment and had students start by turning in a topic and an annotated bibliography. They were instructed on how to use the library catalog to find books by subject or keyword (developing further their catalog skills) and given further instruction on using the library databases to find peer-reviewed articles. They learned how to start with a broad topic and narrow it using different features within the databases, building on the simpler instructions they were given earlier in the semester. The annotated bibliography assignment had some very specific instructions (see Appendix 7). Students were to identify five keywords relevant to their topic, identify some authors who appear to be important in the field, identify five peer-reviewed journal articles and one book reference, and write APA citations for them. The annotation was to have commentary on the relevancy of the article, what kind of dependent and independent variables were used in the experiments, and comments on other concerns, flaws, or missing information. Students were told specifically not to use the annotations that came from the database and were given a sample annotation that was clearly written from a personal level. The assignment contained a request for responses that would indicate evidence of critical thinking regarding possible sources, although no reference to that goal was mentioned.

Many students did complete the assignment appropriately, one quite brilliantly. Unfortunately, at least two students used only the annotations provided by the database. While they wrote their own annotations, a few simply cut and pasted the citation information from the database rather than using APA format. One student failed completely to apply previously learned analogies to the new problem, and, instead, defaulted to using a Web search to find her articles, all of which were published only on the Web, and none of which were peer-reviewed. We took the opportunity in the following class to discuss, again, the use of peer-reviewed journal articles and to educate the students about plagiarism, what constitutes it, and its consequences.

After grading this assignment, it occurred to us that breaking the assignment down even further would have been worthwhile. We did not ask students to turn in their five keywords or the identified authors. Furthermore, we had not explained why these were important steps in the process of developing a research topic, or discuss the amount of time it would likely take to do it properly (CONNECT rubric under "understanding of research strategy"). For about half the class members, reproductive processes and a focus on the superficial aspects of the assignment remained the dominant problem-solving strategy. It was not enough to know that they needed information and to identify keywords (lower-order thinking skills). They needed to understand why it was important to do so, how to refine a search strategy, and that not all sources would be as relevant as others (higher-order critical thinking skills).

Students also turned in two drafts of their papers for comments from their peers and one draft to their instructors. The peer-review process appeared to be quite successful. Using worksheets (developed from Bean) to guide them, student reviewers took their work quite seriously (see Appendix 8).

The individual and group work involved the practice of critical thinking skills in evaluating others' papers. For example, they wrote a brief summary of their peer's thesis, noted the best or worst arguments, commented on the completeness of arguments and the author's clarity of reasoning, assessed strengths and weaknesses, noted any summaries or quotes that were unanalyzed by the author, etc. Unfortunately, there was very little evidence that peer reviews were used constructively to accomplish the revisions expected for the draft due to instructors. It is not clear whether they were unable or unwilling to use the thoughtful responses their peers had provided, but they certainly did not transfer the analogy of analyzing others' papers to the process of analyzing their own.

The drafts completed for the instructors were, without exception, quite poor, and comments included suggestions for considerable revisions. If the problem with peer comments was the unwillingness to convert the sometimes abstract nature of peer responses into substantive changes, or the inability to transfer their learning from peer-review to self-review, then instructor comments should have been more easily translated into revisions. Instructor comments were specific and directly targeted to the student, and individual and small group paper workshop meetings were arranged to clarify comments and discuss expectations for the final draft. The "as-is" (draft) paper was graded (although the grade was not recorded) so that students knew the grade they would receive on the paper if no revisions were made. None of the students were happy with that grade, yet most failed again to use the provided feedback. While instructors are (almost) always disappointed by students' efforts to revise work, we were especially disheartened when some students made no changes at all to their work after receiving their instructor's comments. Explicit instructions regarding the use of skills they practiced in evaluating others' work and later, explicit directions as to how and where those skills should be applied, appeared to be of little consequence. It is tempting to blame laziness and procrastination, but we suspect that it was due in no small part to an inability to critically reflect on their own work, despite previously practiced and demonstrated skills in critical analysis.

WHAT WE LEARNED, WHAT THEY LEARNED

Students were required to turn in a portfolio of all of their work throughout the semester with a cover letter explaining what they learned and how the lessons would apply to their future studies at BSC and/or in their work or private lives. What we did not realize, as instructors, was how important this assignment would turn out to be for us, as well as the students. Students were forced to examine explicitly what they learned in the class and how they would be applied. We learned that although they may not yet be experts able to use the deep analogical thinking we expected of them, requiring them to examine how they might do that in the future could be an important component to the critical thinking process. Students were instructed to discuss both their understanding of how the psychology they learned related to their own academic achievement and how they would apply the information literacy skills they learned to further their studies. A template was provided for their cover letters. It included organizational instructions and a series of questions designed to measure learning outcomes in each of the following areas: journaling (pre- and post-writes); presentations; literature review; knowledge about psychology (and applications to self, thinking, and habits); information literacy; and critical thinking. Although the assignment was personal and informal, students took this work seriously, and their comments showed thoughtful reflection and gave the instructors some significant insight into what the students had learned.

Portfolio letters indicated that students were applying what they learned with respect to learning skills and information literacy. Student comments indicated that, overall, they were pleased with their own progress in their ability to do public speaking, in managing stress, developing better study habits, time management, in working in groups, and in using the library. Comments such as "I didn't even know where the BSC library was" and "I was afraid to ask the librarians for help because I felt stupid and ashamed that I could not find a simple book" were indicative of what our students knew coming into the class. This was particularly important for us to know, especially when considering these students had already spent a semester at BSC before they took our class. This, in turn, made it especially gratifying to read statements such as "I have already used the online searching skills I learned in this class for another research paper I am doing for writing 102"; "I will rely less on Google and Wikipedia"; and [I] "believe I . . . could help others." This last statement is particularly important given that so many students rely on peers for developing their information literacy skills (Latham and Gross 2007, 281). Personal statements also indicated that students did seem to understand and appreciate the value of analyzing resources as well.

Regarding critical thinking, students reported that they had learned how to break down tasks, especially when reading articles. Many students reported that they had learned to apply the lower order skills of reading an article several times, of note-taking, of summarizing, and using a dictionary to look up unfamiliar words. Some reached higher levels of critical thinking and reported that they looked for similarities and differences in articles, or considered how the information applied to their own lives to make it more meaningful to them and to critically analyze the information. Again, students did seem to understand that what they learned was transferable to other classes or aspects of their lives. One reported that she was planning "on keeping . . . class worksheets for reference." Another, when discussing the importance of breaking down tasks, said she "will use this skill in the future studying for tests, doing projects, and managing work and outside school activities."

The cover letter assignment was probably more important than we realized when we created it. In having the students answer specific questions regarding how they would use the library and information skills and how they might apply the psychology and critical thinking skills they learned, we forced students to think explicitly about how knowledge they had learned implicitly might be applied in other settings. In the future, we will make this outcome clear to the students and ourselves when the assignment is given.

LOST IN TRANSLATION

In teaching this course, we learned some valuable lessons about the information literacy skills our students needed when they started, and what they will need to develop as their college careers progress. It was evident to us, both through our own observations and through our students' comments, that they came to our class with few or no library or information skills. Students did not know how to find, much less use, the library catalog or the library databases. They did not understand the difference between a search engine, such as Google, and a subscription database. Bringing them to the library and guiding them in their first assignments is essential in that, for many, this was their very first exposure to an academic library. We can assume neither that students will find their own way to the library nor that students can simply be sent to the library and expect that they will ask for help if needed. They require repeated library instruction and explicit help in translating the reproductive strategies into productive strategies that are not only used for other assignments, but are seen as useful analogies for solving future problems.

It was obvious to us in observing the earliest presentations that those students who presented first actually had the best articles to work with because they had the most guidance. It was also evident to us that lessons needed to be repeated, especially when teaching students about things about which they had no prior knowledge (e.g., peer-reviewed journals). As resource and knowledge limited novices, they were not spontaneously able to make productive use of many of their newly acquired skills. Students seemed to understand our presentation on finding the articles, but reverted to comfortable, quick, and easy searches (e.g., Google and Wikipedia) when under pressure, confused about the nature of the assignment, or not explicitly reminded to apply analogous learning. Perhaps starting with something the students found less foreign, for instance, finding books, would have made the transition to using an academic library less daunting for them.

Ultimately, students did demonstrate an ability to apply the information literacy skills they learned to other tasks, and they believe they can and will use them in other classes, along with the psychological principles they learned. However, it was only through explicit questioning as to how they would apply them that we were able to draw this conclusion. Although students made strides in understanding the use and value of a variety of resources, there is no doubt that this course was only a beginning in developing the students' information literacy and critical thinking skills. Evident in their final literature reviews was some inability to distinguish between opinion and fact (see CONNECT rubric under "what is information?"). Students made uncited claims in their papers, and, when asked where the information came from, answered that this was "common knowledge." There was also a misunderstanding among students that, while psychology experiments may provide convincing evidence, they do not "prove" anything, a point that was made no fewer than five times during the course of the semester.

At the end of a semester-long course centered on information literacy, there was still work to be done regarding when and how to cite and in time management when conducting research. In too many cases, it was apparent that students rushed their projects, even when given shorter assignments to help them break it down, and even though they claimed that they learned this important strategy. (See CONNECT rubric under "citation" and "understanding development of research strategy.") Students' shortcuts to completing assignments led to poorly organized projects. Even when we required the completion of assignments in stages that required various levels of library and critical thinking skills, we did not explicitly explain the derivation of the assignment or overtly illustrate how it moved them closer to the goal state as the instructors understood it. For example, while we regularly referred to the CONNECT rubric ourselves in creating lessons and assignments, our students actually never even saw it. In the future, students in our classes will be made explicitly aware which outcomes from the rubric we are addressing and why.

IN CONCLUSION: WHY ALL THE MYSTERY?

There was a distinct disconnect between what students reported that they understood and what was evident to us in the written work required for presentations, posters, and literature reviews. In their discussions with poster session attendees and in their portfolio cover letters, students seemed able to respond appropriately to thought questions. Their answers indicated they had done, and would be able to do, critical thinking concerning both library and psychological research. In informal venues, students were able to communicate detailed information regarding their knowledge and learning, calling upon examples from reading or previous class discussions. Their formal assignments, however, revealed little substantiating evidence. Perhaps students did learn about psychology, information literacy, and critical thinking skills, but as happened when students were left to choose their own articles, the purpose of the activity (an understanding of which is difficult in the "beginning thinker" stage of critical thinking as defined by Elder and Paul) was overshadowed.

Recall that students used the page-length criteria when choosing articles, making the practice of the next steps of critical thinking (understanding the concepts involved, the question or problem at hand, the point of view, the evidence, and the implications and limits of conclusions accomplished by Elder and Paul's "Practicing Thinkers") nearly impossible. Perhaps students became so distracted by the sub-problems and surface aspects of the formal assignments that the problem space was never clearly in sight, making the feedback and explicit instructions for improvements appear irrelevant at best and as the source of more confusion at worst. To use a well-worn phrase, they could not see the forest for the trees and were forced to rely on reproductive processes to produce work that met surface requirements, but lacked insight.

Still, students' resource and knowledge limitations steadily declined, and although they did not reach the expert status required for building an accurate representation of the problem space and developing production rules that can be transferred from one problem to another, students did practice critical thinking skills in producing their work. Just as students learned how to use the library and search databases while choosing inappropriate articles, portfolio cover letters indicated that they had indeed learned something about psychological research, source and evidence analysis, the identification of assumptions and biases, and the application of deep analogies even while they prepared inferior work. In the course of writing their cover letters, students began to build a representation of the maze they had negotiated during the semester and the labyrinth was (at least dimly) illuminated. However, had we attempted an illustration of the larger problem space and explicitly included descriptions of how their new knowledge and resource management skills would help them negotiate it, the class would have been less of a mystery they didn't even know they were to solve and more of an adventure toward a common goal.

While this course was a fine example of the power of incidental learning on the part of students and instructors, and no doubt will form the foundation for future growth for all, we must do an even better job of making the problem space and the skills necessary to negotiating it more explicitly available to students. This will require hard work on the part of the instructors, as conscious awareness of procedural knowledge is elusive. We were only marginally successful in our efforts to access cues to what we "knew" but could not declare. Even as we focused on critical thinking, and actively attempted to make the importance of those skills explicitly available to students, we leaned heavily on cooperative education and experiential teaching techniques to create valuable analogous learning opportunities that were obvious to the instructors, but elusive to students. In preparing materials for upcoming courses, we are listing on the syllabi the critical thinking skills that will be measured, explicitly referring to them in assignments, and outlining how they will reveal (to the student and instructor) their progress toward the goal and their negotiation of the problem space explicitly defined by the instructor. When it comes to information literacy, enumerating the critical thinking skills is of vital importance. Students (and instructors) are much more likely to identify their initial and goal states regarding content with enough accuracy to keep them from wandering the maze aimlessly. When it comes to seeing how the library skills and the critical thinking involved can be used productively to negotiate any problem space more effectively, students have a more difficult time. Instructors must help students move from reproductively using library resources to productively thinking about the problem restructuring power of information literacy. For all but a few students, the explicit route is the most expedient and efficient one to ensuring the application of this admittedly deep analogy. When teaching information literacy, integrated assignments are a necessary beginning. However, students and instructors must be made explicitly aware of how the lessons and skills modeled, as well as the assignments and activities, can be applied in other classes and settings. We cannot assume students will be able to use our carefully crafted but poorly articulated analogies, and we must be prepared to help them see the relationships. Critical thinking is developed over time. Explicitly discussing the development of these skills will help students make better connections.

REFERENCES

American Library Association. 1989. Presidential Committee on Information Literacy. FinalReport. http://www.ala.org/ala/acrl/acrlpubs/whitepapers/presidential.htm.

Anderson, J. R. 1993. *Rules of the mind*. Hillsdale, NJ: Lawrence Erlbaum.

Bean, J. C. 2001. *Engaging ideas: The professor's guide to integrating, writing, critical thinking, and active learning in the classroom*. San Francisco: Wiley.

Brooke, R. R. and A. J. Ruthven. 1984. The effects of contingency contracting on student performance in a PSI class. *Teaching of Psychology* 11: 87–89.

Carbonell, J. G. 1986. Derivational analogy: A theory of reconstructive problem solving and expertise acquisition. *In:* R. S. Mikalski, T. M. Mitchell, and J. G. Carbonell (eds.) *Machine learning: Vol. II. An artificial intelligence approach*. Los Altos, CA: Morgan Kaufmann, pp. 371–392.

Cohen, N. J. 1984. Preserved learning capacity in amnesia: Evidence for multiple memory systems. *In:* L. R. Squire and N. Butters (eds.) *Neuropsychology of memory*. New York: Guilford, pp. 88–103.

Elder, L. and R. Paul. 1996. Critical thinking development: A stage theory. The Critical Thinking Community Website. http://www.criticalthinking.org/articles/ct-development-a-stage-theory.cfm.

Foos, P. W. 1989. Effects of student-written questions on student test performance. *Teaching of Psychology* 16: 77–78.

Gardiner, J. M and R. I. Java. 1993. Recognizing and remembering. *In:* A. F. Collins, W. E. Gathercole, M. A. Conway, and P. E. Morris (eds.) *Theories of memory*. Hove, UK: Lawrence Erlbaum, pp. 163–188.

Gentner, D., M. J. Rattermann, and K. D. Forbus. 1993. The roles of similarity in transfer: Separating retrievability from inferential soundness. *Cognitive Psychology* 25: 524–575.

Gick, M. L. and K. J. Holyoak. 1980. Analogical problem solving. *Cognitive Psychology* 12: 306–355.

Goldman, G. U. 1978. Contract teaching of academic skills. *Journal of Counseling Psychology* 25: 320–324.

Holyoak, K. J. and K. Koh. 1987. Surface and structural similarity in analogical transfer. *Memory and Cognition* 15: 332–340.

Keane, M. 1987. On retrieving analogues when solving problems. *Quarterly Journal of Experimental Psychology* 31: 29–41.

King, L. A. 2001. The health benefits of writing about life goals. *Personality and Social Psychology Bulletin* 27: 798–807.

Klein, S. B. and J. F. Kihlstrom. 1994. Elaboration, organization, and the self-reference effect in memory. *Journal of Experimental Psychology: General* 11: 26–38.

Koestler, A. 1964. *The act of creation*. London: Picador.

Larkin, J. H., J. McDermott, D. Simon, and H. A. Simon. 1980. Expert and novice performance in solving physics problems. *Science* 208:1335–1342.

Latham, D. and M. Gross. 2007. What they don't know can hurt them. *In:* H. A. Thompson (ed.) *Sailing into the future: Charting our destiny: Proceedings of the ACRL 13th National Conference*, Chicago: Association of College and Research Libraries, pp. 277–286.

Lindstrom, J. and D. D. Shonrock. 2006. Faculty-librarian collaboration to achieve integration of information literacy. *Reference and User Services Quarterly* 46: 18–23.

Newell, A. and H. A. Simon. 1972. *Human problem solving*. Englewood Cliffs, NJ: Prentice Hall.

Ohlsson, S. 1992. Information processing explanations of insight and related phenomena. *In:* M. T. Keane and K. J. Gilhooly (eds.) *Advances in the psychology of thinking*, Vol. 1. London: Harvester Wheatsheaf, pp. 1–44.

Ohlsson, S. 1984. Restructuring revisited I: Summary and critique of Gestalt theory of problem solving. *Scandinavian Journal of Psychology* 25: 65–76.

Paul, R. 1995. *Critical thinking: How to prepare students for a rapidly changing world.* Santa Rosa, CA: Foundation for Critical Thinking.

Reed, J. H. and J. D. Kromrey. 2001. Teaching critical thinking in a community college history course: Empirical evidence from infusing Paul's model. *College Student Journal* 35: 201–215.

Rogers, T. B., N. A. Kuiper, and W. S. Kirker. 1977. Self-reference and the encoding of personal information. *Journal of Personality and Social Psychology* 35: 677–688.

Rooke, S. E. and J. M. Malouff. 2006. The efficacy of symbolic modeling and vicarious reinforcement in increasing coping-method adherence. *Behavior Therapy* 37: 406–415.

Schacter, D. L. 1987. Implicit memory: History and current status. *Journal of Experimental Psychology: Learning, Memory and Cognition* 13: 501–518.

Seger, C. A. 1994. Implicit learning. *Psychological Bulletin* 115: 163–196.

Tufte, E. 2006. *Beautiful evidence*. Cheshire, CT: Graphics Press.

Wharton, C. M., K. J. Holyoak, P. E. Downing, T. E. Lange, T. D. Wickens, and E. R. Melz. 1994. Below the surface: Analogical similarity and retrieval competition in reminding. *Cognitive Psychology* 26: 64–101.

Williams, R. L., R. Oliver, J. L. Allin, B. Winn, and C. S. Booher. 2003. Psychological critical thinking as a course predictor and outcome variable. *Teaching of Psychology* 30: 220–223.

APPENDIX 1.

Common Learning Outcomes for First Year Information Literacy Across the five CONNECT institutions: Bridgewater State College, Bristol Community College, Cape Cod Community College, Massasoit Community College, and University of Massachusetts Dartmouth

Use of online catalog	Citation	Understanding Development of Research Strategy	Evaluation of Sources	Database Use and other online materials	What is Information
Novice					
Cannot identify the catalog; regularly asks for assistance using and locating items.	Does not document sources and does not understand the need. Cannot write or identify the elements of a citation. Does not understand plagiarism.	Unable to identify the formats needed. Does not know who or when to ask for help. Uses one source (probably Google) for everything. Does not understand how much time research takes. Cannot understand research need.	Does not analyze; accepts all information as equally valid.	Cannot identify any database. Relies mainly on Google.	Believes all information to be equally valid.
Practitioner					
Understands what is in the database; knows what the call number is. Can differentiate between reference,	Knows what information is needed to write a citation; knows when to cite. Rudimentary understanding of	Understands that there are different types of formats. Knows when to ask for help. Knows to use more than one	Understands that search engines do not vet web pages, but may not understand that analysis of other resources is	Can identify some database(s), but does not always use them. Asks for help to choose appropriate database. Uses	Understands difference between opinion and fact, may not be able to distinguish that difference.

circulating, and other collections.	plagiarism.	source. Understands that good research takes time. Needs help formulating question.	also necessary.	Google when appropriate.	Understands difference between opinion and fact, may not be able to distinguish that difference.
Expert Understands catalog record. Understands different search skills (e.g. keyword, subject, browse). Understands how to use subject terms.	Can write an appropriate citation in the style needed; understands and respects intellectual property. Understands that they are contributing to the knowledge base of the field.	Selects proper formats for information needs. Uses a variety of resources effectively. Uses Boolean operators (AND, OR, NOT) effectively. Modifies strategy as research progresses; breaks down tasks into manageable timepieces.	Analyzes all resources for accuracy.	Uses appropriate database for research need. Understands the value of a subscription database.	Understands and can identify bias/opinion. Recognizes that there is a difference between popular and scholarly material.

Created by: Ms. Mary Adams, University of Massachusetts Dartmouth; Dr. Gabriela Adler, Bristol Community College; Ms. Susan Berteaux, Massachusetts Maritime Academy; Dr. Marcia Dinneen, Bridgewater State College; Ms. Jean Marie Fraser, Cape Cod Community College; Ms. Pamela Hayes-Bohanan, Bridgewater State College Ms. Jennifer Rudolph, Massasoit Community Collegebased on standards created by the Association of College and Research Libraries
Spring 2006

APPENDIX 2

Reading Research–Guidelines for Evaluating Empirical Studies

Find the answers to the following questions and annotate your article (make notes directly on your hard copy). The exercise will help you find important points in the article, understand the research, aid you in the writing process/presentation process, and help you to identify areas in which the current research has failed to answer important questions. Write directly on your article. Circle and underline and make a note which question below is answered.

Introduction

Does the introduction provide a strong rationale for why the study is needed?

How many studies are cited in the introduction?

How many different perspectives/positions are presented? (While the authors are making their case, do they offer some alternative ideas?)

Are the measures that are going to be used described? If the authors are using a new measure, do you understand why and what the foundation will be?

What are the research questions and hypotheses?

Method/Design

Subject evaluation

What are the subject recruitment and selection methods?

Are there any probable biases in sampling?

Is the sample appropriate in terms of the population to which the author generalizes?

If two or more groups are being compared, are they comparable on demographics, background, intelligence, other variables of importance, etc?

Is this is a correlation study? If so, which variables are expected to be correlated and why?

If this is an experimental study, were subjects randomly assigned to groups? If appropriate, was a control group used, and is it satisfactory?

Is the method described so that replication is possible without further information? What *exactly* did they "do to" the participants and what *exactly* did they measure?

Were procedures constant across subjects in all groups? Were any confounds (errors) introduced through use of different procedures?

Measures

For all measures (measures to classify subjects, dependent variables, etc.), did the authors provide evidence of reliability and validity, either by summarizing data or by referring the reader to an available source that provides the information?

Do the measures match the research questions and hypotheses being addressed?

Were multiple measures used, particularly those that sample the same constructs, but with different methods (e.g., self-report, ratings by others, direct observation)?

If human observers, judges, or raters were involved, was interobserver or interrater agreement (reliability) assessed?

Was administration and scoring of measures done blindly (by someone who was unaware of the hypotheses?

Independent Variables

If an experimental study, was there a check that the independent variable was manipulated as described (e.g., were people really manipulated into being angry, etc.)?

If more than one treatment or condition is being compared, did the authors document that these conditions differ in ways that they are supposed to differ, and are they the same in every other way? If not, are the differences likely to confound the results?

Results

Were tests of significance used and reported appropriately (i.e., with enough detail to understand what analysis was being conducted)?

If there were a large number of statistical tests performed, do the authors adjust the alpha level or report using multivariate techniques to reduce the probability of Type I error?

Are means and standard deviations reported (if relevant) so that the reader can examine whether statistically significant differences are large enough to be meaningful?

Discussion

Do the authors over interpret the data (e.g., use causal language in their discussion of correlation data or interpret self-report data as equivalent to direct observation, etc.)?

Do the authors consider alternative interpretations/explanations?

Do the authors include a "humility section" in which they discuss the limitations of their research. Are there aspects of subject selection, procedures and dependent variables that may limit the generalizability (applicability to other people or populations) of the findings?

APPENDIX 3

As a group (turn in one paper with all your names on it), answer the following short answer questions *in your own words.* If you have two articles, do this for *both.*

1. What are the hypotheses and why do the authors expect them to be supported (on what theories or previous research do the authors base their expectations)?
2. Describe what was done to the participants/what did the participants do, and what was measured?
3. What did the authors find? If the authors say that Group 1 scored better than Group 2, what analysis do they use to support that finding?
4. Did the results match predictions? Did the authors state anything that was not supported by their results? How do authors explain any discrepancies?
5. What are the implications of the results? What do the results mean with regard to academic achievement? What do they mean to you?
6. How do you "feel" about the study? Does anything stand out as problematic or missing? Are you convinced? Are there additional studies you would recommend?

APPENDIX 4

Go over your notes from the last meeting and discuss the articles together. Answer the following short answer questions *in your own words*:

1. Make at least two general statements about the theory or hypotheses that inspired the research. Write your answers in professional language. For example, you might finish the following sentences: According to theory, improved critical thinking skills . . .

It has been hypothesized that emphasizing critical thinking in college courses will . . .

2. Write down at least three sentences that describe how the articles differ, contradict each other or are distinctive. Write your answers in professional language. For example, you might finish the following sentences:
   In an effort to study critical thinking, authors have employed different methods to teach the skill to college students. For example . . .
   Authors have used different measures to measure college students' use of critical thinking. For example . . .
   In two studies, the author (or authors) . . . (describe what they did or something they found out), while in the third the author(s) . . . (describe what they did or something they found out).
   While Williams, Oliver, Allin, Winn, and Booher (2003) found that . . . Foos' (1989) and/or Reed and Kromrey's (2001) results did not support that finding.
3. Write down at least 3 things that the articles' findings (results) have in common. Write your answers in professional language. For example, you might finish the following sentences:
   The results of three recent studies have suggested that . . .
   Based on the results of the three studies, we can conclude that . . .
   Results of three studies indicate that . . .
4. Write down at least three things that follow from the research findings of *all three* articles. Write your answers in professional language. For example, you might finish the following sentences:
   Based on the research reviewed (Foos 1989; Reed and Kromrey 2001; Williams, Oliver, Allin, Winn, and Booher 2003), college students might benefit from employing the following tactics in studying: . . .
   According to recent research (write out the citations), college students should look for professors who . . . if they want to expand their critical thinking skills.
   To enhance learning, research suggests college students should focus on . . . not just . . . (citations).
   Researchers have suggested that students might . . . (citation) . . . (citation), and . . . (citation) to improve their grades in college courses.
5. Write down at least two things that are problematic about or questions that are left unanswered by the studies you read. Suggest a follow-up study in response to your criticism. Your answers should be written in professional language. For example, you might finish the following sentences:

Although recent research (write out the citations) has suggested . . . the problem of . . . was not addressed. A follow-up study might . . .

While three studies have indicated that . . . (citations) none have included . . . so it remains an open question whether . . . . Future work should . . .

APPENDIX 5

Help out your peers! Everyone will be revising and adding to their presentations for the poster assignment. Your input will help. Please keep track of your thoughts and questions.

Group Topic:

Things I didn't understand (terms, ideas, connections, etc.)

Holes in your talk or materials—things that seemed to be missing

Things you did talk about that I wish you had said more about

Things you should think about researching, ideas you might explore

Things you talked about that I wish you had said less about

Applications I thought of while I was listening

What you absolutely should not change

What you absolutely should change

Other advice or ideas

APPENDIX 6

The Abstract is a summary of your project (150 words max) and must include sufficient information for the reader to understand the nature of the topic.

For your purposes, the abstract should contain a concise summary of

(a) the problem under investigation or goal and its significance
(b) brief review of methodology
(c) results of the study, and
(d) implications of the study.

Start by answering the following (on a separate sheet of paper with all of your names on it):

The goal of this study was to

The problem investigated was

The most important finding was that

The findings are important because

Next, try filling in the following blanks to try different wording for your abstract.

As part of a course on academic success, it was revealed that___________ was important to college student achievement because ___________. Researchers completed a review and comparison of the literature and found that___________ . The results indicate that___________.

Research on college academic achievement indicates that ___________ is a problem for many students. In a review and comparison of the literature, researchers identified possible solutions, including ___________. The results are important because___________ .

Researchers investigated the impact of___________ on college student achievement and found___________ was an important factor. The results help clarify___________ and can be used to ___________.

Now, write your own abstract.

APPENDIX 7

Literature Review Assignment Overview

What is a literature review? The purpose of the literature review is to evaluate, synthesize, interpret, and critique information, not just paraphrase prior research, list previous studies, or quote statistics. The literature review begins with a broad statement of the problem under investigation and then proceeds to cover the specifics of interest. The idea is to introduce the reader to the overall issue/problem that is being examined and to provide justification for any recommendations. In order to accomplish these tasks, the author needs to review past research on the same topic, discussing their findings.

Purpose: The literature review paper is your opportunity to do an in-depth exploration of an area of interest and display the research skills and writing skills you have developed over the semester. The paper should demonstrate critical thinking and your ability to write a clear and coherent summary of relevant research. It should introduce the reader to the topic and to the most important work in the area. The literature review assignment will help you develop the academic skills required to communicate effectively about social science research and applications.

What NOT to do:

Present information from each source separately without transition or clarifying the relationships between them.

Present only broad generalizations without any specifics about the research findings, research that contributed to your summary and conclusions.

Assume that your readers understand terms or research details that you do not understand.

Plagiarize in any manner, shape, or form.

What TO do:

Introduce the problem.

The paper should begin by broadly describing the research problem or point of the paper in 1–2 paragraphs that may include a research question or theoretical implication of the research.

Review the background literature.

This section will be the longest, as you will review the background literature based on its relevance to the current topic. Give the reader enough information to understand a previous work and then relate it back to your topic.

Restate the purpose/rationale and mention problems or unanswered questions

In the final section of the literature review you should formally restate the paper's purpose, your rationale, and specific problems or unanswered questions. The previous section should naturally lead up to this point. A reader should be able to understand why the topic is important. There should not be a "surprise ending" or something that was not covered under the background subsection.

Developing Your Literature Review Topic

Identify the question about the effects of psychological variables on academic achievement that you intend to investigate and use your library skills to:

Find at least five keywords relevant to your area of interest.

Identify authors who appear to be "important" (authors that appear to have published several articles or books during their career).

Using APA-style citations, create a resources list that includes at least one book available on your topic and five journal articles you might use.

For each of the above, write a general comment on why you believe it to be relevant. Comment on the hypotheses that have been tested relevant to your area of interest. Include the independent and dependent variables and the operational definitions of each (what did they test and how did they measure it?). Comment on each with regard to a possible flaw, something you believe might be missing, or a concern/thought you have about the study.

For example:

I am interested in how service learning influences college students' involvement and contributions to campus. The Smith and Jones (1999) study is relevant to my topic because it measured whether college students gave money to charity after viewing either a film that included footage of a college student volunteering to work on student government project (modeling) or a film that included a statement about the benefits of getting involved in campus life (statement). The authors measured the success of each film based on the amount of time participants later agreed to spend on a charitable project. They found that the film modeling volunteerism was more effective than the film with the importance statement. They also found that those who had participated in service learning were more likely to donate their time. I wonder whether background information (such as religion or past charitable giving practices) was collected, and I wonder whether participants with service learning history would volunteer even if they saw no movie.

Attach the abstracts of the five journal articles and one book you found useful. Note whether the articles are available or will need to be requested through ILL.

Many journal and book references will not be available in the library and you have to interlibrary loan materials. Complete an ILL form and send a request for one of the articles that the BSC library does not own (if you already know your topic), or simply print the request without sending it to the library (to show me that you know how to do an ILL, but without wasting resources on something you aren't sure you will need).

APPENDIX 8

Guidelines for Peer Evaluations

Do not be afraid to write on each other's papers. As you read the draft, note with a wavy line in the margin all the places where you got confused as a reader, and jot down any questions that come to mind. You don't have to know the answers to make a comment. It is okay to write impressionistic comments such as "this doesn't flow . . ." or "this sounds funny. . . ."

Do not wait until the last minute. You want the person to feel you read the paper with care and attention. Sometimes it helps me to read through papers quickly, set them aside, and go back later. This way I am not judging too quickly, and it gives me time to think about the topic, content, and style.

You should feel free to comment on:

1. Style (is the paper understandable, readable, clear, concise, free of typographical errors, misspellings, does it flow well, etc.).
2. Format (margins, spacing, citations, references, APA style, etc.).

I realize that peer evaluation is a socially awkward situation, but students are always disappointed when they don't get enough helpful feedback. In addition to the above comments (which are useful for quick improvements, but not really helpful for the required comprehensive revisions), you should make at least three constructive comments or questions about the paper you are editing.

For example, do three of the following (wherever possible, back up your comments with specific examples from the draft, and be as precise as possible):

1. Give your peer a brief summary of their thesis as you understand it and the main reasons the author has given for accepting the thesis.
2. Discuss the writer's reasoning process, the completeness of arguments and the research used as support. (Imagine that the writer is a defense lawyer—can the position be defended based on the arguments presented? Is there extraneous information that is distracting and should be removed? Are there concluding remarks that summarize the case?)
3. Write out questions a reader would have about the inclusion of particular research.
4. Write out questions a reader would have about the research studies described.
5. Note the best argument and worst argument included in the paper.
6. Note the best/strongest part of the paper and the worst/weakest part of the paper.
7. Note things in the paper that would likely leave the reader wondering.
8. Comment on organization, clarity of reasoning, or the effectiveness of the author's process of educating the reader.

Refining Your Peer Evaluations

You and your partner should collaborate to give advice to the writer. Answer the following questions (on a separate worksheet for each paper you are reviewing).

Name of writer:
Names of reviewers:

1. Write out the question, problem, or issue that this draft addresses.
2. Write out the writer's complete thesis statement. (Note that if you are having problems with 1 and 2, concentrate on helping the writer clarify these matters.)
3. Write out your assessment of the strengths and weaknesses of the writer's ideas. Assuming that the teacher is interested primarily in the quality of thinking in a paper, how will the teacher respond to the ideas in this draft?
4. Examine the draft for quality of support. Does the writer offer sufficient details to support the arguments? Does the writer need to do more research?
5. Write out at least two things that you think are particularly strong about this draft.
6. Write out at least four recommendations for specific changes the writer should make in the next draft.

Author: Reviewers:

Help your peers determine their potential grade. Start with these four yes or no questions:

1. Does the paper have a clear thesis or statement of purpose that is not too broad given the length of the paper?
2. Is the paper free of summaries (or quotes) that exist only to fill space or that are unanalyzed by the writer?
3. Did the writer produce complete, understandable sentences?
4. Is the paper free from basic grammatical errors?

Before moving on, assign a grade based on your consideration of the four questions above. If the answer to any one of the above is a "no," the grade will be some level of "C." A "no" answer to two results in some level of "D" and so on. Given your answers to the questions above, what is the *highest* grade this paper could receive if it was turned in "as is?"____

Now answer and elaborate on these "style" questions which fine tune the grades and separate the "A's" from the "B's":

1. Does the paper respond to the question or topic of concern in a full and interesting way? Does the paper have an appropriate degree of complexity, or does the problem appear overly simple or tedious? Should the topic be examined from another perspective or could something be added to make it more meaningful, thoughtful, or original?
2. How well organized is the paper? Does it stick to the point? Does every paragraph contain a clear topic sentence? Are transitions well made? Describe problems or suggestions.
3. Does the paper have a real conclusion? The paper should not simply "end." How might the writer formulate a concluding paragraph that sums up the material and helps the reader come to a logical conclusion?
4. Is the writing style "efficient" and not too wordy, or too sparse to be clear? What suggestions do you have?
5. Can you hear a lively, intelligent, interesting human voice speaking to you as you read the paper? Why or why not? Be honest, since this is probably one of the most important grading criteria!

We Won't Be Fooled Again: Teaching Critical Thinking via Evaluation of Hoax and Historical Revisionist Websites in a Library Credit Course

Stephanie M. Mathson
Michael G. Lorenzen

INTRODUCTION

In this era of instant access to information on the World Wide Web, it is crucial for college students to possess solid critical thinking and analysis skills. Far too often, college students bypass their institutions' library collections (print *and* electronic) in favor of finding questionable, less academic resources for papers via Google and other search engines. Using general Web sources, however, is not always an inappropriate choice—provided that students have a thorough understanding of how to evaluate the information they find. For as Bradshaw et al. (2002) posed the question: "What potential does the WWW have to extend and facilitate more progressive educational models that require students to develop and then use complex thinking skills? If educators use the Web simply as a novel way to support traditional instruction, they are missing the point of its potential" (279). Unfortunately, in one-shot library instruction sessions, time is at a premium, and fully utilizing the general Web to teach critical thinking skills—as this article presents—is not always feasible. However, teaching information literacy or research courses for credit affords librarians the opportunity to address the set of skills that students need to successfully navigate online information.

At Central Michigan University (CMU), librarians have the relative luxury of teaching multiple sections of an eight-week, one-credit research skills class (LIB 197) to hundreds of undergraduate students each semester. A majority of students, particularly during fall semester, are freshmen. However, sophomores tend to enroll in sizable numbers both in the fall and spring. Also, during spring semester, instructors often find in their sections several upperclassmen from two degree programs (Family Studies and Social Work), which require the course.

While the main focus of LIB 197 is to teach students how to find, use, and properly cite library resources (both print and electronic), librarians also design lessons to teach World Wide Web organization and how to analyze the information found via search engines. These topics taken together allow librarians to address critical thinking skills. However, the focus of this article will be specifically on how Web analysis helps students to hone those skills. Some instructors choose to evaluate what the students learn through the use of the research readiness self-assessment (RRSA), an online assessment tool created by CMU faculty.

Administered at the beginning of the semester, prior to any formal discussion or teaching in LIB 197, the RRSA provides baseline scores in a variety of areas, including research confidence, knowledge of citation styles and plagiarism, overall reliance on general Web sources, and information evaluation (or critical thinking) skills, which is the emphasis of this article. The questions that assess critical thinking skills focus on brief Website and journal article analysis. The Websites were created for the express purpose of including them in the RRSA, but there is precedence for doing so (Heil 2005) when developing means of evaluation. Upon completion of all the modules in the course, students complete the same assessment again as a post-test. Thus, instructors can evaluate what their students have learned and make adjustments in lesson planning and assignments as necessary.

RESEARCH READINESS SELF-ASSESSMENT PRE-TEST RESULTS

Table 1 summarizes the research readiness self-assessment pre-test results from three sections of LIB 197 (two from fall semester 2006 and one from spring semester 2007). Though as many as ten sections of LIB 197 are taught during fall semester each year, and seven or eight sections are taught during spring semester, only those three sections in which the instructors teach extremely similar lessons on Web evaluation and critical thinking are included in the results given. Since academic freedom in the classroom is highly valued at Central Michigan University, it is up to each

TABLE 1. Research Readiness Self-Assessment (RRSA) Pre-Test Results

LIB 197	Browsing the Internet (Score %)	Evaluating Information (Score %)	Obtaining Information (Score %)
Fall 2006 Sect. 1	45%	54%	65%
Fall 2006 Sect. 2	35%	54%	66%
Spring 2007 Sect. 1	32%	57%	69%

instructor to decide how to customize the master course syllabus and best teach the topics listed therein.

Responses that are tallied in the "browsing the Internet" category are for those questions that score a student's overall reliance on general Web sources for information to meet personal and research needs. Questions that are scored for the "evaluating information" category are those directly related to the analysis of information found for a wide variety of purposes and from a wide number of sources. "Obtaining information" scores refers to answers given in response to questions about how information is found; this category includes use of library resources (i.e., library databases, reference materials, etc.).

In theory, post-test results, which are discussed at the end of this article, should show a decrease in the "browsing the Internet" category because, upon the conclusion of LIB 197, students are familiar with subscription databases and, hopefully, will turn to those resources first when conducting research. The scores for the other two categories ("evaluating information" and "obtaining information") should increase because of the students' growing strengths in those areas.

WEB EVALUATION

By the time we reach the point in our courses to discuss critical thinking skills as related to general Web analysis, we have already covered the use and evaluation of the library Website and materials, including the catalog, subscription databases, and research guides (many of which do include links to free and reputable Web sources selected by bibliographers). How we preface and explain Web evaluation may be quite different. One instructor, for example, likes to informally poll students by starting a discussion with the following questions: How often do you use the Web? What do you use it for? How many of you have created Webpages? For what purpose have you done so? Responses vary, of course, but the majority of students use the Web every day for e-mail, Facebook, shopping, and, yes, even research. Typically, many students also indicate that they have created Websites for everything from class projects to sharing personal interests. If so inclined, we may share with our students statistics on Web usage from a variety of Pew Internet reports. The overall goals of this line of discussion are to make students aware of the fact that Internet usage still continues to grow, and that people can put any information they want online.

Typical Web evaluation criteria covered in class, and, at least in one section, handed out as a guide, include evaluating the authority, accuracy, currency, coverage, and objectivity of Web sites. Most students tend to have at least some prior knowledge of what those concepts entail but are not necessarily familiar with the questions posed for each, such as: Who created the site? What are his/her credentials? What is the purpose of the site? Can the information presented be verified by other sources in any format? Is the subject covered in adequate detail? When was the site last updated? As a rule, we inform students that, while they will not have to answer all of these questions as they complete the day's in-class Web evaluation assignment, they should consider the questions when searching for Websites for personal information or research needs.

A Toronto-based librarian who maintains a variety of library-related blogs, including one he calls "information visualization," has developed his own unique way to examine information found on the Internet—"The 6 A's for Evaluating Web Content" (Taher 2006). The A's stand for: authority, accuracy, approach, age, audience level, and accessibility. Taher argues that the purpose of a Website and its objectivity or subjectivity should be considered under approach, while contemplating accessibility requires Web users to examine the style and appearance of each page within a site. In other words, are the pages of similar style or does the design vary widely? Are pages under construction? The other A's are related to those concepts presented in the previous paragraph with regard to date of last update, adequate coverage, authority of Website creator(s), and so on.

Prior to handing out the in-class Web evaluation assignment, we will show students one or two Websites, which we then discuss in class according to the standards just covered. The choice of sites and means of discussion are left to the discretion of the individual instructor, but our aims remain the same—to prepare students for the day's assignment.

ASSIGNMENT SUMMARY AND DISCUSSION

Prior to handing out the assignment, instructors divide the students into pairs or allow the students to select their own partners. The assignment is hands-on and allows the students to apply what they have just learned about carefully scrutinizing Websites to determine what kind of sources they are: hoax or genuine and reputable or disreputable.

Jacobson and Xu (2002) wrote broadly about how librarians can motivate students in an information literacy course, but this statement certainly applies to the lesson plan discussed here: "Multiple examples, drawn from different settings, should be given to illustrate and clarify the points so that students will not only have a better understanding of the ideas but will also be able to apply them to new situations" (430). To that end, the student teams are given a list of Websites to examine. Each team must first focus on one specific site to answer a number of different questions within a set amount of time (about fifteen minutes). The team will then briefly present its conclusions to the class. However, all of the Websites to be examined and discussed are listed on the assignment sheet everyone receives. Often after analyzing their own sites, students go on to familiarize themselves with others on the list. Appendix 1 presents a list of Websites instructors discuss with students and include on this assignment. Appendix 2 lists the questions that students must answer in analyzing the Websites assigned to each pair.

Upon completion of the in-class assignment, we again briefly review the key Web evaluation criteria discussed earlier in the class and how those points can be used when examining Websites listed on the assignment. Those sites that are obvious hoaxes (i.e., tree octopi, male pregnancy, and gnomes) provide a somewhat entertaining way to reinforce the concepts of critical thinking and analysis for students. Most seem to appreciate our attempts to use humor in the classroom while simultaneously conveying a lesson about the importance of carefully evaluating Websites. It is easy for many students to quickly refute the information on such sites by determining an individual site's purpose and authorship, bias, and even outright absurdity, which is principally determined through a lack of corroborating evidence for what is presented on the given site. For example, with the male pregnancy Website, some student teams try to determine whether or not the "institution" that created the site (RYT Hospital-Dwayne Medical Center) exists. (It does not.) Other teams search for supporting documentation of the phenomena because they know that if a man was really pregnant, legitimate news agencies would certainly report it!

Critical thinking skills as applied to Web evaluation are certainly not a concern only for librarians and other information professionals. Indeed, Buffington (2007), an assistant professor of art at Virginia Commonwealth University, recently published an article about students' use of the Web for art research primarily at the upper elementary and secondary level, in which she noted, "If educational uses of the WWW are to fulfill even a fraction of the claims made when the movement to wire every school was in its heyday, then educators must continually evaluate developing trends with its use" (18). Buffington proposed a working definition of critical thinking for art and reviewed the literature for interesting cases to highlight.

Students in all disciplines certainly need to possess solid critical thinking skills. In addition to covering fantastic and hoax sites in LIB 197, discussion also turns to revisionist social, historical, and political Websites. It is then that students have a more difficult time discerning whether the sites are valid or not. Students err in deeming that the Texas Independence Movement and Dominion of British West Florida sites (see Appendix 1) are hoaxes, but most do correctly decide that the Hawaiian Sovereignty movement is legitimate (in part because of the separatists' extensive media coverage). On the flipside, some students start to think that perhaps the Apollo 11 moon landing really was a hoax perpetrated by the United States government. More frightening to note is that almost all students fail to comprehend that Holocaust deniers and white supremacists are responsible for most of the content on the Website for the Institute for Historical Research.

Critical thinking can be taught by challenging students to analyze Websites that cover history and the social sciences. For example, how should students interpret extreme claims that Hawaii and Texas are illegally occupied by the United States when no international court has ever made such a judgment? How can students interpret the "overwhelming" evidence of historical revisionists that the Apollo Moon Landings never occurred, that the Holocaust is a hoax, or that 9/11 is a CIA conspiracy when the actual evidence for these events indicates the exact opposite? What is most useful in pointing out the flaws of seemingly well documented but one-sided revisionist sites is to contrast the contributors' claims with those facts that are accepted by international courts, historians, and scientists.

There are dangers in exposing students to historical revisionist groups via their Websites, yet it is important to do so in order to convey the necessity to critically analyze information—especially that which is freely available on the World Wide Web. The primary problem is that many undergraduate students are not well versed in history. It is not a subject that is taught in depth in most of the elementary and secondary schools in the United States. Students often can graduate from high school with a single course in the subject. A recent study by Gravois (2006) found that only 47.8% of college students could pass a basic history test. According to Cheney (2001), more than half of the students in a 1999 study believed that Cornwallis surrendered to General Grant after Yorktown during the American Revolution.

Recognizing this deficiency in history education in the United States, the federal government came up with National History Standards in the early

21st century. Included in the five recommendations was a call for teaching critical thinking skills in relation to history. Further, it was recommended that all teachers should be trained in the importance of history as it relates to democratic citizenship (Brown 2003).

Historical Revisionism on the Web

It is hardly surprising then that students have difficulty sorting out good from bad history information on the Web. The massive proliferation and growth of the Web, coupled with weak historical knowledge, makes many students clueless to what is and what is not a credible source of history information. Van Hartesveldt (1998) wrote, "Critical discrimination among sources requires significant knowledge of the subject and a level of sophistication to be expected from an advanced student, not a beginner. Furthermore, the nature of the Web makes such discrimination significantly more difficult than in a library" (54).

Compounding the problem is the ease with which individuals and organizations disseminating suspect historical information have in leading unsuspecting people to their sites. Many of these groups have professional help with search engine optimization, which makes it more likely that their sites will be found by search engines like Yahoo and Google when students type in search terms. When browsing through search results, students enter a history world on the Web where, among other things, the Holocaust never happened, the Apollo Moon Landings were a hoax, large portions of the United States are undergoing prolonged illegal military occupation by the Federal government, 9/11 was a CIA plot, President Kennedy was assassinated in a conspiracy by dozens of different groups (take your pick). FDR knew about the impending Japanese attack on Pearl Harbor and did nothing, the government is hiding the fact that a UFO and aliens were captured after a crash in Roswell, New Mexico in 1947, and so on.

A large portion of bad historical information on the Web is due to historical revisionism. This can be a legitimate academic pursuit, which allows historians to critically reexamine historical facts using newly discovered information. However, some historical revisionists do not use the process in an appropriate manner. Instead, they engage in the revisionist practice of negationism. This is a process by which history is rewritten by minimizing, denying, or ignoring essential facts. In some countries, like Germany, historical revisionism on some topics like the Holocaust is illegal. Orwell's 1984 is a classic example of bad historical revisionism, and in the book, Big Brother revises history to reflect the current political situation. For example, if the nation goes to war with another nation, all history is changed to reflect that the nation has always been at war with the other nation (Orwell 1949).

Examples of Bad Historical Revisionism Online

There are thousands of examples of bad history on the Web. (Appendix 1 lists such sites that are discussed with students in LIB 197.) The movements described below base their arguments on faulty historical analysis. Not one is accepted by the majority of mainstream historians and none is likely to be any time in the future. These movements are also not unified. Often there are multiple and competing groups with different sites on the Web that may argue for the same revisionist view of historical data but may interpret it differently.

Perhaps the best known historical revisionist movement is Holocaust denial. Proponents claim that Nazi Germany's genocide never occurred. The movement denies that Germany ever targeted Jews for extermination, that nine to eleven million people died in concentration camps, and that there were gas chambers in those same camps. It is further argued that the Holocaust was a hoax created to further the aims of Jews or to redirect blame for World War II from the Allies to the Germans.

The Holocaust happened. Despite the claims of the Holocaust deniers, there is no debate about this historical fact. Braham (2000) wrote, "Perhaps no other event in world history has been as thoroughly documented as the Holocaust, the destruction of close to six million European Jews during the Nazi era. Yet, this vast documentation notwithstanding, the authenticity of no other event has so consistently been questioned as that of the Holocaust" (11).

Despite the evidence, Holocaust denial is rampant on the Web. Organizations such as the Institute for Historical Review (IHR) publish countless articles on their sites and in online journals highlighting the evidence for denial. Students have little trouble finding these sites and may not even realize they are at Holocaust denial sites at first, as many of the arguments presented are subtle and only indirectly attack the historical authenticity of the Holocaust. In LIB 197, it is always with trepidation that instructors discuss the IHR Website and invite students to determine its accuracy and bias. As students lack the general knowledge necessary to refute revisionists' claims, emphasizing other means through which a site's validity can be examined becomes critical. For example, though the IHR publishes a journal (*Journal of Historical Review*) and countless leaflets, the articles in those sources are cyclical—authors reference only the works of a select few other scholars and subjects are re-addressed over and over and over again. Equal weight and coverage are not given to dissenters.

A second notable revisionist movement claims that the United States captured a UFO and its alien crew after the UFO crashed in Roswell, New Mexico, in 1947. Further, believers think that the last fifty years of world history (including the Cold War) can be viewed as a consequence of this act, as alien technology and perhaps diplomacy with aliens have strongly influenced recent history.

The believers state that a massive conspiracy is at play and it has suppressed the public's (and historians') knowledge of the true history of the 20th century. Unfortunately, for the UFO revisionists, there is little if any solid proof to their claims. Korff (1997) wrote, "The Roswell mystery has been solved, and there is no credible evidence that the remains of an extraterrestrial spacecraft was involved" (25).

The idea that any government could withhold information of this magnitude for half a century is almost beyond belief, particularly when one considers that other governments, such as the (former) Soviet Union, would have known of this situation, too, if it impacted international relations as is claimed at many Roswell UFO sites. How many hundreds of thousands of people would have had access to this information without once leaking it in a credible manner? Unlike most bad revisionist theory, this case could be proven; all that is needed is a UFO or an alien body. However, in the absence of these items, the numerous sites on the Web portraying recent history through the lens of the Roswell crash cannot be taken seriously.

Another major revisionist movement that is widespread on the Web involves a number of American separatist groups whose members believe that history proves that the United States government is illegally occupying most of what we consider to be the United States. Some of these sites are from racists who claim that the Confederate States of America still exists and has been under illegal federal control since the end of the American Civil War in 1865. Other sites include such fringe groups as the Kingdom of EnenKio, which claims to be the legal government of the American dependency of Wake Island based on its representation of the Aboriginal people of the island, although the island has never been inhabited by an indigenous group. Then there are the residents of the "Dominion of British West Florida" who are loyal to the British Crown and claim West Florida is legally a part of the British Commonwealth. All of these groups cite history and international law as evidence for their claims.

The American separatist sites students are perhaps most likely to find on the Web deal with Alaska, Hawaii, and Texas. All three have groups who claim their area is illegally held by the United States government. The arguments are quite similar, beginning with the premise of illegal occupation, and then working backward in time to only accept evidence, which supports their views while ignoring or misconstruing evidence that does not fit. In the cases of Hawaii and Texas, invasion and invalid annexation by Joint Resolutions of Congress are cited. In Hawaii and Alaska, invalid elections (though huge majorities voted for statehood) are cited despite the United Nations having removed both areas from the list of non-self-governing territories after these elections in the 1950s.

The questions as to whether Queen Elizabeth II should own West Florida, if the Republic of Texas or Kingdom of Hawaii should return, or whether the Confederacy should be restored are political issues that everyone has a right to debate. Political boundaries change and there is nothing wrong with discussing whether a particular area of the United States should be independent. Further, it is valid to debate whether the United States should have annexed Texas, Hawaii, and other regions in the first place. However, claiming that history shows these areas to be illegally occupied today is bad revisionism, it is counter to history and international law, and it ultimately renders the phrase "illegal occupation" meaningless when it is used inappropriately in these cases.

The last major revisionist movement we cover centers on what proponents argue is the Moon Landing Hoax. In 1969, NASA landed men on the moon; however, several vocal groups on the Web are trying to use historical evidence to prove that the entire event was a hoax concocted to give the United States a symbolic victory in the Cold War. They claim that the entire moon landing was filmed in a studio and that a moon landing may be scientifically impossible for humans due to radiation in space. These arguments were featured sympathetically on a FOX television program in 2003, which had fifteen million viewers.

Like the Roswell UFO, such a historical hoax would require a massive conspiracy not only by the government but by the scientific community. According to Villard (2004), "The scientific samples, photographic evidence, and telemetry from the moon are incontrovertible. For this to be otherwise, the world's foremost planetary scientists would have to be dead wrong (imagine the book: *Moon Rock Analysis for Dummies*). Or even more fantastic, scientists have their own international conspiracy to pawn off phony data—an idea even more impossible than a government conspiracy" (50).

Refutations of the moon landing hoax theory, no matter how historically or scientifically sound, are irrelevant to the moon revisionists. These Websites remain up and the authors keep spinning new arguments. Their use of history is bad, and it could easily confuse students who do not take the time to think critically or explore the topic in more credible sources—as students in LIB 197 are taught to do. To refute historical revisionists well requires students to find evidence to the contrary using reputable sources in print or online.

Skewing History on the Web

There is a variety of ways that bad history sites on the Web go about attacking legitimate history and try to sell their version of the past to Web surfers. However, the steps librarians and teachers normally teach students on how to evaluate a Web resource will not always help in identifying them. Many of these bad history sites are well designed, with proper spelling and grammar, are hosted on servers at educational institutions, have current copyrights, list authors with legitimate credentials on the sites, and provide unbroken links to what often are credible sources. Yet, despite passing most or all of the tests that are taught to students on how to identify a bad Website, these sites are still full of questionable material.

There are dozens of tactics that can be used to skew history in writing. Many of them are used frequently on the Web. These can include claims of conspiracy theories, the selective use of facts, the denial of known facts, the fabrication of facts, the use of hard to understand jargon, irrelevant conclusions, and the use of *ad hominem* attacks against those who dispute the revisionist's version of history. Teaching students to recognize these techniques and think critically when they see them will help them to better determine if a site is a good one for historical information (or, for that matter, any other purpose).

Conspiracy theories are a mainstream of bad history online. Such claims allow proponents of a particular view to avoid providing evidence such as written primary sources or oral histories regarding an event. Instead, proponents can claim that such evidence existed but that someone (usually some shadowy government agency) destroyed the documents relating to the event and harassed, threatened, or murdered people who took part in the event or witnessed it. Proponents can also claim that any evidence or testimony that disagrees with them is a product of the same conspiracy. Claims of conspiracy are used by Holocaust deniers, those who claim the Apollo moon landings were faked, 9/11 skeptics who blame the event on the CIA or any other group except Al-Qaeda, and the Roswell UFO believers, for example.

The selective use of facts and sources is another common trick. An author will cite and praise two articles in the history literature which seem to agree with some of the bad history claims being made on the site. However, the author will neglect to cite or acknowledge in any way the several hundred articles in the same literature, which clearly disagree with the author's views. Facts can also be manipulated by selective use. It may be true that a highly regarded professor at an Ivy League institution once made a statement that would appear to support the revisionist author. However, the author will fail to mention that that same Ivy League professor clarified the statement later in ways that do not support the site author's views. Examples of this include the many Hawaiian separatist sites that extensively cite and link to copies of the Blount Report, which appears to support their claims, but at the same time are silent on and do not link to the congressionally authored Morgan Report that many believe refutes most of the conclusions of the Blount Report (Twigg-Smith 1998). In another example regarding the 9/11 conspiracy advocates, Eagar, an engineering professor at MIT, suggested they "use the reverse scientific method. They determine what happened, throw out all the data that doesn't fit their conclusion, and then hail their findings as the only possible conclusion" (Watch 2006).

Denying proven facts is another technique, which can serve to confuse Website visitors. If the facts do not fit the version of history that the revisionist is presenting, the facts are often denied. This can be subtle denials of small pieces of evidence, which help to distort the larger picture, or it could be the denial of something major. For example, historians have proven beyond any doubt that the Ottoman Empire under the Young Turks participated in a genocide of Armenians that may have resulted in as many as a million deaths. The response of the current Turkish government is to deny that the Armenian Genocide ever happened and to make it illegal for any one to say or write that it did (Crampton 2006). Likewise, Holocaust deniers refuse to accept that the Holocaust happened despite the proven fact that nine to eleven million people died in Europe in Nazi death camps.

Inventing "facts" is another way that bad history can be supported. In many cases, someone will invent bogus information and it will be passed around extensively in the community that believes in a particular historical fallacy. Most in the community will not know that the information was fabricated, as they usually judge the validity of facts based on how well the information supports what they already believe. The creation of the *Protocols of the Elders of Zion*, which purports to be a Jewish plan for world domination, is a good example of this (United States Senate 1964). The existence of video footage purporting to be an autopsy of an alien from Roswell is another (Bauer 1997). Though both the *Protocols* and the alien autopsy have been proven to be fraudulent, many students may still believe in both as true and factual.

Bad historical revisionism often can be advanced by the use of confusing jargon. Needlessly convoluted, scientific, or legalistic terminology is presented for the purpose of conferring legitimacy on an author or to confuse the site visitor with words they may not understand or may misinterpret. For example, the Texan separatists often use the terms *de facto* and *de jure* in describing American ownership of Texas in an attempt to convey that the U.S. owns Texas in practice but not legally. By using Latin legal terminology, they are hoping to raise doubts of American ownership despite the fact that no American or international court has ever ruled anything other than that Texas is indeed under the *de jure* control of the United States. As *de jure* means what is legal, which is ultimately determined by courts, the United States does have jurisdiction over Texas, and the use of that phrase by separatists suggests a historical or legal controversy that does not actually exist.

Irrelevant arguments are often advanced by bad history sites as well. The conclusions that accompany these arguments do not follow from the evidence being presented. For example, Holocaust deniers often point to the Allied firebombing of German cities such as Berlin and Dresden as being war crimes comparable to anything Nazis may or may not have done to Jews, with the suggestion being that these acts balance each other out and keep the Allies from being able to claim the moral high ground. Deniers even claim one of the reasons that the Allies fabricated the Holocaust was to hide their moral culpability in the death of German citizens. That argument, however, has no bearing on whether the Holocaust happened and is irrelevant to the question being asked.

In another example, Texan, Alaskan, and Hawaiian separatists often point to international laws passed in the 20th century under the League of Nations or the United Nations (such as the Montevideo Convention of 1933) and then apply them retroactively to events of the 19th century. However, this is an *ex post de facto* application of international law and cannot be applied to American actions in 1845 (Texas), 1867 (Alaska), or 1898 (Hawaii). The backward use of applying 20th century law to 19th century events is irrelevant since only international law that existed at the time of these events is applicable to the legality of the annexations of these regions to the United States.

Finally, *ad hominem* attacks on those who disagree with bad history sites are quite common. Attacking the character and intelligence of opponents is often the only recourse authors of these sites have when well-educated individuals question and can disprove the version of history being presented by partisans of a suspect history claim. For example, those who argue that the Holocaust did indeed happen are labeled as Zionists out to create a worldwide Jewish state. Similarly, those who challenge the claims of Hawaii being illegally occupied by the USA are accused of being racist toward native Hawaiians. People who disagree with revisionist attempts at history about 9/11 or Roswell, New Mexico, are called foolish sheep who have successfully been duped by their government. *Ad hominem* attacks can be found on many history sites, but they appear to be a staple on revisionist sites and are often a dead giveaway that something is amiss.

TEACHING CRITICAL THINKING IN HISTORY

There is no way to prepare students for every suspect history claim they will find on the Web. It seems that no matter how bizarre a claim may be, someone believes it and has a well-done Website about it. The only way to teach this is by going over methods for evaluating a site, instructing students to double check all claims on the Web against more credible sources, and asking the students to critically think about what they read. If a claim is wild, outrageous, and depends on conspiracies to work, it probably is not history.

In a 1997 book, Sagan and Druyan asked readers to turn on their baloney detectors to help detect false claims. It is important to teach students to do the same in history (and other fields). As Windschuttle (2006) noted, "The overwhelming majority of people who read history want it to be true . . . my opponents are now falling all over themselves to deny any connection with postmodernist relativism about the truth. They have found they cannot win any public debate by appeals to multiple truths or relativist perspectives" (34).

Although history will always be open to multiple interpretations and subject to fresh looks based on new information, many facts can be determined and are not open to debate. The use of outrageous sites on the Web, which offer up bogus historical data in a serious manner, can be a powerful teaching tool. Although there is a danger in students being mislead by these sites, with firm direction, students can learn to recognize arguments and techniques that can indicate a site is not grounded in good historical analysis.

Suggest that students visit some of the Websites listed in this paper or find similar sites to use as examples. Compare these to more mainstream sites on the same subjects. Have groups of students evaluate revisionist sites by looking for conspiracy theories, missing or misused facts, conclusions that do not follow the arguments, *ad hominem* attacks, etc. It could be helpful to bring in articles from respected history journals to which students can compare the revisionist sites.

In short, be prepared to ask hard questions. If the Holocaust never happened, why does the overwhelming amount of evidence indicate that it did? Why do few serious historians take Holocaust denial seriously? If Alaska, Texas, and Hawaii are illegally occupied by the U.S., why has no court ever backed these claims? Why does the United Nations recognize American claims to these areas if the U.S. possesses them illegally? Why has no one involved in the Apollo moon landing hoax ever come forward to set the record straight? Why did the Soviet government, which monitored all the radio transmissions from the moon to the earth, not expose the hoax as it occurred? If the U.S. government could not keep Watergate or Monica Lewinsky from public scrutiny, how in the world could it preserve aliens for more than half a century and keep the matter a secret? These types of questions will help students really think about historical information they find on the Web and hopefully equip them to probe further when their baloney detectors sound.

RESEARCH READINESS SELF-ASSESSMENT POST-TEST RESULTS

If students can grasp the difficult concepts presented in the previous section, then they should certainly be able to use their analysis skills in evaluating and thinking critically about any kind of Website. Web evaluation is covered by most LIB 197 instructors near the end of the eight-week course. At that point, students are once again—at the instructors' discretion—assigned to complete the research readiness self-assessment (RRSA), this time as a post-test. The critical thinking skills discussed in the Web analysis unit are fresh in the minds of the students at the time they complete the RRSA.

As explained at the beginning of this article, results that are tallied in the "browsing the Internet" category are for those questions that score a student's overall reliance on general Web sources for information to meet personal and research needs. Questions that are scored for the "evaluating information" category are those directly related to the analysis of information found for a wide variety of purposes and from a wide number of sources. "Obtaining information" scores refer to answers given in response

TABLE 2. Research Readiness Self-Assessment (RRSA) Post-Test Results

LIB 197	Browsing the Internet (Score %)	Evaluating Information (Score %)	Obtaining Information (Score %)
Fall 2006 Sect. 1	27%	70%	74%
Fall 2006 Sect. 2	29%	57%	72%
Spring 2007 Sect. 1	25%	61%	76%

to questions about how information is found; this category includes use of library resources (i.e., library databases, reference materials, etc.) (see Table 2).

In theory, post-test results, should reflect a decrease in the "browsing the Internet" category because students are now familiar with subscription databases and know how searching them is different than using the general Web for research. On the other hand, in the post-test results, the scores for the remaining two categories ("evaluating information" and "obtaining information") should increase because of the students' growing strengths in those areas. As Table 3 shows, the scores did decrease and increase exactly as expected. Notably, the students in Section 1 during Fall Semester 2006 showed the greatest increase in the category of "evaluating information"—16.25%! The differences in scores are reflections upon the individual instructors' styles.

TABLE 3. Comparison of the Averaged Scores from the Research Readiness Self-Assessment (RRSA) Pre- and Post-Test Results

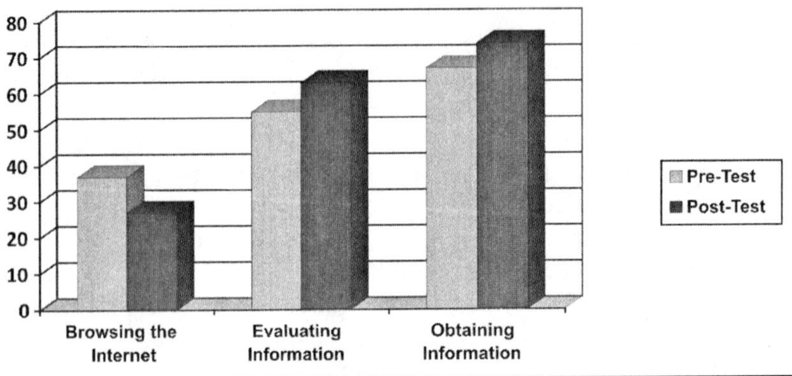

Our lesson plans in Web analysis, while similar, do allow for us to each employ our own unique teaching methods; hence, this could explain some of the differences in the post-test scores. The fact remains, however, that students do show improvement in how they obtain and evaluate information after completing the LIB 197 course. By examining pre-and post-test scores, instructors can better determine how to tweak lesson plans and assignments in the future and hopefully see wider changes in scores across the board.

CONCLUSIONS AND FUTURE RESEARCH

Using the Web to teach critical thinking skills to university underclassmen is clearly a challenge. It simply is not enough to show them hoax sites on subjects like male pregnancy, fictional languages, or tree octopi, and ask students to determine why such information is farcical. Instead, in order to fully convey the importance of critiquing information found via the Internet, instructors must be willing to tackle difficult topics such as historical revisionism and government conspiracies.

Many, if not most, of today's college students lack basic knowledge of United States and world history. Thus, discussing whether or not the Holocaust took place or the Apollo 11 moon landing really happened can present problems for teachers. One does not have to be a history expert to refute preposterous claims. Providing students with basic knowledge to ask thought-provoking questions and tips for evaluating Websites can go a long way in lessening students' beliefs in false information they find on the Web.

In the future, the authors hope that more colleagues in the Central Michigan University Libraries will use the research readiness self-assessment to evaluate what students learn in the LIB 197 course. The more students who take the assessment, the better we can determine how our teaching methods and activities impact students' learning. Library instruction, whether in one-shot sessions or in eight-week courses, is fluid and requires our constant attention to changing trends in teaching methods. We must also continue to keep abreast of hoax and historical revisionist sites on the Web and work closely with teaching faculty to ward off students' use of such information when conducting research.

REFERENCES

Bauer, J. A. 1997. A surgeon's view: Alien autopsy's overwhelming lack of credibility. *In:* K. Frazier, B. Karr, and J. Nickell (eds.) *The UFO invasion: The Roswell incident, alien abductions, and government coverups*. Amherst, NY: Prometheus Books.

Bradshaw, A. C., Bishop, J. L., Gens, L. S., Miller, S. L. and Rogers. M. A. 2002. The relationship of the World Wide Web to thinking skills. *Educational Media International* 39: 275–284.

Braham, R. L. 2000. The assault on historical memory: Hungarian nationalists and the Holocaust. *East European Quarterly* 33: 411–425.

Brown, S. D. 2003. *History standards in the fifty states*. Bloomington, IN: ERIC Clearinghouse for Social Studies/Social Science Education.

Buffington, M. L. 2007. Contemporary approaches to critical thinking and the World Wide Web. *Art Education* 60: 18–23.

Cheney, L. 2001. Mrs. Cheney's remarks on "Teaching for freedom" at Princeton University. http://www.whitehouse.gov/mrscheney/news/20011130.html.

Crampton, T. 2006. French pass bill that punishes denial of Armenian genocide. *The New York Times,* October 13, Section A, 10.

Gravois, J. 2006. Condemned to repeat it. *Chronicle of Higher Education,* http://chronicle.com/weekly/v53/i14/14a02101.htm.

Heil, D. 2005. The Internet and student research: Teaching critical evaluation skills. *Teacher Librarian* 33: 26–29.

Jacobson, T. E. and L. Xu. 2002. Motivating students in credit-based information literacy courses: Theories and practice. *Portal: Libraries and the Academy* 2: 423–441.

Korff, K. 1997. What really happened at Roswell—Truth behind the July 1947 UFO crash in Roswell, New Mexico. *Skeptical Inquirer* 21: 24–31.

Orwell, G. 1949. 1984. London: Secker and Warbug.

Sagan, C. and A. Druyan. 1997. *The demon haunted world: Science as a candle in the dark.* New York: Ballantine Books.

Taher, M. 2006. The six A's for evaluating Web content. http://www.geocities.com/drmtaher/SixAsWebEvaluation.pdf.

Twigg-Smith, T. 1998. *Hawaiian sovereignty: Do the facts matter?* Honolulu, HI: Goodale Publishing.

United States Congress, Senate. 1964. Committee on the Judiciary.*Protocols of the Elders of Zion: A fabricated "historic" document. A report prepared by the Subcommittee to Investigate the Administration of the Internal Security Act and Other Internal Security Laws.* Washington, DC: U.S. Government Printing Office.

Villard, R. 2004. Did NASA fake the moon landing? *Astronomy* 32: 48–53.

Van Hartesveldt, F. R. 1998. The undergraduate research paper and electronic resources: A cautionary tale. *Teaching History: A Journal of Methods* 23: 51–59.

Watch, T. 2006. Controversy dogs Y.'s Jones. *Deseret News,* September 9. http://findarticles.com/p/articles/mi_qn4188/is_20060909/ai_n16723280.

Windschuttle, K. 2006. National identity and the corruption of history. *New Criterion* 24: 29–34.

APPENDIX 1. SAMPLE WEBSITES DISCUSSED AND EVALUATED IN LIB 197 SECTIONS

Website Name	URL
Alaskan Independence Party	http://www.akip.org/
Apollo 11 Hoax Conspiracy	http://www.geocities.com/apollo11conspiracy/
A Concise Grammar of Feorran	http://www.lib.montana.edu/-bcoon/feorran.html
Endangered Blondes	http://news.bbc.co.uk/1/hi/health/2284783.stm
The Dominion of British West Florida	http://dbwf.net/
EnenKio Online Network	http://www.enenkio.org/
The Flat Earth Society	http://www.alaska.net/~ clund/e_djublonskopf/ Flatearthsociety.htm
Free the Gnomes	http://www.freethegnomes.com/
Hawaii: Independent & Sovereign	http://www.hawaii-nation.org/
Havidol	http://www.havidol.com/index.php
Institute for Historical Review	http://www.ihr.org/
Pop! The First Male Pregnancy	http://www.malepregnancy.com/
Roswell UFO Crash of 1947	http://www.roswellufocrash.com/
Save the Pacific Northwest Tree Octopus	http://zapatopi.net/treeoctopus/
Texas Independence Movement	http://www.texasrepublic.com
The Voluntary Human Extinction Movement	http://www.vhemt.org./

APPENDIX 2. WEB ANALYSIS QUESTIONS ASKED ON IN-CLASS ASSIGNMENT

1. What is the site about? For what purpose was it created?
2. What evidence do you see that would indicate this is a valid site for information?
3. What evidence do you see that would indicate that this might not be a good site for finding valid information?
4. In your opinion, is this a hoax site? If you believe it is, why? If you think the site is legitimate, would it be an acceptable source of information (for a paper or other assignment) even if you think the content is strange or out of the mainstream?

Learning More About How They Think: Information Literacy Instruction in a Campus-Wide Critical Thinking Project

Corey M. Johnson
Elizabeth Blakesley Lindsay
Scott Walter

INTRODUCTION

When *Time* announced its "Person of the Year" for 2006, a shot was fired across the bow of scholarly authority that still echoes across both our popular culture and the halls of academe. "You," *Time* proclaimed, were the "Person of the Year" in 2006 because "you" (i.e., "we") made use of technology like never before to build community, encourage discourse, and to "[wrest] power from the few" in order to "[found and frame a] new digital democracy" in which traditional forms of authority are suspect, and the key to the future lies in harnessing the power of "mass collaboration" (Grossman 2006; Tapscott and Williams 2006). What does this pronouncement, if true, mean for libraries? And what does it mean for higher education? How do academic librarians help to prepare students to conduct research in an information environment defined by "digital democracy?"

"Mass collaboration" and "Web 2.0" technologies (Wikis, blogs, social networking tools, etc.) have been embraced as landmarks on the contemporary information terrain by many, but others have raised concerns about the quality of the information created by the "hive" (Stephens 2006). Stephen Colbert, for example, has skewered the basic assumptions behind one of the most successful social networking sites for information creation and sharing, *Wikipedia*<http://www.wikipedia.org/>, in commentaries and interviews conducted on his hit television show, *The Colbert Report* (Colbert 2007). In one of his most widely shared commentaries, Colbert defined "wikiality" as "a reality where, if enough people agree with a notion, it becomes the truth" (2006). For librarians and classroom faculty alike, the idea that "wikiality" may reflect our students' view of the research process is a challenge (Jensen 2007). For first-year students, especially, whose experience with "research" may have been defined since junior high school by openly available, participatory, Web-based resources such as *Wikipedia*, our instructional goals must include not only the mastery of subject matter, but also the mastery of the process by which one determines which resources are most appropriate for the information need and the academic task at hand.

Colbert, it should be noted, is a comedian and an author who has proven very successful in using social networking sites to promote both his opinions and his products. Less amusing are comments and criticism of the emergent information environment by those who appear genuinely concerned by the rise of information resources created, vetted, and reviewed popularly, rather than through a scholarly apparatus that has changed little in centuries (Guédon 2001). In their view, resources such as *Wikipedia* are inherently suspect, never appropriate for serious inquiry, and a reflection not of a means to challenge elite mechanisms of information production and control, but rather of a "cult of the amateur," or, in the case of the most overheated rhetoric, "digital Maoism" (Gorman 2007a, 2007b; Keen 2007).

The information environment faced by our students today is a volatile one, and it is unlike almost anything those of us currently employed in higher education experienced at their age (Frand 2000; Prensky 2001a, 2001b). It is an environment in which there is no consensus on the boundaries of which information resources are "acceptable" for academic purposes. For many of us in libraries, this is nothing new. We remember similar concerns raised a decade ago about the quality of information found on what was then a similarly "emergent" information technology—the World Wide Web. Then, as now, academic librarians were charged with helping both students and faculty to see that (with apologies to Marshall MacLuhan) the medium is not always the (only) message, and that high-quality content can sometimes be found in unexpected places. Just as we have for the past 30 years, academic librarians can help faculty and students to adjust to the shifting information environment and the increasingly blurry boundaries between popular and scholarly information by fostering critical thinking about information through information literacy instruction (Jacobson 2000; Jayne and Vander Meer 1997; Smalley 1998; Walter 2000).

At Washington State University, a unique organizational culture has fostered the ongoing integration of information literacy instruction across an array of instructional initiatives over the past twenty years, including general education, writing across the curriculum, first-year experience, and critical thinking instruction (Elliot and Spitzer 1999; Johnson, McCord, and Walter 2003; Lindsay 2003; Ursin, Johnson, and Lindsay 2004; Walter 2007). This article will explore the integration of critical thinking instruction and information literacy instruction at Washington State over the past decade and the evolving relationship between these two complementary instructional initiatives. At Washington State University, three of the most active partnerships in support of the application of critical thinking skills to the contemporary information environment can be found in collaboration with the freshman seminar program (a first-year experience course) and in the evolution of the freshman seminar teacher training section of Gen Ed 300, accessing information for research, a one-credit course offered by academic librarians under the aegis of the general education program. Finally, another significant area of collaboration at the crossroads of critical thinking and information literacy involves the development of the information literacy education project, a program where librarians and classroom instructors work together to create a series of tutorials and assessment tools to aid in the completion of research assignments for the instructor's course.

INFORMATION LITERACY INSTRUCTION AT WASHINGTON STATE UNIVERSITY

Washington State University (WSU) is one of two comprehensive research universities in the state of Washington. Established in 1890 as the state's land-grant institution, the university maintains a flagship campus in Pullman, a city in the rural southeastern corner of the state, as well as three regional campuses in Spokane, Richland ("Tri-Cities"), and Vancouver. In addition to these academic campuses, the university supports ten learning centers located around the state, as well as cooperative extension offices in each of Washington's 39 counties. In 2006–2007, the Pullman campus enrolled approximately 19,000 students, while thousands more participated in undergraduate, graduate, and continuing education programs held at the regional campuses, learning centers, or extension offices, or delivered through such distance learning options as teleconferencing and Web-based instruction (WSU-Statewide).

The WSU libraries provide a full range of collections, services, and electronic resources to the university community through a network of six libraries on the Pullman campus (agricultural sciences, architecture, education, health sciences, humanities/social sciences, and science and engineering), in addition to libraries on each of the regional campuses. Each Pullman library is supported by at least one subject specialist responsible for reference, collection development, and instructional services in relevant disciplines. Although subject specialists are responsible for providing instruction to liaison departments and programs, they are supported by an independent library instruction department, which is comprised of four FTE librarians, and supported by an instruction coordinator housed in the two largest public service units. Even after thirty years of attention to the increasing importance of the instructional services provided by librarians to faculty, staff, and students across campus, relatively few satellite libraries maintain an independent instructional services unit (Johnson and Fountain 2002). Even more unusual is the degree to which the library instruction department at WSU maintains formal liaison responsibilities to campus programs for which collection development is not a key concern (e.g., athletics, multicultural student services, and residence life (Cummings 2007; O'English and McCord 2006; Walter 2005).

Among the most long-lasting and successful of these liaison relationships are those between the library instruction department and general education (Gen Ed) programs such as freshman seminar (Gen Ed 104) and world civilizations (Gen Ed 110/111). These courses are tied together not only by their place in the general education curriculum, but by their participation in WSU's ground-breaking critical thinking project <http://wsuctproject.wsu.edu/>, which will be described later in greater detail.

Support for an independent library instruction department and for the coordination of academic liaison programs by that department reflect the high priority that the library administration and the library faculty have placed on the provision of instructional services over the years. This support has been earned by the evidence of success provided by the program's growth. During the 2006–2007 academic year, over 11,000 faculty, staff, and students took part in instructional programs provided or coordinated by the WSU Libraries (doubling the number who took part in similar programs during the 1996–1997 academic year). The degree to which information literacy instruction has been recognized as a significant campus priority is also a testament to the success of the instruction program and its faculty, who have been awarded funding three times for program development through the Provost's "improving undergraduate teaching and learning" grant program, and who have been recognized as campus instructional leaders by selection for membership in the president's teaching academy. Most importantly, information literacy has been recognized as one of the six learning goals of the baccalaureate that lie at the heart of undergraduate education at the university.

As one of the six learning goals, information literacy joins critical and creative thinking, quantitative and symbolic reasoning, and communication (including written communication), among the chief learning outcomes for undergraduate education at the university and its academic programs. As important for discussions of the impact librarians may have on student learning, information literacy instruction joins critical thinking and writing as learning outcomes that must be regularly assessed among our students. Building on earlier work across Washington to articulate an effective approach to the assessment of information and technology literacy, the WSU libraries have collaborated with campus partners in the freshman seminar program to make use of ongoing assessment of critical thinking as an opportunity for the assessment of information literacy skills (House Bill 2375, Washington State House of Representatives 2000). Moreover, the campus' successful experience in developing the critical thinking project has informed the ongoing evolution of the instructional services program in the library.

CRITICAL THINKING AND INFORMATION LITERACY INSTRUCTION

Along with "writing across the curriculum" (WAC), critical thinking instruction in college classrooms represents one facet of a wide-ranging effort to reform the undergraduate curriculum since the 1960s (Gaff and Radcliff 1997). Bean (2001) has articulated how these separate initiatives can be brought together to spur student learning inside and outside the classroom. Like its sibling initiatives, information literacy has become a recognized component of the undergraduate curriculum over the past thirty years, and several studies have explored the connections, both theoretical and practical, between information literacy instruction and broader programs focusing on writing instruction and critical thinking instruction. Elmborg (2003) and Elmborg and Hook (2005), for example, have articulated the ways in which the lessons of the WAC movement can inform the movement to integrate information literacy instruction across the curriculum. The connection between information literacy and critical thinking is clear. Both, for example, focus on evaluating the credibility of an information source and on evaluating evidence of the authoritative nature of a source. Pedagogical similarities between information literacy instruction and critical thinking instruction exist as well in that both are effectively taught through attention to active learning, and both have been highlighted as skills well suited for problem-based learning (Bean 2001; Cheney 2004; Gradowski, Snavely, and Dempsey 1998).

One of the earliest pieces of scholarship to make these connections visible appeared in Bodi (1988), who explored the connections between critical thinking in higher education and the goals of library instruction. Bodi noted that the goals of library instruction are to help students find information and foster their evaluation skills as they face materials with differing viewpoints, bias, and expertise, which fits in well with the goals of critical thinking. Bodi advocated the inclusion of library research and instructional sessions for courses striving to improve students' critical thinking skills.

Bodi defined critical thinking as evaluative and exploratory, noting that creative thinking, problem solving, and logical approaches are part of critical thinking but do not entirely comprise it (150). She called upon a number of educational theorists, including John Dewey, Allan Bloom, John McPeck, and Walter Perry, in her definition of the stages of development of critical thinking. Bodi saw these stages as dualism, multiplicity, relativism, and finally a commitment to relativism that marks a student's ability to analyze, synthesize, be objective, recognize bias, and be open to the possibility of changing one's views based on new evidence (151).

In addition, in 1992, Bodi provided librarians with an example of how library instruction could be delivered to meet these goals. She later expanded on this topic in her discussion of collaborations between librarians and faculty for teaching critical thinking skills. Bodi based her model of collaboration on Engeldinger's argument that librarians acting as mere suppliers of information do a great disservice to learners, and that librarians, even though they may not have a PhD in a particular subject, are well suited to "[providing] assistance with evaluating" information resources (1992, 70). By reaching out to teaching faculty, and by working with them to help them to recognize the information needs and information skills of their students (as well as their own information needs and skills), Bodi's library instruction program tripled in number of sessions offered (73).

This connection has been seen in the international arena for some time. In 1992, the *Australian Library Journal* published an extensive article by Henri and Dillon that provided an overview of the history of educational reform in both Australia and the United States in the 1980s, including the rising interest in critical thinking instruction and active learning (resource-based enquiry). Henri and Dillon linked information literacy and critical thinking through a curricular model of research involving concept maps and other processes of doing research, and concluded that while all teachers need to be involved in teaching critical thinking, librarians are in a unique position to see a broader view of the curriculum across disciplines. From this vantage point, they argued, librarians are well positioned to provide valuable training in critical thinking and the use of information resources.

Gibson published a useful overview of critical thinking theory, particularly as it related to the educational reform of the early 1990s. Gibson's work also raised several crucial questions about library instruction and critical thinking that helped many librarians rethink and reshape their instructional efforts. Among these issues were an examination of applying critical thinking across all parts of the research process, strategies for teaching critical thinking within the confines of a single 50-minute library class session, and exploring broader issues of assessment and impact of technology (Gibson 1995).

Over the past several years, a wide array of articles has appeared in library and education journals exploring the links between critical thinking instruction and information literacy instruction. Nowicki (1999), for example, examined information literacy and critical thinking within the electronic information environment. Nowicki noted that the explosion in information resources led to the increased need for students to hone their critical thinking skills, particularly for evaluating Web sites and for formulating effective search strategies. Describing an instructional program provided as part of a first-year experience program similar to WSU's, Harley (2001) concluded that successful teaching and learning of information literacy and critical thinking come when the concepts are related to the students' lives. Albitz (2007) explored the links between information literacy and critical thinking as she tackled the issues involved with defining and building the necessary partnerships between librarians and teaching faculty to deliver instruction in these two areas.

Much of the research and practice surrounding information literacy during this time has focused on the application of the Association of College and Research Libraries' (ACRL) *Information Literacy Competency Standards for Higher Education* (2000). The majority of these standards for student learning outcomes focus on aspects of critical thinking, either directly or indirectly. For example:

- Standard One states that "the information-literate student determines the nature and extent of the information needed";
- Standard Three puts forth that "the information-literate student evaluates information and its sources critically and incorporates selected information into his or her knowledge base and value system"; and,
- Standard Five asks that "the information-literate student understands many of the economic, legal, and social issues surrounding the use of information and accesses and uses information ethically and legally" (ACRL 2000).

All of these standards require that students apply critical thinking skills to their definition of the research question, their evaluation of information that they find, and their use of the information. A key aspect of critical thinking is that students address not only their own perspectives, but also fully understand and address the perspectives of other people involved or affected, as well as the perspectives of the authors of any supporting materials. It is hard to imagine achieving significant information literacy skills without also demonstrating effective critical thinking skills.

THE CRITICAL THINKING PROJECT AT WASHINGTON STATE UNIVERSITY

The close connection between writing instruction, critical thinking instruction, and information literacy instruction has already been noted. And, while Weimer (as cited in Bean 2001, xvii) has called writing across the curriculum "[one] of the most successful movements to sweep through American higher education" in the late 20th century, Halpern (1993, 2003) has noted the simultaneous success of the critical thinking movement. "The ability to think critically," Halpern wrote, "is almost always listed as one of the desirable outcomes of undergraduate education" (1993, 238). Let us not split hairs; being both an effective writer and a critical thinker are valuable skills for undergraduate students. Moreover, as noted earlier, both of these skills have been the subject of scrutiny at Washington State University, and both have joined information literacy as part of the six learning goals of the baccalaureate. As important as each of these learning goals is, however, they remain difficult to assess. At WSU, we have based our assessments of student learning on the review of portfolio projects in writing and the application of a rubric for the assessment of critical thinking. To fully understand the development of the information literacy instruction program at WSU, a brief introduction to the decade-old "critical thinking project"—a collaborative project designed initially by the center for teaching, learning, and technology, the general education program, and the writing program—is appropriate.

The *Guide to Rating Integrative and Critical Thinking* (formerly known as the *Critical Thinking Rubric*) is a seven-dimension rubric originally designed in 1996 "to provide a process for improving and a means for measuring students' higher-order thinking skills during the course of their college careers" (critical thinking project). Following its most recent revision in 2006, the rubric helps instructors to rate students across a spectrum of "emerging," "developing," and "mastering" critical thinking skills. According to the rubric, a student should demonstrate mastery of the following skills as evidence of growth as a critical thinker:

- Identifies, summarizes (and appropriately reformulates) the problem, question, or work assignment;
- Identifies and considers the influence of context and assumptions;
- Develops and communicates own perspective, hypothesis, or position;
- Presents, assesses, and analyzes appropriate supporting data or evidence;

- Integrates issue using other perspectives and positions;
- Identifies and assesses conclusions, implications, and consequences;
- Communicates effectively.

For over a decade, faculty across the curriculum have applied versions of the *Critical Thinking Rubric* in their classrooms and have demonstrated that student critical thinking skills can be measurably increased through the use of the rubric and conscious attention to integrating clear expectations for critical thinking to their students.

The success of the Critical Thinking Project on campus has provided opportunities for substantive discussions of information literacy at WSU over the past decade owing to the clear connections between the critical thinking skills identified in the rubric and several facets of information literacy identified by the "Information Literacy Competency Standards for Higher Education." For example, while the rubric asks for evidence that students can "identify, summarize, and reformulate" a research question or work assignment, Standard One challenges students to "define and articulate the need for information" and to "determine the nature and extent of the information need." Likewise, Standard Three suggests that a student should demonstrate the ability to "[evaluate] information and its sources critically and [to incorporate] selected information into his or her knowledge base and value system." If mastered, those skills might help students to provide evidence that they have increased mastery of the critical thinking skills identified as part of the second, third, fourth, and fifth dimensions of the *Critical Thinking Rubric*. For several years, faculty choosing to take part in the project received an introduction to critical thinking instruction and assessment through workshop programming provided by experienced project members. These workshop programs provided a valuable opportunity for librarians to interact with faculty with a demonstrated interest in instructional innovation, and information literacy was among the topics discussed in workshop and brown bag sessions with faculty from across the curriculum.

Finally, a distinctive feature of the *Critical Thinking Rubric* is its mutability—the rubric can be (and has been) adapted for use in a variety of disciplines, including history, physics, and crops and soils. Given the fact that the general education program was a founding partner in the critical thinking project, it is no surprise that one of its flagship programs—freshman seminar—would include demonstration of critical thinking among the learning outcomes for its students. Designed to measure student critical thinking as demonstrated through a multimedia course project, the freshman seminar version of this instrument has been called the *Multimedia Critical Thinking Rubric*. Both the rubric and the freshman seminar program have evolved since both were first launched, but both have demonstrated how information literacy instruction can become integrated (and assessed) as part of campus-wide instructional initiatives. The remainder of this article will describe the evolution of the library contribution to these programs and suggest both the opportunities and the challenges that can come from a commitment to collaboration.

FRESHMAN SEMINAR AND INFORMATION LITERACY INSTRUCTION

Freshman seminar (Gen Ed 104) is a first-year-experience (FYE) program that has been offered in various formats at Washington State University since 1996. First-year students who join the program enroll in a section of freshman seminar that is linked either to a section of world civilizations (Gen Ed 110/111) or to a first-year course in disciplines such as animal sciences, anthropology, biology, communications, and sociology. Each student enrolled in the freshman seminar becomes part of a learning community comprised of the students in his or her section of Gen Ed 104 and the staff of the Student Academic Learning Center (SALC) who coordinate the program and design each semester's curriculum. In addition, faculty teach the linked courses drawn from the general education curriculum, and librarians introduce the first-year students to library resources and to the research process.

The focal point of the freshman seminar experience is a research project that students design, conduct, and present under the guidance of the undergraduate peer facilitators (PFs) who lead the semi-weekly meetings of each section. The PFs are sophomores, juniors, and seniors who prepare for their new role in the program by completing an upper-division course in "peer leadership" (ED AD 497) (Henscheid 2001). The PFs are assisted in their instructional work by graduate facilitators (GFs) drawn from programs across the curriculum and employed by SALC. The final results of this semester-long research process are presented at a research symposium for which student groups must prepare a poster presentation and answer questions about their research process and product posed by faculty, librarians, academic staff, and other students. Projects are assessed by teams of faculty, librarians, and SALC staff using (among other tools) the *Multimedia Critical Thinking Rubric*.

Instruction in library use has long been a component of FYE programs, and librarians have become increasingly integrated into them across the country in recent years (Hardesty 2007; Pierard and Graves 2002). While some librarians are recent additions to their campus FYE programs, the librarians at WSU have been part of the FYE program since its beginning.Librarians work with freshman seminar sections to introduce students to library resources and to assist with the design and development of student research projects. Instruction librarians and subject specialists have worked together to provide instruction on subjects ranging from the use of the online catalog to evaluating Web-based information resources for use in academic research to identifying appropriate forms of citation for print and electronic sources. In each case, the librarian's overarching concern has always been to introduce students to resources and access tools that would help them to move forward on their research projects. Like other faculty involved in the program, librarians have had the opportunity to be involved in all phases of project development, from initial proposals to evaluation of the final product.

In the early years of the collaboration between freshman seminar and the libraries, the parameters of the relationship were loosely defined, and few attempts were made to coordinate the work of the many librarians involved in the program each semester. All aspects of the collaborative work varied widely from section to section and from semester to semester. This situation began to change in early 2002 when a more programmatic approach to the collaboration between the library instruction department and freshman seminar began to take form (Johnson, McCord, and Walter 2003). The head of library instruction, the director of the freshman seminar program, along with representatives from both groups, devised a new collaborative model based on:

- The need to institutionalize an approach to information literacy instruction that could survive any change in program personnel;
- The desire for librarians to have greater input into curriculum development; and,
- The interest in instruction librarians to provide a greater range of instructional support services to PFs.

This new approach to instructional collaboration had three main components: PF enrollment in Gen Ed 300, an improved communication structure between librarians and the freshman seminar staff, and design of curriculum for new instructional sessions.

In addition to changes in the Gen Ed 300 course to assist in the development and training of the PFs, changes were also made to the instructional content and pedagogical method of the freshman seminar library sessions. Freshman seminar faculty and librarians alike concluded that a key complaint students had regarding the information literacy instruction was that it rarely followed the model of discussion and active learning that freshman seminar students experienced throughout the rest of the program. More broadly, the instruction provided in the library was tool-oriented and did not reflect the emphasis on critical thinking instruction that is central to the freshman seminar program. Although the librarians were eager to provide active learning opportunities, they reported that they felt consistently pressed for time during the single instruction session scheduled each semester. Currently, freshman seminar librarians meet more frequently with their students, and opportunities for active learning and critical thinking about information searches and sources have become a part of each lesson. Also, librarians now have more opportunities to provide feedback on the students' research proposals.

TRAINING PEER FACILITATORS AND INFORMATION LITERACY INSTRUCTION

Freshman seminar and library instruction leaders agreed that each new cohort of PFs would enroll in a specially designed section of the libraries' one-credit information literacy course, Accessing Information for Research (Gen Ed 300). While this section of the course meets the same instructional objectives of other sections (i.e., an introduction to information literacy skills and the research process in a given discipline), its focus is not only on preparing students to be information literate themselves, but also on their becoming effective mentors for their future students in freshman seminar. Taught for the first time in Fall 2002, this new section of the course incorporates specific instructional elements with which future PFs must be familiar if they are to assist first-year students in the research process (e.g., critical evaluation of Web-based information resources). It also introduces them to professional concepts such as process models of information literacy instruction and to resources they might use to develop their own information literacy instruction activities. Requiring participation in this course not only helps assure baseline information literacy skills among all PFs, but provides PFs with a better understanding of information literacy instruction.

One area of course revision involved the development of active learning components on Web evaluation, plagiarism, and citation styles. Students are given a tool kit of criteria for evaluating Web sites, not only for their own use, but for helping teach their future students about the importance of critically evaluating information sources, particularly those freely available on the Internet. Students are taught, for example, to evaluate the degree to which the author of a Web document represents a credible authority in the field in question. Likewise, they are taught to carefully review Web-based documents for potential bias and to evaluate both the currency and the scope of the information presented. A complete outline of these issues is available online at <http://www.systems.wsu.edu/bin/libdocs/instruction/web_evaluation.pdf>.

Teaching about Web-site evaluation exemplifies the dual nature of the Gen Ed 300 course, as students are able to hone their own evaluation and critical thinking skills with regard to the Internet and to gain ideas for how to teach this to others in the future. Although mostly sophomores and juniors, these students benefit greatly from the content. In addition, an approach to helping FS students understand these issues is modeled for them by their instructors. Rather than an extensive discussion or lecture about the evaluation criteria, the class examines a number of Web sites, applying the evaluation criteria to the live samples. Sites visited range from the absurd (Pacific Northwest Tree Octopus <http://zapatopi.net/treeoctopus>) to the tricky (Dihydrogen Monoxide <http://www.dhmo.org>) to the repugnant (Stormfront's Dr. Martin Luther King, Jr., site <http://www.martinlutherking.org>). Each a challenge in its own way, sites such as these serve as a sobering reminder (even to students who have grown up with the Web) that, indeed, critical thinking is an essential research skill in the 21st century.

As in many courses, plagiarism and correct citation practice are issues of concern in freshman seminar. A series of activities designed to foster discussion and learning about plagiarism is completed in class. In addition to instructing or reminding the Gen Ed 300 students about the issues surrounding plagiarism, the activities also provide them with discussion questions and Web resources they can use with their future students. Recently, classes were given a series of hands-on citation exercises, asked to create citations for the information use article they had presented to the class, and evaluated each other's citations as a group.

Activities and discussion of research models were also formally incorporated into the course. Students begin with a creative activity in which they are asked to draw, chart, diagram, or otherwise visually represent their own research style. The discussion then moves into examining various process models of information use, including those developed by Eisenberg and Berkowitz (1990) and Kuhlthau (1993). Eisenberg and Berkowitz's "Big 6" gives the students a framework for the process of research that they can use as future PFs, whereas the introduction to the Kuhlthau model reminds them of the emotional aspects of the process.

The freshman seminar program at Washington State has long been distinctive owing to its extensive use of peer facilitators as classroom instructors. The evolution of the libraries' approach to meeting the needs of this program demonstrates an increasing degree of collaboration and a more nuanced view (developed over time) by librarians of the unique information needs of each new cohort of peer facilitators.

Critical Thinking in Gen Ed 300

As noted earlier, the students in Gen Ed 300 prepare a paper dealing with issues regarding the use of information. Several class sessions are devoted to readings and discussions about how students seek and use information and the role of the Internet in research and communication. The students are given the chance to examine their own views and approaches, and to consider how those have changed during their own educational careers. The readings have included the report by the Pew Internet and American Life Project report on college students' use of the Internet (2002), which not only provides interesting statistics on how students use the Web for communication, learning, and recreation, but also provides an excellent opportunity to discuss issues regarding survey methodology and validity (Jones 2002). Our students have also read Leckie's (1996) article on faculty assumptions about undergraduate research, Davis' (2003) study of the impact of the availability of Web-based information resources on student bibliographies, or Thompson's (2003) article about student attitudes toward research. Each of these readings has led to engaging class discussions. Other materials include a newspaper article on student and teacher attitudes toward using the Internet that paints a portrait of students as generally lazy but also refers to the infamous case of the Johns Hopkins physician whose failure to search beyond MEDLINE and Yahoo resulted in the death of a patient (Frand). This study regarding the "information age mindset," which explores generational differences in the use of technology for communication, brings many discussion points to the class. Students also locate additional articles related to these topics and facilitate discussion of them in class.

After these discussions, students write a paper addressing their views on how the information age and technology have affected education and will affect their future teaching. This assignment (Appendix 1) asks students to consider such questions as, "How would you describe the information use habits of today's students based on class readings?" and "Do you find the descriptions provided in the readings to be accurate based on your own knowledge and experience (why, or why not)?" Most students also choose to address the question posed regarding what skills or knowledge they think they will need to have as a peer instructor in order to help students meet the challenges of doing research in the information age. During the years the program was active, these papers, with the students' permission, were submitted to WSU's critical thinking project for analysis.

This writing assignment requires students to employ information literacy skills such as determining their focus, locating and using information to bolster their argument, and evaluating the different sources. They also need to demonstrate critical thinking skills such as recognizing and addressing other's perspectives in addition to their own. When it comes to reading articles written by older researchers about how millennial students act and think, this can be a particularly crucial and interesting aspect of the papers the students write. The information literacy—critical thinking rubric provides grounds for assessing this writing on a number of levels.

The collaborative work with the freshman seminar program has been successful in many ways. First, it represents a team-oriented and proactive approach to outreach from the academic library as librarians identified problems with an existing instructional collaboration and approached their partners in the freshman seminar program to rethink how they could be more effectively involved in both curriculum design and delivery of instruction. Second, it represents the development of a new version of a for-credit information literacy course aimed specifically at training the undergraduate peer facilitators, who are at the front line of freshman seminar instructional efforts. Finally, it represents an opportunity taken by librarians to use their expertise in information literacy instruction to redefine the ways in which first-year students enrolled in freshman seminar are introduced to library resources and to the research process—an opportunity that has been used to integrate critical thinking instruction into the broader effort to provide first-year students with an effective introduction and orientation to academic research at the college level.

In the summer of 2007, a major overhaul of the freshman seminar program was launched, and a year-long course of revisions is set to take place. The name of the program will be changed to a title as yet unknown that will reflect a course more closely tied to academic research. The course will also be offered at the sophomore instead of freshman level as WSU has a specific goal of curbing its sophomore level dropout rate. Librarians are slated to be intimately involved in the revision process and are excited about the enhanced focus on research for the course.

CRITICAL THINKING IN THE INFORMATION LITERACY EDUCATION PROJECT

The information literacy education project (ILE) is a unique program developed by the library instruction department in the spring of 2007. Through the ILE, librarians collaborate with classroom instructors to create an online information literacy course page <http://www.wsulibs.wsu.edu/ile/>. This page divides research assignments into a series of component processes students do to complete their work. Each component area, which correlates to an information literacy standard, features a customizable set of online tutorials and assessment tools. Students learn how to better define a research question or thesis, access scholarly information in a variety of formats, critically evaluate information quality, and ethically and legally use information to accomplish a specific purpose. By completing the ILE course page, students strengthen their research skills and produce better final products.

Historically, the library instruction department has concentrated on developing relationships with partner programs (e.g., freshman seminar), teaching in-person one-shot classes based on arrangements with these partner programs, and developing online tutorials. In recent years, we have also begun to systematically evaluate student learning and to quantify the level of information literacy among our students. Thus far, we have assessed:

- Tutorial and guide usage with the aid of statistical software packages;
- Student learning by using electronic summary surveys and questionnaires;
- Tutorial effectiveness through usability testing and summary quizzes;
- The overall success of our online learning presence by providing instructors with student assessment services, a site where instructors can create online quizzes or select from an existing bank of assessment tools that they can use to evaluate student learning via our online tutorials <http://www.wsulibs.wsu.edu/usered/sas/>;

- Overall student orientation to and satisfaction with WSU library instruction through the administration of LibQual+, a national survey about library use and development of research skills <http://www.libqual.org/>.

While we have been encouraged by the growth in the increasing number of classes we have taught, and by the rising use of our online learning tools, we are largely disappointed at the results of our assessment activities, which indicate underdeveloped student information literacy skills. Our findings (Lindsay, Johnson, Cummings, and Scales 2006) confirm an expansive set of national research illustrating that students do not thoroughly investigate library resources to provide a quality framework for their scholarly writing. At the same time, we are often hard pressed to find venues for teaching students valuable research skills. Classroom faculty often do not have time in their syllabi to devote to a library session or they believe that students became information literate in another class as well as at an earlier stage in their education.

The ILE project addresses these issues in a number of ways, while also placing a greater emphasis on critical thinking as well. First, this project affords librarians an opportunity to work with teaching faculty members in the creation or revision of their research assignments. We have typically created our lessons based solely as a reaction to assignments instructors had already crafted. These assignments often have mistakes in them in regard to library resources or services because teaching faculty do not have time to keep up with changes in the library and information environment. We help correct these problems before they have a chance to confuse students. Also, teachers tend to focus primarily on the end product when it comes to evaluating research projects. The ILE project helps instructors think about more equal emphasis on all parts of the research process and the critical thinking involved in each step. Second, by moving our curriculum online, we are now able to provide instruction at a greater breadth and depth than we can in a one-shot session. We break the assignment down into manageable pieces based on the five information literacy standards. Third, although our tutorials seem to be getting a lot of use (they average about 100 hits per month each), patrons often likely use them out of context or at least not to their full potential. Through an ILE project course page, tutorials are placed in the context of the students' research assignment(s) and the information literacy standards. In addition, instructors can opt to activate objective quizzes to test for achievement of the outcomes of the tutorials and/or develop an assignment specific assessment directly asking students to apply the information literacy skills honed in the tutorials to a subpart of their research assignment(s). By illuminating parts of the research process, we are asking students to think more critically. For example, by completing an ILE course page section about evaluating information (Standard 3), students will be equipped and disciplined to take the time and make the effort to thoughtfully assess potential resources in relation to authority, accuracy, currency, comprehensiveness, and objectivity.

CONCLUSION

The connection between critical thinking instruction and library instruction is evident across college campuses everywhere. Thinking critically about how to access, evaluate, and use information has become a necessity in light of the information explosion of the last 25 years. While this exponential proliferation of information has served to increase the complexity of the information landscape significantly, college students are more apt than ever before to overestimate their ability to find and assess quality information. The expanded use of Web 2.0 technologies has also raised important questions about information authority and quality. In light of these challenging developments, academic librarians have collaborated with colleagues from all corners of the university to help students effectively apply critical thinking skills to the location, selection, evaluation, and management of information in all its forms.

At Washington State University, we created a critical thinking rubric as part of the critical thinking project. Use of this rubric has aided in the curricular development of freshman seminar and the freshman seminar teacher training section of Gen Ed 300. At the same time that critical thinking elements were more deeply infused into these courses, it became clear that stronger ties to information literacy instruction were a natural course of action as well. Partnerships between the freshman seminar officials and librarians were advanced on a number of fronts. Most recently, the information literacy education project was launched. The aims of this program are to create curricula under the joint guidance of librarians and teaching faculty that will allow students to concentrate more fully (and thus think more critically) about the component parts of the research process. The future looks bright for even more meaningful collaborative efforts that build the information literacy skills of students and inspire them to think more critically.

REFERENCES

Albitz, R. S. 2007. The what and who of information literacy and critical thinking in higher education. *Portal: Libraries and the Academy* 7: 97–109.

Association of College and Research Libraries. 2000. *Information Literacy Competency Standards for Higher Education* [updated 2007]. http://www.ala.org/ala/acrl/acrlstandards/informationliteracycompetency.htm.

Bean, J. C. 2001. *Engaging ideas: The professor's guide to integrating writing, critical thinking, and active learning in the classroom.* San Francisco: Jossey-Bass.

Bodi, S. 1988. Critical thinking and bibliographic instruction: The relationship. *Journal of Academic Librarianship* 14: 150–153.

Bodi, S. 1992. Collaborating with faculty in teaching critical thinking: The role of the librarians. *Research Strategies* 10: 69–76.

Cheney, D. L. 2004. Problem-based learning: Librarians as collaborators. *Portal: Libraries and the Academy* 4: 495–508.

Colbert, Stephen. *The Colbert Report: Wikiality* [updated 2006]. http://www.comedycentral.com/shows/the_colbert_report/videos/the_word/index.jhtml?playVideo=72347.

Colbert, Stephen. *The Colbert Report* [updated 2007]. http://www.comedycentral.com/shows/the_colbert_report/index.jhtml.

Cummings, L. U. 2007. Bursting out of the box: Outreach to the millennial generation through student services programs. *Reference Services Review* 35: 285–295.

Davis, P. M. 2003. Effect of the web on undergraduate citation behavior: Guiding student scholarship in a networked age. *Portal: Libraries and the Academy* 3: 41–51.

Eisenberg, M. B. and R. E. Berkowitz. 1990. *Information problem-solving: The big six skills approach to library and information skills instruction.* Norwood, NJ: Ablex.

Elliot, P. and A. Spitzer. 1999. Lessons of a decade: An instructional experiment matures. *The Reference Librarian* 64: 53–66.

Elmborg, J. K. 2003. Information literacy and writing across the curriculum: Sharing the vision. *Reference Services Review* 31: 68–80.

Elmborg, J. K. and S. Hook. 2005. *Centers for learning: Writing centers and academic libraries in collaboration.* Chicago: Association of College and Research Libraries.

Frand, J. L. 2000. The information-age mindset: Changes in students and implications for higher education. *Educause Review* 35: 15–18+.

Gaff, J. G. and J. L. Ratcliff (Eds.). 1997. *Handbook of the undergraduate curriculum.* San Francisco: Jossey-Bass.

Gibson, C. 1995. Critical thinking: Implications for instruction. *RQ* 35: 27–35.

Gorman, M. 2007a. Web 2.0: The sleep of reason, part 1. *Britannica Blog* [updated 2007]. http://blogs.britannica.com/blog/main/2007/06/web-20-the-sleep-of-reason-part-i/.

Gorman, M. 2007b. Web 2.0: The sleep of reason, part 2. *Britannica Blog* [updated 007]. http://blogs.britannica.com/blog/main/2007/06/web-20-the-sleep-of-reason-part-ii/.

Gradowski, G., L. Snavely, and P. Dempsey (Eds.). 1998. *Designs for active learning: A sourcebook of classroom strategies for information education.* Chicago: Association of College and Research Libraries.

Grossman, L. 2006. *Time*'s person of the year: You. December 13. http://www.time.com/time/magazine/article/0,9171,1569514,00.html.

Guédon, J.-C. 2001. *In Oldenburg's long shadow: Librarians, research scientists, publishers, and the control of scientific publishing* [updated 2007]. http://www.arl.org/resources/pubs/mmproceedings/138guedon.shtml.

Halpern, D. F. 1993. Assessing the effectiveness of critical thinking instruction. *Journal of General Education* 42: 238–254.

Halpern, D. F. 2003. *Thought and knowledge: An introduction to critical thinking*. 4th ed. Mahwah, NJ: Lawrence Erlbaum.

Hardesty, L. (Ed.). 2007. *The role of the library in the first college year*. Columbia, SC: National Resource Center for the First-Year Experience and Students in Transition.

Harley, B. 2001. Freshmen, information literacy, critical thinking and values at San Diego State University. *Reference Services Review* 29: 301–306.

Henscheid, J. 2001. Peer facilitators as lead freshman seminar instructors. *In:* J. E. Miller, J. E. Groccia, and M. S. Miller (eds.) *Student-assisted teaching: A guide to faculty-student teamwork*. Bolton, MA: Anker, pp. 21–26.

Henri, J. and K. Dillon. 1992. Learning to learn: Reflections upon enquiry, information literacy and critical thinking. *Australian Library Journal* 41: 103–117.

Washington State House of Representatives. 2000. House Bill 2375 [An Act Relating to Information and Technology Literacy in Higher Education]. [updated 2000]. http://www1.leg.wa.gov/documents/billdocs/1999-00/Htm/Bills/House%20Passed%20Legislature/2375.PL.htm.

Jacobson, T. E. (Ed.). 2000. *Critical thinking and the Web: Teaching users to evaluate Internet resources*. Pittsburgh, PA: Library Instruction Publications.

Jayne, E. and P. Vander Meer. 1997. The library's role in the academic instructional use of the World Wide Web. *Research Strategies* 15: 123–150.

Jensen, M. 2007. The new metrics of scholarly authority. *Chronicle of Higher Education* 53(41): B6. http://chronicle.com/weekly/v53/i41/41b00601.htm.

Johnson, C. M., S. K. McCord, and S. Walter. 2003. Instructional outreach across the curriculum: Enhancing the liaison role at a research university. *The Reference Librarian* 82: 19–37.

Johnson, K. and K. C. Fountain. 2002. Laying a foundation for comparing departmental structures between reference and instructional services: Analysis of a nationwide study. *College and Research Libraries* 63: 275–287.

Jones, S. 2002. *The Internet goes to college: How students are living in the future with today's technology*. http://www.pewinternet.org/pdfs/PIP_College_Report.pdf.

Keen, A. 2007. *The cult of the amateur: How today's Internet is killing our culture*. New York: Doubleday/Currency.

Kuhlthau, C. C. 1993. *Seeking meaning: A process approach to library and information services*. Norwood, NJ: Ablex.

Leckie, G. 1996. Desperately seeking citations: Uncovering faculty assumptions about the undergraduate research process. *Journal of Academic Librarianship* 22: 201–208.

Lindsay, E. B. 2003. A collaborative approach to information literacy in the freshman seminar. *Academic Exchange Quarterly* 7: 23–27.

Lindsay, E. B., C. M. Johnson, L. Cummings, and B. J. Scales. 2006. If you build it, will they learn? Assessing online information literacy tutorials. *College & Research Libraries* 67: 429–445.

Nowicki, S. 1999. Information literacy and critical thinking in the electronic environment. *Journal of Instruction Delivery Systems* 13: 25–28.

O'English, L. and S. McCord. 2006. Getting in on the game: Partnering with a university athletics department. *Portal: Libraries and the Academy* 6: 143–153.

Pierard, C. and K. Graves. 2002. The greatest problem with which the library is confronted: A survey of academic library outreach to the freshman course. *In:* M. C. Kelly and A. Kross (eds.) *Making the grade: Academic librarians and student success*. Chicago: Association of College and Research Libraries, pp. 71–89.

Prensky, M. 2001a. Digital natives, digital immigrants. *On the Horizon* 9: 1–6.

Prensky, M. 2001b. Digital natives, digital immigrants, part 2: Do they really think differently? *On the Horizon* 9: 1–6.

Smalley, T. N. 1998. Partnering with faculty to interweave internet instruction into college coursework. *Reference Services Review* 26: 19–27.

Stephens, M. 2006. *Web 2.0 and libraries: Best practices for social software*. Chicago: American Library Association.

Tapscott, D. and W. D. Williams. 2006. *Wikinomics: How mass collaboration changes everything*. New York: Portfolio.

Thompson, C. 2003. Information illiterate or lazy? How college students use the Web for research. *Portal: Libraries and the Academy* 3: 259–268.

Ursin, L., C. M. Johnson, and E. B. Lindsay. 2004. Assessing library instruction in the freshman seminar: A citation analysis study. *Reference Services Review* 32: 284–292.

Walter, S. 2000. *Engelond*: A model for faculty-librarian collaboration in the information age. *Information Technology and Libraries* 19: 34–41.

Walter, S. 2005. Moving beyond collections: Academic library outreach to multicultural student centers. *Reference Services Review* 33: 438–458.

Walter, S. 2007. Using cultural perspectives to foster information literacy instruction across the curriculum. *In:* S. C. Curzon and L. Lampert (eds.) *Proven strategies for building an information literacy program*. New York: Neal Schuman, pp. 55–75.

APPENDIX 1

Gen Ed 300

Uses of Information:

Attitudes and Implications for Teaching and Learning in Higher Education

In class, we will read and discuss a number of articles addressing issues such as:

- the nature of the research process for students in the Information Age,
- the challenges faced by both students and teachers in learning how to make use of electronic information,
- the "generation gap" that may exist between faculty and students regarding these basic academic issues (and how this may affect faculty expectations of student work),
- the possibility that the Internet has given rise to entirely new ways of dealing with information ("net think").

In your opinion, what impact has the availability of Internet-based information sources had on the way students conduct academic research? What challenges do students conducting academic research today face that may be different from those they faced before? What challenges remain the same? How has the rise of information technology given rise to some of these challenges, and how has it helped overcome others?

For this paper, you should draw on the resources we have used in class, any related material that you may have used in ED AD 497, and any relevant material that you may find as the result of an article database search. Draw also (but not exclusively) on your own experiences as a student. Be sure to identify key ideas from at least 3 sources that help to illustrate your points or support your answers. Address 2–3 of the questions below:

1. How would you describe the information use habits of today's students based on class readings (or other resources you choose to use)?
2. Do you find the descriptions provided in the readings to be accurate based on your own knowledge and experience (why or why not)?
3. How would you define "net think"?
4. What challenges do these "net think-ing" students face in coming to Washington State University?
5. What instructional challenges do these "net think-ing" students present to faculty?

6. What skills or knowledge do you think you will need to have as a peer instructor in order to help students meet the challenges of conducting academic research on today's campus?

Your paper should be 4–5 pages in length, double-spaced, using standard margins and an 11- or 12-point font. You may use either MLA or APA citation style for your in-text citations and works cited page.

Index